The Art of
Architectu

A Provisional Report

The Temple Hoyne Buell Center
for the Study of American Architecture
Graduate School of Architecture, Planning,
and Preservation, Columbia University

Reinhold Martin, Director
Jacob Moore, Program Coordinator
Susanne Schindler, Adjunct Associate
Research Scholar

The Temple Hoyne Buell Center for the
Study of American Architecture was founded in 1982. Its mission is to advance the
study of American architecture, urbanism,
and landscape. Located within the Graduate
School of Architecture, Planning, and
Preservation at Columbia University, it
sponsors programs and research projects
focusing on issues of both scholarly
and general interest. See buellcenter.org.

This report was produced as a part of *House
Housing: An Untimely History of Architecture
and Real Estate*, a multi-year research
project conducted by the Temple Hoyne
Buell Center for the Study of American
Architecture. The initiative seeks to encourage a public, historically informed conversation about the intersection of architecture
and real estate development. *House Housing*
consists of a diverse body of research that
draws on multiple types of media. It appears
in numerous locations in the form of exhibitions, panel discussions, and publications,
among others, and relates to different
institutional frames. Objects of inquiry range
from architect-designed houses to prefabricated apartment blocks to suburban
gated communities. These architectures are
analyzed in light of their position at the
intersection of design, policy, and finance.

Bracketed references have been made
throughout the text not only to relevant
sections within the report, but also to
"episodes" of the larger *House Housing*
project. See the final pages of the report and
house-housing.com for more information.

Research Team
Alissa Anderson, Erik Carver, Adele Cassola,
Ryan Meehan, Nabila Morales Pérez, Cezar
Nicolescu, Julie Pedtke, Pollyanna Rhee,
Manuel Shvartzberg Carrió, Sonya Ursell

Image Credits
Photographs: Emily Kloppenburg,
Ilaria Ortensi, with Thomas Roma, editor
Plans: Nabila Morales Pérez

Design Team
MTWTF: Glen Cummings, Aliza Dzik,
Michela Povoleri

Special thanks go to colleagues who provided
valuable insight in an early workshop on
this undertaking: Robert Beauregard, Clara
Irazábal, Catherine Fennell, Jesse Keenan,
Leah Meisterlin, Richard Plunz, Sara Stevens,
and Mabel Wilson. We're also grateful to
Elizabeth Blackmar, Jordan Carver, Anne
Kockelkorn, William Morrish, Thomas Roma,
and Juliette Spertus, who provided critical
feedback on the project's general scope and
on matters of detail.

1st Edition, Printed in EU by ORO grafisch
projectmanagement, in September, 2015.

Copy Editor
Ryan Meehan

The Art of Inequality:
Architecture, Housing, and Real Estate

A Provisional Report

Reinhold Martin, Jacob Moore, Susanne Schindler
Editors

The Temple Hoyne
Buell Center
for the Study of
American Architecture

B

▲

Preface

The Art of Inequality: Architecture, Housing, and Real Estate belongs to a long-term research project on architecture, housing, and socioeconomic inequality begun in 2008 by Columbia University's Temple Hoyne Buell Center for the Study of American Architecture. The project sought first to enlarge the discursive frame around housing in response to the 2007–2008 mortgage foreclosure crisis by pointing out the sleight-of-hand by which public housing had been removed from consideration as a viable policy option. This was not, as the project emphasized, the result of urban renewal's injustice or failure, but a thoroughgoing privatization of the imagination for which the only admissible approaches were market-oriented. The Buell Center's collaboration with the Museum of Modern Art in New York on the exhibition *Foreclosed: Rehousing the American Dream* (2012) was among the outcomes of this endeavor. *The Buell Hypothesis*, which pointed out the near impossibility of using the word "public" *in public* any longer when it came to housing, served as a prompt for the architect-led design teams participating in the exhibition. This report extends that research into the real-world impact of cultural imaginaries.

As an academic study center, we aim to examine the terms of debate in order to test the conventional wisdom determining "realistic" options in policy and design. Among the many realities that have come sharply into focus is the hegemony exercised by real estate development in defining those terms. In light of the much wider neoliberal turn that has shaped global discourse, this should not be surprising. Its specifically American aspects represent only one part of a transnational formation that is shaped, in a non-linear fashion, by national and municipal factors. Recent critical scholarship, undertaken mostly by urbanists, geographers, and social theorists, has done a great deal to map this turn's steep embankments as they relate to cities and to spatial politics. By and large, however, the more specific terrain on which architecture and real estate development interact daily has not received much in-depth treatment, perhaps because the relationship between the two is thought to be obvious: architecture, whether as a cultural artifact or a professional service, merely reflects or (at best) reproduces an underlying economic logic. Though undeniable at one level, such a perspective has seemed to us insupportable when confronted with the vast, heterogeneous field called "housing" on which the architectural, the economic, and the social have traditionally met.

This report offers facts related to that field that we hope will deepen the discussion. Necessarily incomplete, it stops short of systematic conclusions. Instead, together with its companion exhibition series, *House Housing: An Untimely History of Architecture and Real Estate*, it offers glimpses into the operating systems that, in effect, run beneath our discourse and shape its terms. The report's title refers to one of these terms: inequality. The Buell Center's earlier work sought to rehabilitate another: public. When we took stock of that effort by collecting and publishing, in a searchable database, every word that had been written in response to the MoMA exhibition, from *The New York Times* to Twitter, our Columbia colleague Peter Marcuse pointed out that the word "race" appeared only once in all of the discussions on housing, suburbanization, and architecture that we had collected. That is reason enough to ask why, even (or especially) when shaken by a historic crisis, public discourse (including our own) finds certain truths unspeakable. Our response here attempts to enunciate some of those truths, by directing attention to the subtle ways in which architecture—through housing—lays the groundwork for our present dilemmas, not simply by casting them in concrete, but by concretely laying out their terms.

We have compiled this report as a group, divided its contents amongst ourselves, met regularly to compare notes, and shared work in progress. Several other colleagues have been especially generous as interlocutors on various subjects: Dianne Harris, Chair of the Buell Center Advisory Board; as well as Robert Beauregard and Mabel Wilson, both Buell Center Advisory Board members. The report itself exists largely due to the work of a research team made up of students and scholars from a variety of disciplines located at Columbia's Graduate School of Architecture, Planning, and Preservation: Alissa Anderson, Erik Carver, Adele Cassola, Ryan Meehan, Nabila Morales Pérez, Cezar Nicolescu, Julie Pedtke, Pollyanna Rhee, Manuel Shvartzberg Carrió, and Sonya Ursell. Ryan Meehan applied the copyeditor's judicious knife, and Ilaria Ortensi and Emily Kloppenburg contributed the photographs intercut throughout Part 1. The report's particular form is due in no small part to the talents and imagination of our design collaborators at MTWTF: Glen Cummings, Aliza Dzik, and Michela Povoleri. Finally, very special thanks go to Jacob Moore and Susanne Schindler who, in addition to co-authoring the opening section of the report, organized the research and convened the discussions. Even more, in his capacity as Buell Center Program Coordinator, Jacob Moore has overseen the entire project, including the *House Housing* exhibitions, with the care, sensitivity, and dedication worthy of such a difficult topic, and of the many open minds we hope the result will continue to challenge.

— *Reinhold Martin*, Director

Introduction

What is inequality? Or better, how does it work? This report sketches a partial answer to these questions in architectural terms, specifically those related to housing. By "inequality" we mean not only the measurable socioeconomic gap that separates the very wealthy from the very poor, but also a seemingly endless chain of inequities around which both individuals and social groups hold conflicting interests. This report only addresses a small subset of these, mostly centered on economic disparities, but with a close eye on how they link with others: structural racism, gender discrimination, and other exclusions or expulsions that are internal (that is, *built-in*) to the American housing system.

We focus on the United States, leaving implicit the many ways in which specific forms of socioeconomic inequality predominant in American cities, suburbs, and towns fundamentally relate to others elsewhere. As its subheading suggests, this is by no means a definitive document. It is a provisional report compiled on behalf of colleagues and students in the field of architecture, but it is for anyone who may be struggling to grasp concretely certain key facts that shape social and economic life. Among the facts we have outlined are the numbers, captured in the slogans referring to "the 1%" (the ruling elites) or "the 99%" (everyone else), that reveal the starkest of disparities. At the same time, these numbers conceal others that run up, down, and sideways across the socioeconomic spectrum. Housing, understood as the material, social, institutional, and economic process that determines where members of a society sleep at night—where they live and love, and perhaps where they die—cuts an important cross-section through the dominant patterns. But like other instances of inequality, housing is not just an indicator of deeper trends; it consists of techniques that contribute to and perpetuate the very conflicts that it might seem only to reflect. In other words (to misuse a well-known phrase), housing is a verb; it does things as well as represents them. This is what allows us to speak of something like a housing system: a dynamic set of relations, a portion of which this report sketches via the logic and the "laws" of real estate development.

We therefore aim to show some of the ways in which real estate development effectively writes the laws that govern the American housing system. The report's title, *The Art of Inequality*, emphasizes that far from being objectively given, these laws are pieces of artifice that amount to a way of governing, as in the expression "the art of governing." Insurmountable housing disparities are not a historical accident, nor are they merely the unintended side effect of well-meaning policies and practices. They are designed, built into the system by which housing is produced and maintained in the first place. Architecture matters here precisely for this reason. For it too does not come after economic forces (those mysterious representatives of "the economy") have done their work. Architecture actively participates at every step, simply because there is no housing without architecture, however humbly defined or constrained its authors—architects, designers, policymakers, developers, bankers, residents, etc.—may feel.

Yes, it does seem today that everyone is talking about inequality. But perhaps that is because inequality is everywhere. Political standoffs between incentivized luxury development and rent regulation run parallel with a litany of racial violence that, in turn, reflects the role of both race and space in determining economic outcomes. Newspapers lament gentrification while featuring lush advertisements for improbable dwellings populated by two-parent, three-child families who seem only ever to be waiting for the guests to arrive. Housing is analyzed daily for its role in construction starts, mortgage interest rates, and home values' growth or decline, with its artfulness largely relegated to sidebar commentary in lifestyle magazines. The housing system is all of this and more. Understood most blatantly as the form given to real estate, but also as an arrangement of material things that makes real estate possible, architecture thus becomes both evidence and instrument of growing socioeconomic divides.

In its format and subject matter *The Art of Inequality* refers indirectly to a historical document featured in the series of exhibitions that form another part of the Buell Center's ongoing project, *House Housing: An Untimely History of Architecture and Real Estate*. Released in 1968, *The Report of the National Advisory Commission on Civil Disorders*, better known as the "Kerner Report," was the result of an official investigation into the racially charged unrest occurring in cities throughout the United States beginning in 1965. Against the backdrop of a military and foreign policy debacle, implicitly acknowledging the limitations of his domestic "Great Society" programs, President Lyndon Johnson asked the commission writing the report to answer three basic questions: 1) *What happened?* 2) *Why did it happen?* and 3) *What can be done?* But if, in the refusal of African Americans to accept police violence in Ferguson, Missouri, Staten Island, New York, Baltimore, Maryland, or elsewhere, this unrest seems to be repeating itself, such pre-emptive questions as those in the Kerner Report must not repeat along with it. Instead, alluding only to their style, we modify these questions to confront assumptions shared among many policy makers, real estate developers, architects, and others regarding the rule of the markets and the inability (or unwillingness) to link racial justice with economic and spatial justice. We therefore began by asking, in the present tense: 1) *What is happening?* 2) *Why is it happening?* and 3) *How is it happening?*

The report's three-part structure reflects these questions. Part 1 describes different conceptions of inequality today, some expected and others not. In particular, we focus on the roles of and interdependencies among real estate development, housing, and architecture, and outline a number of key ways in which inequality is produced in the wider socioeconomic field that housing helps construct. Part 2 reverses the perspective and considers inequality not as a consequence but as an agent, describing its *own* techniques of governance in architectural terms. Part 3 then breaks down some of the specific tools required by real estate development and architecture, both as discourses and practices within this domain, comprising among others: legal documents, marketing images, educational materials, and terminology.

To further convey a sense of how inequality plays out visually and spatially today, the report includes commissioned photographs of the 125th Street corridor in Manhattan (Columbia's own immediate environs), as well as representative floor plans of recent residential developments across the United States. Throughout, the report also points to the episodes in the *House Housing* exhibitions to illustrate how policy, finance, and the design of housing have intersected across the last one hundred years. These brief stories are supported by graphic, audio, and video artifacts that are accessible via the *House Housing* website (house-housing.com). At no point, however, did we conduct field studies or compile and analyze primary data; our method has been to synthesize. If the result is incomplete, that is partly due to the scope of the subject, and partly because our aim is to point toward productive questions rather than to definitive conclusions.

Our focus on architecture in relation to economic inequalities enables a more cogent connection with other disparities, including those related to race. We aim to complement existing scholarship even as we draw on it, and to enrich the current academic and public debate by offering a slightly different frame. We have tried to limit what falls within this frame to facts drawn from credible sources, and to tangible evidence drawn from readily available documents. Rather than speaking with the authoritative voice of expertise or recommending future action prematurely, we have sought only to put these facts and this evidence—numerical, textual, and visual—on the table, to demonstrate that nothing is self-evident as it may appear. Implicitly, this report asks a simple question: How might anyone with a vested interest in architectural design *and* a commitment to addressing our time's most pressing social concerns reconcile the two, if at all?

— *Reinhold Martin, Jacob Moore,* and *Susanne Schindler*

Notes on Photography

From East 125th Street to West 125th Street, New York, June, 2015

Emily Kloppenburg, Ilaria Ortensi, photographers
Thomas Roma, editor

For the commissioned photographs included in Part 1 of this report, the goal was not to illustrate projects mentioned in the text, but to convey the ever present, often banal, and seemingly self-evident faces of inequality, which can be found anywhere, anytime. Together with their advisor Thomas Roma, Emily Kloppenburg and Ilaria Ortensi—current and former Master of Fine Arts candidates at Columbia University, respectively—proposed Manhattan's 125th Street as a site of investigation. One of Harlem's commercial and cultural arteries in an area long characterized by disinvestment, this important east-west corridor has, in recent years, been the site of charged debates prompted by the rapid demographic and physical changes. If the art of inequality is visible anywhere, it is most certainly here, at our doorstep.

In my work, I use photography as means of visually mapping subliminal states of various "architectures" within their environs. For The Art of Inequality, *I traversed the horizontal axis of 125th Street in New York City. Systematically moving from west to east, I sought to locate abstruse instances of our current urbanity that surpass the known and the preconceived. My pictures reveal the "concealed" as pertinent examples of the delicate, complex realities that surround our contemporary structures as well as the visual and social landscapes that they inform.*
— Emily Kloppenburg
(pages 26, 27, 38, 39, 50 bottom, 52, 64, 65, 74, 75, 77, 89)

I'm interested in the possibility of exploring architecture as a product of political, social, and aesthetic conditions. Through my work I want to communicate the conflicting ideas and feelings that emanate from contemporary space. I believe that the way we construct and perceive ourselves has a strong affinity with the way we construct space. Growing up in Rome I developed a sensitivity toward space that is strictly connected to time. Photography is, for me, the ideal medium through which to describe the rapidity that characterizes urbanism today.
— Ilaria Ortensi
(pages 28, 40, 41, 50 top, 51, 53, 62, 63, 86, 87)

Part 1 Concepts

1.1 Defining Inequality
Jacob Moore and *Susanne Schindler*

What is inequality? Typically, inequality is defined by a combination of economic measures referring to income and wealth. Such inequality is inseparable from social disparities of other kinds, however, an interdependency that is particularly apparent in the provision of housing. More than just a building type or a market sector, housing is a primary architectural act. It begins when a line is drawn that separates inside from outside, and ultimately, one house from another. Under the rule of real estate development, that relation is structurally unequal. This is the art of inequality.

1.1.1 Affordability, Income, and Wealth

Following the neoliberal turn in the early 1970s and the "Great Recession" more recently, inequalities of all types have become increasingly legible in exclusively financial terms. These terms, including their inherent occlusions and limitations, occupy an outsize proportion of our collective imagination. Speculative real estate development—just such a concept—is premised on differences in value, particularly in housing [See HH: 1952, 1978, 2000]. The notion of affordability, therefore, is one of several possible openings into the complex relationship to architecture and the primary vehicle through which housing is produced and priced in the United States—real estate.

Affordability is generally determined by whether one's income can pay for essential goods and services without causing undue financial hardship. Housing is one of these essential goods. Income inequality describes the relative difference in income between specific groups. It is no accident that both affordability and income inequality are much discussed in the United States today: incomes are diverging at an accelerated rate, and housing is increasingly unaffordable not only for those people on the (expanding) lower end of the spectrum. According to U.S. tax data in 1976, the 1 percent of households earning the highest pre-tax incomes received 9 percent of the nation's total income. By 2012, their share had increased to over 22 percent.[1] In 2014, according to the National Low-Income Housing Coalition, 49 percent of renters across the United States had a housing cost burden, and for 27 percent it was deemed "severe."[2]

Another example that brings together growing income inequality and unaffordability, this one focusing on individuals within a single company as opposed a nation's households, is perhaps more telling. As the business magazine *Quartz* put it in 2014: "It takes the average McDonald's worker seven months to earn what its CEO makes in just a single hour."[3] This calls to mind studies comparing the purchasing power, measured in Big Macs, of McDonald's hourly wages around the globe. McDonald's entry-level workers in the United States earned 2.41 Big Macs per hour of work, while their counterparts in India earned 0.35 of a Big Mac hourly, and those in Japan earned 3.09.[4]

In parallel, inequality of wealth—including assets such as real estate—is reaching new heights. In the U.S. in 2013, upper-income families' median wealth was almost seven times that of middle-income families, and almost 70 times that of low-income families. These are the highest levels of wealth inequality that have been recorded by the Federal Reserve since they began collecting data thirty years ago.[5] On a global scale, according to a 2014 study, the wealth of the world's eighty-five most affluent individuals is equivalent to that of the poorest 3.5 billion.[6] Accordingly, in the realm of housing, discussions of inequality in the United States no longer refer primarily to physical factors—inadequate size or a lack of basic services like running water or electricity—but to financial aspects—affordability, and the unequal distribution of wealth according to housing ownership.

Today, in the United States, housing constitutes roughly half of all household wealth.[7] Both through private investment and expenditures on utilities and rent, housing contributes 17 percent of GDP.[8] Geographers Manuel Aalbers and Brett Christophers write: "It is of immense significance that in many capitalist societies residential property is the largest individual wealth/asset class although at the same time many—in some countries most—households own no residential property whatsoever. As such, it is in housing that the vast wealth inequalities of capitalist societies . . . are often most visible and most material."[9]

1.1.2   Real Estate Development
The concept and practice of real estate development are based on certain assumptions. If these assumptions are less than a surprise, it reveals the extent to which the logic of real estate development under capitalism has taken hold of the way we see the world. This logic has led us to consider principles constructed over time and under specific historical circumstances as axiomatic, self-evident truths [See 3.1, 3.2, HH: 1910]. The first hegemonic assumption is that space and its underlying land can be subdivided and owned: that individuals or corporations can hold a title to a circumscribed piece of the planet's surface, along with the space above or below it. This ownership,

then, entitles one to occupation, use, and exploitation of any natural resources in that space. A second assumption fundamental to real estate is that space can be sold and traded [See 3.2.3]. In other words, space is a commodity like any other—such as a car, a sweater, or a gold ingot. As property, space is not passed on solely through familial bonds, but is freely tradable through contractual arrangements [See 3.1]. A third assumption is that the price of a piece of space to be sold, or the rent to be charged for its use, is determined by a market, i.e. by supply and demand, and not through other mechanisms [See 3.2.4]. Only more recently has a fourth and final assumption developed that, as a property, land can become a financial instrument [See 3.2.3]. That is, by establishing space as collateral to be borrowed against, as the security for a loan, and allowing for the debt on that property to be resold to other creditors, what is in principle the most tangible and real form of property, has become the most fungible.

Under this hegemony, real estate development is fundamentally speculative. It is premised on the rise in value in a piece of land or property, in the expectation that its resale value be higher than the original payment made [See 3.2.5]. Thus, for most forms of real estate development, a property's exchange value (how much its sale will bring on the market) is more important than its use value (what functional benefit it brings to its residents). These categories are not clearly separable, and in the case of an owner who occupies the property, the two goals overlap.[10] Because market value is nevertheless considered of principal importance, homeownership has often been promoted as a key defense against both income and wealth inequality. The premise is that the value of property is expected to appreciate, enabling households to accumulate wealth and borrow against said wealth to provide liquidity.[11] In practice, this has not always played out positively. In the United States, which has a comparatively high homeownership rate, this became especially conspicuous during the mortgage crisis of 2009. Between 2005 and 2010, US housing wealth decreased by $8.2 trillion, by which time mortgage debt stood at 163 percent of home equity.[12] This loss of housing wealth disproportionately affected low-income homeowners.[13]

1.1.3 In Terms of Housing

A largely unregulated housing market will not serve those households who are unable to pay market rent. The state, therefore, remains the de facto guarantor, both directly and indirectly, of a social safety net. In the United States, federal, state, and local governments have taken up numerous strategies in the attempt to guide or define the intersection of real estate development and housing: building codes and zoning, rent regulation, anti-discrimination legislation, direct provision, direct and indirect subsidies, vouchers, insured mortgages, and more.

The ambiguities and contradictions of these strategies are best illustrated by governmental programs' use of the term "affordable housing" itself [See 3.5]. The U.S. Department of Housing and Urban Development defines housing as affordable when rent or mortgage payments as well as utilities are not higher than 30 percent of a household's pre-tax income. By this definition, only 37 percent of U.S. households lived in affordable housing in 2010.[14] As with the "Big Macs per hour" example, the link between income and affordability can be illustrated through the concept of a housing wage—that is, the minimum hourly wage a full-time worker would need in order to spend no more than 30 percent of his or her income on a rental unit at Fair Market Rent (FMR).[15] In 2015, the average national housing wage for a two-bedroom unit was $19.35 while the national minimum wage was $7.25. In other words, a household earning minimum wage would need to work more than two and a half full-time jobs to afford an average two-bedroom rental.[16] In the San Francisco and New York City metropolitan areas, where levels of income inequality are some of the country's highest, it takes more than three.[17]

Despite technically pertaining to all income levels, "affordable housing" is used in practice to describe housing produced and priced through governmental incentives, usually targeted to groups below the Area Median Income or AMI.[18] "Affordable housing" can be developed by for-profit and non-profit entities, and is often also described as "workforce housing" or "subsidized housing." Among other initiatives, funding can come through state or municipal bonds, housing trust funds, or Low-Income Housing Tax Credits (LIHTC) allotted by the Internal Revenue Service to the states [See HH: 1986]. Given the market-driven nature of the programs, the income- and price-restrictions (elements of the perceived "affordability") are not permanent. Their expiration can come as early as 15 years after completion (the minimum stipulated by LIHTC), or as late as 50 years (the goal set by the state of Oregon).

"Affordable housing" is typically contrasted with "market-rate housing," housing that is developed and sold or leased—ostensibly—without governmental regulation or subsidies. While neither price nor eligibility is regulated, market-rate housing benefits from tax breaks which amount to governmental subsidies of their own. The Mortgage Interest Deduction, for instance, allows homeowners an income tax deduction of interest paid on the debt on their primary residence; in 2014, this amounted to a tax expenditure of $101.5 billion and, since lower-income households do not make enough to afford this deduction, primarily benefitted upper-income households.[19]

In contrast to the malleable and highly contingent terms affordable and market-rate, "public housing" refers specifically to that which is developed, owned, and operated by the public sector. In the United States, municipal housing authorities take the local lead, but are regulated and funded by the federal government. This model of housing provision was formalized in the 1937 Housing Act. It was originally conceived to counterbalance the private market and help alleviate the housing shortage through supply, with the additional ambition of demonstrating higher design and construction standards [See 1.3.2, HH: 1934]. Due to pressure from a private sector in fear of competition, however, the program ended up exclusively targeting households at the low end of the income spectrum, today generally defined as making not more than 60 percent of the AMI.[20] This led in many cases to the financial and social problems (and their consequent stigmas) with which the program has become associated.[21]

In the early 1970s, federal policy regarding public housing shifted from new construction to a voucher system allowing eligible households to rent from private landlords [See HH: 1973]. The aim was not only to work against the concentration of poverty in public housing developments, but to support market-driven initiatives and end the federal government's direct role in housing development. A further restriction to public housing was introduced by the Faircloth Amendment to the broader welfare reforms implemented in the Quality Housing and Work Responsibility Act of 1998. This amendment outlawed federal funding for housing authorities who sought to expand their public housing stock.

The term "social housing," common in Europe and familiar across the world, has rarely been used in the United States. Yet some scholars argue that the term applies to this country's necessarily hybrid and codependent nature of funding sources for non-profit and publicly owned housing, where it constitutes about 5 percent of total stock.[22] This codependency, along with a political preference for a "return" of social housing to market rules after a certain time, has also affected efforts to establish non-profit forms of housing provision, both as rental and cooperative developments. For instance, in 1959, New York State's Mitchell Lama program, established only four years prior, abandoned its original goal to keep developments regulated in perpetuity, allowing owners to opt out once the mortgage was paid.[23]

For these and many other government programs, the "household" is the central social unit of measurement. The U.S. Census defines the "household" architecturally: "A household consists of all the people who occupy a housing unit." This is directly linked to a more circumscribed definition of "family" [See 1.2.1, 1.2.2, 2.1.4, 3.5]. Again citing the U.S. Census, "There are two major categories of households, family and nonfamily." While a "family" is defined as two or more individuals "related by birth, marriage, or adoption and residing together," a "nonfamily household" is defined as a single person living alone or exclusively with non-related others.[24] Reading definitions of family and household reminds us that these social constructs are also central to our understanding of what is "decent." Whether that is considered morally (in terms of who should be cohabiting and what should occur within and between dwellings); in terms of fairness (and access to "adequate" construction and amenities); or with regard to its implications for public health and the protection of private property (historically the key driver for housing regulations), notions of what is decent have always pertained to what was considered socially acceptable, and thus credit worthy [See 1.2.1, HH: 1939].[25] As one of the most striking examples, upon their founding as a part of the New Deal, guidelines from the Federal Housing Administration (FHA) to evaluate candidate properties for mortgage insurance stipulated that neighborhoods be racially homogenous.[26]

1.1.4   Race in Place

Since the late 1980s, scholars have analyzed housing's relationship to various other basic necessities—from education, to transportation, to employment—in their assertion that "place matters."[27] A person's exposure to poverty and crime, or their prospects for health, education, and income, as well as other indicators of "well-being," are not only measurable, but predictable, according to the neighborhood in which he or she lives [See 1.2.1].[28] The racial dimensions of wealth inequality remain striking and have direct spatial implications as well. In 2013, the median-income white household's net worth was ten times that of the median-income Hispanic household, and 13 times that of the median-income black household. And even with higher incomes, according to a 2015 study, middle-income black households are more likely to live in low-income areas than white households of comparable incomes, turning the primacy of economic inequality on its head.[29]

The principles underlying real estate development play a central role in establishing these relationships. Property taxes collected annually on the assessed value of land and buildings are local governments' single most significant source of revenue for supporting public services.[30] Accordingly, local real estate values—and not the overall wealth of a city, state, or nation—are one of the clearest predictors of the quality of education, amenities, and safety in U.S. neighborhoods. In turn, the quality of those public services is often the strongest predictor of the real estate prices [See HH: 1995]. In 2010, the average cost of homes near high-achieving public schools in the 100 largest metropolitan areas of the U.S. was 2.4 times higher than those near schools whose achievement was deemed low.[31]

In this way the housing market distinguishes itself from other markets. Its commodities are fixed; its rootedness in place inextricably links it to vital aspects of life beyond simply providing shelter; its production occurs over extended periods of time and is cost intensive; and there are highly emotional values attached to it. It differs from other sectors of the real estate market through one key factor: for the overwhelming majority of people, participation is not optional, since the result would be homelessness. This last point creates a decided imbalance of power and choice between the providers of housing—developers or large-scale owners—and those needing housing. This imbalance of power within the housing market translates fiscal concerns into material ones, highlighting the necessarily permeable borders that define the set of concerns related to what we call the "economy." After all, the root of the word itself, the Greek *oikos* or household, indicates an interplay of forces at work that reaches beyond a financial frame without negating it. So, upon closer inspection, we recognize that many of the conditions and qualities more conventionally relegated to the world of culture are not simply affected by economic inequality, but rather that they actively assist in its design and reproduction [See HH: 1949]. In this sense, the spaces of house and housing—the *oikos*—are not just coincidentally instructive examples of inequality; they define it.[32]

1. Thomas Piketty and Emmanuel Saez, "Income Inequality in the United States, 1913–1998," *The Quarterly Journal of Economics* 118, no. 1 (2003): 1–39. Tables and figures updated to 2013, accessed June 16, 2015, http://eml.berkeley.edu/~saez/.

2. National Low-Income Housing Coalition, "Affordable Housing is No-where to be Found for Millions," *Housing Spotlight* 5, no. 1 (2015): 4.

3. Richie King and Roberto Ferdman, "How Many Months It Takes an Average Worker to Make What the CEO Makes in an Hour," *Quartz*, December 23, 2013, accessed April 20, 2015, http://qz.com/156522/how-many-months-it-takes-an-average-worker-to-earn-what-the-ceo-makes-in-an-hour/.

4. Orley C. Ashenfelter, "Comparing Real Wages," *NBER Working Paper 18006* (2012), accessed June 12, 2015, http://www.nber.org/digest/aug12/w18006.html.

5. Richard Fry and Rakesh Kochhar, "America's Wealth Gap Between Middle-income and Upper-income Families is Widest on Record," Pew Research Center, December 17, 2014, accessed June 2, 2015, http://www.pewresearch.org/fact-tank/2014/12/17/wealth-gap-upper-middle-income/. Here upper income is defined as household incomes, adjusted for size, that are more than twice the national median.

6. Further, "The top 1 percent controls almost 50 percent of global wealth and the top 10 percent owns 83 percent of the world's wealth. In contrast, the bottom half of the

population together possess less than 2 percent of global wealth." See Peter Dreier, John Mollenkopf, and Todd Swanstrom, *Place Matters: Metropolitics for the Twenty-First Century*, 3rd ed. (Lawrence: University Press of Kansas, 2014), 14.

7. See, for instance, Matteo Iacoviello, "Housing Wealth and Consuption," The Federal Reserve Board, *International Finance Discussion Papers*, no. 1027 (2011), http://www.federalreserve.gov/pubs/ifdp/2011/1027/ifdp1027.htm.

8. "Housing's Contribution to Gross Domestic Product (GDP)," National Association of Home Builders (NAHB), accessed May 1, 2015, http://www.nahb.org/generic.aspx?genericContentID=66226.

9. Manuel Aalbers and Brett Christophers, "Centring Housing in Political Economy," *Housing, Theory and Society* 31, no. 4 (2014): 380.

10. The concepts of exchange value and use value are generally associated with the work of Karl Marx. They are still valuable today, despite the fact that the two concepts are perhaps not so easily separable, but rather codependent. For a recent elaboration in terms of housing, see Douglas S. Massey, Len Albright, Rebecca Casciano, Elizabeth Derickson, and David N. Kinsey, *Climbing Mount Laurel: The Struggle for Affordable Housing and Social Mobility in an American Suburb* (Princeton: Princeton University Press, 2013), 8.

11. This premise presumes that ownership provides a greater degree of insulation from rising housing costs than renting. See "The Homeownership Experience of Low-Income and Minority Families: A Review and Synthesis of the Literature," U.S. Department of Housing and Urban Development, Office of Policy Development and Research, http://www.huduser.org/publications/pdf/hisp_homeown9.pdf.

12. Joint Center for Housing Studies, *The State of the Nation's Housing 2010*, 3, http://www.jchs.harvard.edu/sites/jchs.harvard.edu/files/son2010.pdf. Statistics were taken from the 2010 study due to its proximity to the housing crisis and focus therein. For more recent statistics, see the 2015 study at http://www.jchs.harvard.edu/sites/jchs.harvard.edu/files/jchs-sonhr-2015-full.pdf.

13. Joint Center for Housing Studies, *The State of the Nation's Housing 2010*, 8.

14. According to HUD, affordable housing is "In general, housing for which the occupant(s) is/are paying no more than 30 percent of his or her income for gross housing costs, including utilities." "Glossary," U.S. Department of Housing and Urban Development, accessed July 22, 2015, http://www.huduser.org/portal/glossary/glossary_a.html. Housing scholars have suggested that this measure of affordability is too limited to address the implications of the cost of housing on overall household budget. See Michael E. Stone, "What Is Housing Affordability? The Case for the Residual Income Approach," in *The Affordable Housing Reader*, ed. J. Rosie Tighe and Elizabeth J. Mueller (New York: Routledge, 2013), 103. For a discussion of how affordability criteria have evolved and what their limits are, see Gary Pivo, "The Definition of Affordable Housing: Concerns and Related Evidence" (2013), http://www.fanniemae.com/resources/file/fundmarket/pdf/hoytpivo_mfhousing_affordablehousingdef_122013.pdf.

15. Fair Market Rent represents the 40th percentile of rents (including contract rent and utilities) for typical units of standard quality. They are set annually by the U.S. Department of Housing and Urban Development (HUD) for different metropolitan areas.

16. Megan Bolton, Elina Bravve, Emily Miller, Sheila Crowley, and Ellen Errico, "Out of Reach 2015," (Washington, D.C.: National Low Income Housing Coalition, 2015), http://nlihc.org/sites/default/files/oor/OOR_2015_FULL.pdf.

17. Information on income inequality in these areas comes from Alan Berube and Natalie Holmes, "Some Cities Are Still More Unequal than Others—An Update," Brookings Institute, accessed June 2, 2015, http://www.brookings.edu/research/reports2/2015/03/city-inequality-berube-holmes.

18. Each year, HUD publishes household income limits that are used to determine eligibility for housing subsidies administered at various levels of government. These limits are based on estimates, adjusted for family size, of the median family income for designated metropolitan and non-metropolitan areas. The resulting Area Median Income (AMI) estimates enable families' incomes to be expressed as a percentage of the median for their area. Families earning no more than 80 percent of AMI are typically considered to be low-income and those earning no more than 50 percent of AMI are considered extremely low-income. U.S. Department of Housing and Urban Development, "FY 2015 HUD Income Limits Briefing Material," accessed July 14, 2015, http://www.huduser.org/portal/datasets/il/il15/IncomeLimitsBriefingMaterial_FY15_Rev_2.pdf.

19. Office of Management and Budget, "Fiscal Year 2014 Analytical Perspectives of the U.S.

Government," *Budget of the U.S. Government*, 244, https://www.whitehouse.gov/sites/default/files/omb/budget/fy2014/assets/spec.pdf. Of the estimated $270 billion the federal government spends annually on housing, approximately $195 billion is spent on tax subsidies for homeowners. In comparison, the government spends approximately $40 billion annually on means-tested housing subsidies (such as the public housing and Housing Choice Voucher programs) and $6 billion on the LIHTC program. See Robert Collinson, Ingrid Gould Ellen, and Jens Ludwig, "Low Income Housing Policy," March 1, 2015, 1, accessed August 24, 2015, http://www.nber.org/chapters/c13485.pdf.

20. For a definition of AMI, see footnote 18.

21. "To overcome opposition from the real estate industry, advocates for public housing agreed to have the program designed so that it would not compete with the private housing market. This meant that families eligible for public housing would have incomes far below the level necessary to secure decent housing in the private market. The concentration of very low-income families in public housing is widely considered a source of many of public housing's most dire problems, including its difficulty meeting operating costs and the myriad issues associated with concentrated poverty." Alex F. Schwartz, *Housing Policy in the United States: An Introduction*, 2nd ed. (New York: Routledge, 2010), 105.

22. Rachel G. Bratt, "The Quadruple Bottom Line and Nonprofit Housing Organizations in the United States," *Housing Studies* 27, no. 4 (2012): 438.

23. Hilary Botein, "New York State Housing Policy in Postwar New York City. The Enduring Rockefeller Legacy," *Journal of Urban History* 35, no. 6 (September 2009): 839; 845–846.

24. "Definitions." U.S. Census, Current Population Survey (CPS), accessed June 14, 2015, http://www.census.gov/cps/about/cpsdef.html.

25. "Decency" is rarely defined, but is central to many housing programs. From Mayor de Blasio's *Housing New York: A Five-Boro, Ten-Year Plan*, released in mid-2014: "to make this a city where everyone rises together, and everyone has a safe and decent home." Message from the Mayor, accessed June 12, 2015, http://www.nyc.gov/html/housing/pages/home/index.html; or from the City's Housing Quality Standards (HQS) Inspection, administered to all Section 8 housing: "This inspection is required to confirm that a HPD Section 8–subsidized apartment is decent, safe, sanitary, and meets minimum physical standards set by the U.S. Department of Housing and Urban Development (HUD)," accessed June 12, 2015, http://www1.nyc.gov/nyc-resources/service/1870/housing-quality-standards-hqs-inspection. See also the Social Science Research Council's "Decent City" initiative: http://citiespapers.ssrc.org/.

26. Among other governmental and non-governmental organizations, the Federal Housing Administration was instrumental in enforcing segregated cities according to not only stylistic and economic criteria, but also racial ones—namely through supporting the practice of redlining and preferential treatment of developments with racially restrictive covenants. This type of institutional discrimination was the primary motivation for the 1968 Fair Housing Act. FHA (Federal Housing Administration), *Underwriting Manual. Underwriting and Valuation Procedure Under Title II of the National Housing Act*, 1934 (Excerpts in Richard C. Stearns, "Memorandum. Racial Content of FHA Underwriting Practices, 1934–1962," n.d.). For a broader reflection on this matter, see, for instance, Kenneth Jackson, *Crabgrass Frontier* (New York: Oxford University Press, 1995).

27. William Julius Wilson was among the first to expose how the structural economic changes of the 1970s and 1980s, including the declining industrial base of cities, the bifurcated low-wage and high-wage economy, and the geographic shift of jobs to the suburbs, manifested in spatial concentrations of poor, minority communities in inner-city neighborhoods with high rates of unemployment. Because past discrimination had led African Americans to be concentrated in the central-city neighborhoods and manufacturing occupations that were especially hard-hit by economic restructuring, these economic changes had a particularly deleterious impact on this group, whose socio-spatial isolation from the economic mainstream reached critical levels through the movement of middle- and higher-income African American families to the suburbs after the passage of fair housing laws. Wilson argued that this exodus deprived inner-city communities of critical resources and role models. William Julius Wilson, *The Truly Disadvantaged: The Inner City, the Underclass, and Public Policy* (Chicago: University of Chicago Press, 1987). Though emphasizing a different causal mechanism—racial segregation itself rather than middle-class flight—Douglas Massey and Nancy Denton also examined the socioeconomic dislocation and disadvantage associated with growing up in racially segregated areas of concentrated poverty. Douglas Massey and Nancy Denton,

American Apartheid (Cambridge, MA: Harvard University Press, 1993). Following these seminal works, the turn of the century witnessed a burgeoning literature focused on inequality of neighborhood conditions and their impacts on residents' life chances. For a review, see Ingrid Gould Ellen and Margery Austin Turner, "Do Neighborhoods Matter? Assessing Recent Evidence," *Housing Policy Debate* 8, no. 4 (1997): 833–866. While acknowledging the racial dimension of poverty concentration, many of these subsequent works have focused more broadly on how living and growing up in low-income neighborhoods affects a number of different economic and social outcomes. For example, Dreier, Mollenkopf, and Swanstrom demonstrate how rising economic segregation, combined with jurisdictional fragmentation and the devolution of responsibility for service provision to localities, has left many low-income neighborhoods struggling to provide the services their residents need to survive and get ahead in life. Peter Dreier, John Mollenkopf, and Todd Swanstrom, *Place Matters: Metropolitics for the Twenty-First Century.* 3rd ed. (Lawrence: University Press of Kansas, 2014). In his comprehensive study of neighborhood effects in Chicago, Robert J. Sampson demonstrated the powerful effect of concentrated poverty on behaviors and outcomes ranging from violence and incarceration to verbal skills and employment chances. Robert J. Sampson, *Great American City: Chicago and the Enduring Neighborhood Effect* (Chicago: University of Chicago Press, 2012).

28. As just one example of the renewed interest in studies done around the Moving to Opportunity pilot project, a series of articles were published in *The New York Times* this year. See, for instance, David Leonhardt, Amanda Cox, and Claire Cain Miller, "The Upshot: An Atlas of Upward Mobility Shows Paths Out of Poverty," *New York Times*, May 24, 2015, and the linked interactive feature published on the same date, "The Best and Worst Places to Grow Up: How Your Area Compares," http://www.nytimes.com/2015/05/04/upshot/an-atlas-of-upward-mobility-shows-paths-out-of-poverty.html?_r=0&abt=0002&abg=1.

29. Sean F. Reardon, Lindsay Fox, and Joseph Townsend, "Neighborhood Income Composition by Race and Income, 1990–2009," *Annals of the American Academy of Political and Social Science* 600, no. 1 (2015): 78–92.

30. "[P]roperty tax-based local finance can also produce inequalities, and in particular can produce paths that worsen these inequalities. Consider a distressed city with low property values per person. In order to provide basic services, the city will need to charge very high property tax rates. This in turn could lead businesses (which typically pay more in taxes than they use in services) to migrate away, which in turn reduces the tax base, which in turn worsens services. This leads to an unvirtuous cycle." Richard K. Green, "Housing Markets, Prices, and Policies," in Nancy Brooks, Kieran Donaght, and Gerrit-Jan Knapp, eds., *The Oxford Handbook of Economics and Planning* (New York: Oxford University Press, 2012), 431.

31. Jonathan Rothwell, "Housing Costs, Zoning, and Access to High-Scoring Schools," (Washington, D.C.: The Brookings Institution, 2012), http://www.brookings.edu/research/papers/2012/04/19-school-inequality-rothwell.

32. Thomas B. Foster and Rachel Garshick Kleit, "The Changing Relationship Between Housing and Inequality, 1980–2010," *Housing Policy Debate* 25, no. 1 (2014): 16–40.

1.2 Narrating Inequality

Inequality is more than the series of interconnected facts laid out in the previous section; it is a discourse, for which housing is a central term. This discourse is of a dual nature: numeric and narrative. Here we summarize some of the key paths the discourse on inequality has taken—focusing on a short but telling governmental history of "middle-class economics" in the United States—and place them in relationship with other, seemingly unrelated facts to show how this discourse works.

1.2.1 Producing Data

Whether the facts collected and used in this discourse are quantitative or qualitative depends partly on who is measuring. Not surprisingly, different kinds of facts—here largely in the form of data sets—can be put to different kinds of uses. While private, for-profit organizations are more likely to collect and evaluate data as it relates to purchasing power and consumption habits, data are collected by governmental or non-governmental entities in order to define and legitimate policy options. For example, the Gini Coefficient—which ranges from 0 for a country where all citizens have identical incomes to 1 where all income goes to a single individual—is an important international comparative measure of inequality in this respect.[1] Certain trends however, described below, are pushing this type of data collection from long-established quantitative metrics into a more qualitative direction, with potential implications for the discourse on inequality, both nationally and internationally.

The Organization for Economic Co-operation and Development (OECD), an organization of leading industrialized nations known for measuring the gross domestic product (GDP), has recently added to its otherwise quantitative analysis of "income inequality and poverty" the more subjective layer of "well-being."[2] On the occasion of its fiftieth anniversary in 2011, the organization released a compendium of eight new indicators focused on this self-reported state of mind, all to further its mission of supporting not only economic growth, but "better policies for better lives."[3] In the United States, the Social Science Research Council has also taken up this search for alternative measures to the GDP. Its "Measure of America" initiative, launched in 2006, measures inequalities by congressional district, and focuses on three main indicators of the United Nations' Human Development Index.[4] It combines indicators of health, education, and standard of living into a single number between 0 and 10. Health is measured by life expectancy at birth; education by level of education; and standard of living by median income.

In contrast to the OECD, the World Bank—one of the main international organizations focused primarily on funding long-term development projects in high-poverty countries—has traditionally opted for a more straightforward approach. Its measure of poverty is not relational but absolute, premised on purchasing power parity: extreme poverty is defined as living with $1.25 a day or less, moderate poverty at $2 a day.[5] Since 2013, however, the World Bank's goal has also been framed in less absolute terms. The heading "Inequality and Shared Prosperity" has dominated its publications since the Bank launched its "Shared Prosperity Indicator" to measure income growth at the bottom 40 percent in each country, and its "Visualize Inequality" program to focus on childrens' "inequality of opportunity" [See HH: 2009].[6]

Perhaps predictably, the practices of US government agencies conform to these trends as well. The United States Census Bureau, part of the Department of Commerce, is the nation's key source of public data on demographic and economic change. Though it deals largely in quantitative data, the Census Bureau does cite the "middle class" as a prominent part of their narrative on inequality, despite or because of the difficulty in defining it [See HH: 1978].[7] Such a term lends a degree of productive ambiguity to the Bureau's data, since a vast majority of U.S. citizens self-define as middle class.[8]

Putting all of this and additional data to use, academic scholarship on inequality has recently proliferated, with Thomas Piketty's *Capital in the Twenty-First Century* receiving much attention. Though it contains a wealth of analysis, Piketty's decision to sidestep the potential problems associated with the term "middle class" is telling of a singular focus.[9] Given this emblematic bracketing out of cultural variables on the part of the economist, alongside the previously outlined implication of the state in the housing market and the similar patterns visible in the private sector, we choose to focus here on the discursive techniques used by governmental institutions.

1.2.2   Framing Data

Appropriately then, it is widely accepted that inequality, especially when construed as a threat to the "American Dream," is a defining issue of our time, as the following quotations related to the 2016 presidential campaign indicate:

> *Millions of our fellow citizens across the broad middle class feel as if the American Dream is now out of their reach. . . . Too many of the poor have lost hope that a path to a better life is within their grasp. While the last eight years have been pretty*

good ones for top earners, they've been a lost decade for the rest of America.[10]
—Jeb Bush, 2015

Today, more people are getting by, but they are still not getting ahead. At the same time, the top 25 hedge fund managers make more than all the kindergarten teachers in the country combined, and the top CEOs earn 300 times more than a typical American worker. It's time for everyday Americans to share in growth and prosperity.[11]
—Hillary Clinton, May 2014

Income inequality is a symptom of a bigger problem: opportunity inequality.[12]
—Marco Rubio, 2015

We live in one of the wealthiest countries on earth, yet children go hungry, veterans sleep out on the streets and senior citizens cannot afford their prescription drugs. This is what a rigged economic system looks like.[13]
—Bernie Sanders, 2015

Taken at face value, the exhortations of scholars and the talking points for would-be presidents evince a common understanding of inequality as a principally economic issue whose explanations are best framed by considerations of a nebulously defined middle class. Though finer points are debated, a consensus emerges about the basic nature of the problem at hand, which in turn dictates the nature of any possible solutions. This rhetorical loop defines the current limits of the discourse on inequality. But the fact nevertheless remains—as demonstrated quite specifically by housing—that understandings and usages of "inequality" as a call-to-action cannot be uniformly or exclusively filtered through an economic sieve; doing so presupposes the "economy" as an isolated phenomenon that takes precedence over all else.

1.2.3   Historicizing Data

Closer to the current policy-makers themselves, underlining this focus in its 2015 Annual Report, the Executive Office of the President's Council of Economic Advisors (CEA) highlights income inequality as a fundamental analytic required to understand and promote what the Obama Administration has called "middle-class economics."[14] The Economic Report of the President, intended primarily for a Congressional audience, is released annually by the CEA in order to explain, contextualize, and justify the Administration's domestic and international priorities for fiscal policy. In 2015, alongside productivity and participation, according to the CEA, inequality is a force to be reckoned with for those in charge of managing the United States of America's "well-being."[15]

In this, their mandated frame of mind, the CEA has characterized "A Brief History of Middle-Class Incomes in the Postwar Period" as fitting neatly into the following stages: "The Age of Shared Growth (1948–1973)," "The Age of Expanded Participation (1973–1995)," and "The Age of Productivity Recovery (1995–2013)."[16] Representative of dominant narratives on inequality today in both its content and its structure (where a "brief history" of four pages ostensibly provides sufficient context for a 414-page manual of contemporary policy assessments and proposals), a very particular story emerges in the CEA report—one that has been told and retold in different forms. Upon further inspection, however, its limiting assumptions are revealed.

1.2.3.1   "The Age of Shared Growth (1948–1973)"

The report's periodization picks up in 1948, just

two years after the CEA was founded as part of the Employment Act of 1946. This was precisely the time when the idea of "the economy" was beginning to be discussed at all as an object of analysis in its own right.[17] [See HH: 1933] This is an unlikely coincidence, since, as the CEA indicates, the newly networked field of technology, materials, and presumptively shared understandings of the middle-class road ahead facilitated a veritable explosion of growth for the U.S. economy immediately after the war.

In response to unprecedented rates of urbanization, and framed by a perceived communist threat abroad, the federal government crafted a series of policies meant not only to manage but also to distribute this growth—both spatially and financially—among the members of the aspirational middle class.[18] Though the 1956 Interstate Highway Act is the most well known, the U.S. Housing Act of 1949 was perhaps the most comprehensive and far-reaching of these efforts. Principally known for its emphasis on the reform of urban housing conditions through slum clearance and urban renewal programs, the act also drastically increased the federal backing of mortgage insurance, ramping up the government's long-standing policy of homeownership promotion above other types of housing tenure [See HH: 1944, 1949, 1952, 1962, 1973, 2009].[19] By most economic measures (although importantly not by others) income inequality was soon at an all-time low.[20] In the 1950s and 1960s, Americans' average annual incomes increased. However it was the lowest-earning fifth of families that experienced the highest average increases, while the top 5 percent experienced the lowest.[21] The homeownership rate, accordingly, increased from 44 percent in 1940 to 55 percent in 1950 and 62 percent in 1960.[22] Due in part to this expansion of access to homeownership, the share of total wealth held by the least wealthy 90 percent of the population increased from 22 percent in 1940 to 32 percent in 1976.[23]

According to the CEA's narrative, this rising tide of shared growth continued until 1973. But the shape of inequality during this period begs closer scrutiny, as post-war growth put increasing pressure on the idea of the middle class as an attainable aspiration for all. The report's authors acknowledge that they exclude "non-economic dimensions" in favor of a focus on productivity, income inequality, and participation, and that those crafting domestic policy should take this into account.[24] Nevertheless, the discursive segregation persists. Record low levels of income inequality during the 1950s did not exist in economic isolation. Instead they must be thought of together with inequalities based on gender, race, and sexuality— the separate-but-equal cul-de-sacs, highways, and lunch counters that made "shared growth" with one's middle-class neighbors imaginable at all [See HH: 1949, 2012].

In marked contrast to the generally positive picture painted by the CEA, discrimination and segregation in the housing market not only persisted, but were produced and maintained by governmental programs. Redlining in loan distribution meant that mixed-race or all-black neighborhoods were considered high-risk in governmentally insured mortgage programs, which effectively meant that no loans were available in those areas.[25] On a private level, restrictive covenants in housing developments placed limits on who could live where and how they could do so on individual parcels.[26] Accordingly, the post-war expansion of access to housing wealth largely excluded black households, with strong repercussions for the intergenerational transmission of wealth inequality.[27] In 1950, 57 percent of white households owned their homes compared to 35 percent of non-white households. By 1970, these numbers were 65 percent and 42 percent, respectively.[28] Among all housing units financed by Veterans' Affairs and FHA loans between 1946 and 1959, less than 2 percent were bought by black households.[29]

In public housing, which was shrinking in avail-ability during this period, access to shared growth was not only more limited, it was increasingly segregated as well.[30] In Los Angeles, the composition of public housing ten-ants shifted from 55 percent white and 30 percent black in 1947, to 14 percent white and 65 percent black (with 19 percent of Mexican origin) by 1959.[31] In Chicago, 60 per-cent of Chicago Housing Authority tenants were black in 1948, compared to 95 percent in 1984 [See HH: 1954, 1962]. These post-war spatial arrangements were also di-visive along gender lines. Inner-city public housing pop-ulations in large cities like Chicago were quickly shifting from mainly two-parent families to households headed by females and receiving public assistance.[32] Meanwhile, suburban environments were criticized for isolating wom-en physically and socially by distancing them from jobs, childcare services, and opportunities for social interaction and support, while tying them to traditional norms of do-mesticity.[33] These segregations simultaneously reinforced comparable discrimination against people of any gender with non-normative sexual orientations. Though the nar-rative of shared growth and decreasing income inequali-ty in the postwar U.S. economy is accurate in many ways, the contours of the middle class among whom this growth was distributed were in flux, and embedded inequalities of all kinds were far from mitigated by over-determined notions of economic growth.

1.2.3.2   "The Age of Expanded Participation (1973–1995)"
As a result of cultural shifts responding to some of these very inequalities, the CEA points toward "expand-ed participation" as the dominant economic paradigm for the period from 1973 to 1995.[34] With the legal incorpora-tion of women, racial minorities, and other historically marginalized groups into the market economy, globaliza-tion was coming into focus as a phenomenon pertaining to

all, and the terms through which it was beginning to be articulated were largely ecological in nature [See HH: 1970]. Despite attention paid to environmental causes, as well as the Cold War's geopolitical repercussions, the techniques of globalism—namely deregulation and management of the worldwide recession—were increasingly relegated to the realm of finance. The CEA paints expanded participation as exclusive to the market economy, bracketing out the other sociocultural transformations that facilitated it. President Richard Nixon's moratorium on federal subsidies for the construction of public housing and the introduction in 1974 of a precursor to the contemporary housing voucher program are two of the more obvious signs of this shift [See HH: 1973].[35]

President Ronald Reagan continued this move from brick-and-mortar subsidies to tenant-based housing allowances—a shift taking place across advanced industrialized countries, in line with generally decreased faith in welfare-state services, an increased reliance on the private market to fulfill this role, and a growing emphasis on consumer choice [See HH: 1986].[36] Precisely at this time, when low-income households lacked the financial security that had made housing a sound investment for the middle class before them, the U.S. and other advanced industrialized countries began to promote low-income homeownership.[37]

Taking these factors into account generates friction with received narratives of baby-boomer prosperity as reinforced by the CEA. Not only was the underclass in a more precarious position than it had been in previous generations, but its ever more limited options were increasingly determined through according to the metric of security. If, during this era as defined by the CEA, participation was expanding in the middle-class workforce, for those less fortunate it was also expanding in the nascent prison-industrial complex. Increasingly, housing in the

United States included not only single family homes and multi-family apartments, but cellblocks—with the incarceration rate increasing fourfold since the early 1970s.[38] The institution of punitive drug laws, beginning in New York State in 1973 and spreading across the country, was a major contributor to the trend. Drug convictions were heavily concentrated in inner cities—spaces largely excluded from the "shared growth" of the immediate postwar era.[39] African American men born between 1945 and 1949—a demographic concentrated in said areas—had a 10 percent probability of being imprisoned by the age of 34. Among those born thirty years later, this likelihood rose to 27 percent. For white men, the probabilities were, respectively, 1.4 percent and 5.4 percent.[40]

The CEA does not once use the words "crime," "prison," or "incarceration" in its report. Admittedly, these issues fall outside their stated purview. And yet, this purview—assuming an economy with a traceable exterior—is itself historically informed by inequalities of all kinds. Received narratives of increasing participation in the market should be read not simply alongside, but rather within narratives of decreasing participation in civic life.

1.2.3.3   "The Age of Productivity Recovery (1995–2013)"

After decades of decreasing productivity and increasing participation, the CEA credits the incorporation of information technology for its most recent era of "productivity recovery" and the concomitant improvements in the stagnating economy. However, the CEA also notes that income inequality worsened during this period—a trend which began during the financialized, deregulated "Age of Expanded Participation."[41]

Following through on tendencies from the previous decade, welfare reform in the U.S. was one way that the federal government sought to better capitalize on the recent expansion of the marketplace while avoiding any

additional direct provision of aid to those who fell outside of its assumed embrace.[42] This move was complemented by adjustments to housing policy. HOPE VI legislation ("Homeownership Opportunities for People Everywhere"), launched by the Clinton administration in 1992, aimed to reduce concentrated poverty through the public-private redevelopment of distressed public housing projects into lower-density, mixed-income communities [See 1.3.3.4, HH: 1994].

Reinforcing the implications of this policy, new mechanisms emerged within lending practice for increased productivity in the expanded, financialized market. Subprime loans are designed to provide borrowing opportunities to individuals with low credit ratings who are unable or have difficulty obtaining prime (conventional) loans. Because lenders perceive these borrowers as more likely to default on their loans than borrowers with higher credit ratings, subprime mortgages typically impose higher interest rates and steeper fees and penalties than conventional mortgages.[43] The subprime loan market increased in value from around $43 billion in 1994 to $385 billion in 2003.[44] In low-income, predominantly minority communities—the same ones largely marginalized from CEA's "shared growth" and, subsequently, cajoled into participating in a less-and-less regulated market—the share of home-buying loans that were sub-prime increased from around 2 percent in 1993 to 13 percent in 2001.[45] There also, the share of refinanced loans that were sub-prime was 20 percentage points higher than the share for affluent, predominantly white neighborhoods in 2001.[46] Black and Hispanic households were nearly two times as likely to experience or be at serious risk of foreclosure compared to white households during the housing crash.[47]

Accordingly, for a contemporary audience, the CEA's use of the word "recovery" for a period bridging the "Great Recession" of 2008–2013 deserves a second look [See HH: 2010]. With the implication being that productivity, understood in its established technological, growth-oriented postwar frame, can or should be "recovered," one is again reminded of the suburban communities heralded during the "Age of Shared Growth"—which are now more widely distributed, diverse in size and demographic makeup, and yet increasingly divided along economic lines.[48] The country is seeing a decline in the proportion of suburbs that can be categorized as middle class—cleaving from the imaginary undergirding of the CEA's narrative. Instead there exists a growing disparity between affluent and poor suburbs. Between 2000 and 2011, in the suburbs of the largest metropolitan areas, the number of people living below the poverty line grew by 64 percent. In comparison, the impoverished population in cities grew by 29 percent.[49] Whereas thirty years ago, these cities and their suburbs hosted equal shares of immigrants, by 2010, more than half of the country's immigrants were living in suburbs (compared to 33 percent living in cities).[50]

Though it helped get Bill Clinton elected to the U.S. presidency just before this period began, it turns out that the central issue was not just, as he famously said, "the economy, stupid."[51] With growth, participation, and productivity also comes marginalization. But this story does not fit neatly into the narrative given within the CEA report.

In a period that has now been labeled "The Great Acceleration," in reference to human-generated climate change, this suffusion of the sociocultural and environmental context with economic thinking must be understood as constitutive of the changing—and accelerating—nature of inequality as such.[52] Seeing income inequality as both an egregious and insufficient marker of contemporary conditions cannot be dismissed as self-contradicting. Gay rights, seemingly improving at a rate unforeseen by many, counts as its most influential champions the same multinational corporations that emerged out of and for the suburbanized, reurbanized, and deregulated middle-class economics–driven conditions; conditions that enforced segregation and persecution in the first place.[53] This is the nature of many contemporary structural contradictions. In its seemingly pragmatic focus on middle-class economics, the CEA's oft-repeated narrative ultimately makes today's most pressing problem more, not less, difficult to understand. Inequality is complex, and complex stories are not easy to tell. Given its continued emphasis on homeownership, the story of "the American Dream" shows how design—traditionally brought in as a solution to problems—helps elucidate them as well. Unfortunately, in this elucidation, the agents of design themselves are often implicated.

1. "GINI index (World Bank Estimate)," The World Bank, accessed June 15, 2015, http://data.worldbank.org/indicator/SI.POV.GINI; "OECD Income Distribution Database (IDD): Gini, Poverty, Income, Methods and Concepts," Organisation for Economic Co-operation and Development, accessed June 15, 2015, http://www.oecd.org/social/income-distribution-database.htm; "Income: Narrative (Middle Class)," U.S. Census Bureau, accessed June 15, 2015, http://www.census.gov/hhes/www/income/data/inequality/middleclass.html.

2. OECD, *Better Life Initiative: Compendium of OECD Well-Being Indicator*, OECD, 2011.

3. The criteria range from housing, to civic engagement, to work-life balance. Through a web-based interactive tool, "Your Better Life Index," users can weigh the criteria according to what's important to them, and then compare their country's to other countries' performance. www.oecd.org/betterlifeindex.

4. Sarah Burd-Sharps and Kristen Lewis, *Geographies of Opportunity: Ranking Well-Being by Congressional District*, The Measure of America Series of the Social Science Research Council, April 2015, www.measureofamerica.org/congressional-districts-2015.

5. The United States, too, uses an absolute measure to define a poverty level, mainly to determine eligibility for certain government programs. It builds on a definition set up by the Department of Agriculture in 1963/64, which multiplies the cost of adequate nutrition/food by three. See "Frequently Asked Questions Related to the Poverty Guidelines and Poverty," U.S. Department of Health and Human Services, accessed April 24, 2015, http://aspe.hhs.gov/poverty/faq.cfm#share.

6. "Visualize Inequality," The World Bank, accessed June 15, 2015, http://www1.worldbank.org/poverty/visualizeinequality/.

7. "The Census Bureau does not have an official definition of the 'middle class,' but [it] does derive several measures related to the distribution of income and income inequality. These are the shares of aggregate income received by households (or other income recipient units such as families) and the Gini index (or index of income concentration)." "Income: Narrative (Middle Class)," U.S. Census Bureau, accessed August 10, 2015, http://www.census.gov/hhes/www/income/data/inequality/middleclass.html.

8. "Nearly nine out of 10 people consider themselves middle class, as a recent survey by the Pew Research Center found, regardless of whether their incomes languish near the

poverty line or skim the top stratum of earners." Pew Research Center, "Most Say Government Policies Since Recession Have Done Little to Help Middle Class, Poor," March 2015, cited in Patricia Cohen, "Middle Class but Feeling Economically Insecure," *New York Times,* April 11, 2015.

9. "It is not my purpose to police dictionaries of linguistic usage. When it comes to designating social groups, everyone is right and wrong at the same time. Everyone has good reasons for using certain terms but is wrong to denigrate the terms used by others. My definition of "middle class" (as the "middle" 40 percent [of total income]) is highly contestable, since the income (or wealth) of everyone in the group is, by construction, above the median for the society in question. . . . [T]he definition I have given seems to me to correspond more closely to common usage: the expression 'middle class' is generally used to refer to people who are doing distinctly better than the bulk of the population yet still a long way from the true 'elite.' Yet all such designations are open to challenge, and there is no need for me to take a position on this delicate issue, which is not just linguistic but also political." Thomas Piketty, *Capital in the Twenty-First Century* (Cambridge, MA: Harvard University Press, 2014), 251.

10. This is an excerpt from the mission statement of the PAC Right to Rise, which was founded by former Florida Governor Jeb Bush, who declared his candidacy for the Republican nomination on June 15, 2015. "What we Believe," Right to Rise, accessed June 15, 2015, https://righttorisepac.org/what-we-believe/.

11. This is an excerpt from Hillary Clinton's website Hillary for America. The former Secretary of State declared her candidacy for the Democratic nomination for president on April 12, 2015. "The Four Fights: Building an economy for tomorrow, " Hillary for America, accessed June 15, 2015, https://www.hillaryclinton.com/the-four-fights/economy-of-tomorrow/.

12. This is quoted from "Transcript: Freedom Partners Forum: Ted Cruz, Rand Paul and Marco Rubio in Conversation with ABC's Jonathan Karl." *ABC News,* January 26, 2015, http://abcnews.go.com/Politics/transcript-freedom-partners-forum-ted-cruz-rand-paul/story?id=28491534. Florida Senator Marco Rubio announced his candidacy for the Republican nomination for president on April 13, 2015, about four months after this forum took place.

13. This is an excerpt from the website of New Hampshire Senator Bernie Sanders who announced his candidacy for the Democratic nomination for president on May 26, 2015. "Issues: Income and Wealth Inequality," Bernie 2016, accessed June 15, 2015, https://berniesanders.com/issues/income-and-wealth-inequality/.

14. Council of Economic Advisers (CEA), *Economic Report of the President* (Washington, D.C., 2015), https://www.whitehouse.gov/sites/default/files/docs/cea_2015_erp_complete.pdf.

15. In the CEA Report, "well-being" appears in seven places, not always economically speaking. In fact it seems to be one of the principal semantic routes out of economics and into broader discussions (or at least hints therein) for the authors. Re: Middle Class, see page 29: "The ultimate test of an economy's performance is the well-being of its middle class".

16. CEA, *Report,* 29.

17. Timothy Mitchell, "Economentality: How the Future Entered Government," *Critical Inquiry* 40, no. 4: 483. It is telling that the section of the Employment Act of 1946 that authorized the CEA doesn't use the noun "economy" once; instead, the qualifier "economic" is used repeatedly.

18. In 1950, 59 percent of housing units in the U.S. were located in metropolitan areas; 59 percent of these units were in central cities and 41 percent in suburbs. By 1973, 67 percent of housing units were in metropolitan areas; 47 percent of these were in central cities and 53 percent were in suburbs. See U.S. Census Bureau, *Statistical Abstract of the United States: 1976* (97th ed.), Table No. 1269: Housing Units, by Geographic Region: 1950 to 1974 (Washington, D.C., 1976).

19. Manuel Aalbers and Brett Christophers, "Centring Housing in Political Economy," *Housing, Theory and Society* 31, no. 4 (2014): 376.

20. Incomes rose among all economic classes between 1947 and 1979. See, for instance, Peter Dreier, John Mollenkopf, and Todd Swanstrom. *Place Matters: Metropolitics for the Twenty-First Century,* 3rd ed. (Lawrence: University Press of Kansas, 2014), 16.

21. Pew Research Center, *Fewer, Poorer, Gloomier: The Lost Decade of the Middle Class* (Washington, D.C.: Pew Social & Demographic Trends, 2012), 59. http://www.pewsocialtrends.org/files/2012/08/pew-social-trends-lost-decade-of-the-middle-class.pdf.

22. U.S. Census Bureau, *Statistical Abstracts Section 31: 20th Century Statistics*, Table No. 1428: Housing Units – Historical Trends for Selected Characteristics: 1940 to 1997 (Washington, D.C., 1999), accessed June 5, 2015, https://www.census.gov/prod/99pubs/99statab/sec31.pdf.

23. Among other factors, increased access to pensions also played a role in this growth in wealth, which reached a high of 36 percent in 1986 before eventually declining to 23 percent in 2012. Emmanuel Saez and Gabriel Zucman, "Wealth Inequality in the United States since 1913: Evidence from Capitalized Income Tax Data," *NBER Working Paper 20625* (2014), accessed June 5, 2015, http://gabriel-zucman.eu/files/SaezZucman2014.pdf.

24. CEA, *Report*, 31.

25. For a general history of suburbanization and its racial components, see Kenneth Jackson, *Crabgrass Frontier: The Suburbanization of the United States* (New York: Oxford University Press, 1985).

26. For histories of restrictive covenants, see Marc Weiss, *The Rise of the Community Builders: The American Real Estate Industry and Urban Land Planning* (New York: Columbia University Press, 1987); Richard R.W. Brooks and Carol M. Rose, *Saving the Neighborhood: Racially Restrictive Covenants, Law, and Social Norms* (Cambridge, MA: Harvard University Press, 2013).

27. "African-Americans were frozen out of the greatest wealth building opportunities in American history. From the Homestead Act in the 1860s, to education and homeownership opportunities provided by the GI Bill and the Federal Housing Administration, to redlining through contemporary discrimination in housing markets, to the segregation tax on housing appreciation, major government sponsored wealth building opportunities helped foster America's middle class and created much wealth. Meanwhile, these same policies and practices left the African-American community behind at the starting gate. Inheritance of our racial past thus becomes an integral part of the wealth narrative." Thomas M. Shapiro, "Race, Homeownership and Wealth," *Washington University Journal of Law & Policy* 20 (2006): 67–68.

28. U.S. Census Bureau, *Statistical Abstract of the United States: 1973* (94th ed.), Table No. 1167: Occupied Housing Units – Tenure, and Population per Occupied Unit, by Race of Household Head and by Residence: 1900 to 1970 (Washington, D.C., 1973).

29. Dreier et al., *Place Matters*, 129.

30. Though the 1949 Housing Act authorized the construction of 810,000 units of public housing by 1955, only 320,000 had been constructed by 1960. Raymond A. Mohl, "Shifting Patterns of American Urban Policy since 1900," Arnold R. Hirsch and Raymond A. Mohl, eds. *Urban Policy in Twentieth Century America* (New Brunswick: Rutgers University Press, 1993), 15.

31. Richard Rothstein, "Race and Public Housing: Revisiting the Federal Role," *Poverty & Race* 21, no. 6 (2010): 1–16.

32. For histories of this trajectory, see Bradford D. Hunt, *Blueprint for Disaster: The Unraveling of Chicago Public Housing* (Chicago: University of Chicago Press, 2009) and Lawrence J. Vale, *Purging the Poorest: Public Housing and the Design Politics of Twice-Cleared Communities* (Chicago: University of Chicago Press, 2013).

33. Susan S. Fainstein, "Feminism and Planning: Theoretical Issues," in *Gender and Planning: A Reader*, eds. Susan S. Fainstein and Lisa J. Servon, 120–138 (New Brunswick, NJ: Rutgers University Press, 2005).

34. CEA, *Report*, 31.

35. Sandra J. Newman, "Housing Allowances American Style: The Housing Choice Voucher Program" *Housing Allowances in a Comparative Perspective*, ed. P.A. Kemp (Bristol: Policy Press, 2007), 87–106.

36. Reagan cut the budget for public and Section 8 housing by half in his first year in office alone. Dreier et al., *Place Matters*, 154.

37. For histories of this shift toward policies promoting home-ownership for low-income households, see for example, Michael Harloe, *The People's Home? Social Rented Housing in Europe & America* (New York: Wiley, 1995); Peter Malpass, *Housing and the Welfare State: The Development of Housing Policy in Britain* (New York: Palgrave MacMillan, 2005).

38. "From 1973 to 2009, the state and federal prison populations that are the main focus of this study rose steadily, from about 200,000 to 1.5 million, declining slightly in the following 4 years. In addition to the men and women serving prison time for felonies, another 700,000 are held daily in local jails.... The U.S. penal population of 2.2 million adults is

the largest in the world.... The U.S. rate of incarceration, with nearly 1 of every 100 adults in prison or jail, is 5 to 10 times higher than rates in Western Europe and other democracies....The growth in incarceration rates in the United States over the past 40 years is historically unprecedented and internationally unique." Jeremy Travis, Bruce Western, and F. Stevens Redburn, *The Growth of Incarceration in the United States: Exploring Causes and Consequences* (Washington, D.C.: The National Academies Press, 2014), 1–2.

39. H.A. Thompson, "Why Mass Incarceration Matters: Rethinking Crisis, Decline, and Transformation in Postwar American history," *The Journal of American History* 97, no. 3 (2010): 703–734.

40. The inequalities produced by high incarceration rates among African American men is often called "invisible inequality" as this population is isolated from mainstream society while incarcerated and often not counted in conventional measures of unemployment. Bruce Western and Becky Pettit, "Incarceration and Social Inequality," *Daedalus* 139, no. 3 (2010): 8–19.

41. CEA, *Report*, 31–32.

42. In 1996, the Temporary Assistance for Needy Families (TANF) was introduced to reduce previous entitlements while instituting work requirements for welfare recipients. The number of recipients decreased by 58 percent between 1995 and 2010; and in 2010, only a quarter of children living in poverty lived in households receiving cash transfers. Dreier et al., *Place Matters*, 290.

43. Alex F. Schwartz, *Housing Policy in the United States*, 1st ed. (New York: Routledge, 2006), 236.

44. Joint Center for Housing Studies, *The State of the Nation's Housing 2004* (Cambridge, MA: Harvard University, 2004), 16.

45. Sub-prime loans accounted for 28 percent of refinancing loans to these borrowers in 2001. Joint Center for Housing Studies, *The State of the Nation's Housing 2004*, 19.

46. Ibid.

47. Debbie Gruenstein Bocian and Robert G. Quercia, *Lost Ground, 2011: Disparities in Mortgage Lending and Foreclosures* (Center for Responsible Lending, 2011), 4, http://www.responsiblelending.org/mortgage-lending/research-analysis/Lost-Ground-2011.pdf. Further, in 2000, high-income black households were more likely to receive subprime refinanced loans (35 percent) than low-income white households (24 percent). Schwartz, *Housing Policy in the United States*, 237.

48. Dreier et al., *Place Matters*, 38–47.

49. The poverty threshold is established by the U.S. Census Bureau. Elizabeth Kneebone and Alan Berube, "Confronting Suburban Poverty in America: Executive Summary," Metropolitan Policy Program at Brookings, 2013, accessed June 7, 2015, http://confrontingsuburbanpoverty.org/wp-content/uploads/2013/05/Brookings_Toolkit_Executive-Summary.pdf.

50. Audrey Singer, *Migration and the Metropolis* (Washington, D.C.: The Brookings Institution: 2013). http://www.brookings.edu/research/articles/2013/04/migration-metropolis-singer.

51. Michael Kelly, "The 1992: The Democrats – Clinton and Bush Compete to Be Champion of Change; Democrat Fights Perceptions of Bush Gain," *New York Times*, October 31, 1992.

52. See Will Steffen, Paul J. Critzen, John R. McNeill, "The Anthropocene: Are Humans Now Overwhelming the Great Forces of Nature?" *AMBIO* 36 (December 2007): 614–621.

53. New York Times Editorial Board, "Big Business's Critical Role on Anti-Gay Laws," *New York Times*, April 4, 2015. For more detailed information about this case, see the court's final decision for "Obergefell v Hodges" at http://www.supremecourt.gov/opinions/14pdf/14-556_3204.pdf."

1.3 Designing Inequality

The narratives and data that make inequality intelligible are made tangible through architecture. That architecture both reflects and helps produce the prevailing social and economic order is not surprising. Buildings embody the rules, regulations, and imaginations that called this order into being. Here we aim to identify some of the ways in which architecture has intersected with political and financial efforts through program and form, types and styles. If architecture contributes to socioeconomic disparities, might it also do the reverse?

1.3.1 Easy Explanations

No building type or architectural style creates inequality as such. Assuming so would be to grossly over-estimate architecture's power. The Pruitt-Igoe public housing complex in St. Louis, designed in 1951 by Leinweber, Yamasaki & Hellmuth and demolished beginning in 1973, serves us well to make this point. Recent scholarship has shown that it was not the high-rise elevators or the open-air galleries that led to "failed architecture." Rather, it was the unemployment, racial segregation, and the concentration of single-parent households among its residents, as well as—among other factors—severe cost limits in construction and operations dependent on minimal rents which all led to its demise.[1]

If architecture does not create inequality as

such, however, it does have the power to naturalize it. As was the case with Pruitt-Igoe, architecture can provide an "easy explanation," and an excuse for the inequalities that exist within it. Creating new architecture thus also provides a relatively easy, if illusory, solution to social and economic problems.[2] Projecting a new building is much simpler than solving problems of poverty, substance abuse, unemployment, and crime. Physical determinism of this sort, common during the urban renewal of the 1950s and 1960s, is no different than the assumptions underlying the earliest New Deal clearance projects, where the eradication of "slums" or "blighted areas" was imagined to solve the social, economic, and public health problems of the people living therein. In this sense they were no different than the more recent redevelopments of high-rise public housing superblocks as low-rise neighborhoods.[3] Although few of the people displaced by redevelopment ever actually move into the new buildings, the proposed new models of housing—based on minimum dimensions, natural light and ventilation, and access to open space, to cite just a few design indicators—have repeatedly been envisaged as solutions to inequality in their own right.[4]

So while new or modified architectural types are often suggested as an easy response to inequality, in reality the uses, associations, and meanings of building types change. The story of the loft building is a well-known example. A space for industrial production in the late nineteenth-century, the high ceilings, large windows, and open floor plans became not only the symbol of, but the model for new construction of high-end residential projects.[5] Another telling example: seen as a sign of bourgeois decadence in the postwar period, ornament was stripped from nineteenth-century façades, only to return a few decades later as a sign of human scale, friendliness, and community values.[6] Even the high-rise tower and the slab enjoy a new popularity. Had Pruitt-Igoe been privatized

and renovated instead of demolished, it might today be a site of relatively affluent residents enjoying well-planned apartments and excellent views. This is precisely what has been happening through the privatization of some of London's council (or public) housing, for instance with the Trellick Tower. Once known as the "tower of terror," its Brutalist design is now a site of "authentic" inner city living for young professionals who can afford the price.[7] Some will see rising real estate values in formerly off-market housing as a positive development leading to improved quality of life and financial empowerment for its residents. Others will object to this as discriminatory and unfair gentrification, undermining a project's original goal of providing housing in central locations for those unable to pay market rate. In either case, what is clear is that architecture cannot be considered independently of the policies, social relations, and financial arrangements to which it is attached and through which it is made.

1.3.2   Standards
One of the key ways in which the policy, finance, and design of housing intersect is in the writing of zoning regulations and building codes. Zoning rules, which govern permissible land uses, were first legalized in the United States through a Supreme Court ruling in 1926. Codes, regulations, standards, and guidelines were drafted to protect private property and public health. Hence, most are premised on what was, and often still is, considered decent and sanitary: the division of public and private spaces, the separation of parents' and children's rooms, or the integration of a full bathroom and kitchen into the dwelling. These protections were subsequently incorporated into underwriting standards used by banks [See HH: 1939].[8] The legal language of regulations and standards regarding what a dwelling unit is and how it is to be used pertains to us all, irrespective of income, cultur-

al background, or lifestyle, to this day [See 1.1.3]. On one level, these standards have thus led to far greater equality (in terms of homogeneity) in how the rich, poor, and all those in between, live. A legal bedroom in the United States is required to meet certain criteria, irrespective of whether its construction was financed through tax credits or through a cash payment made via overseas shell companies: it may not be narrower than 9'-4" feet, or less than 110 square feet in area, must have access to natural light and air, and contain a closet 2 feet deep and 5 feet wide.[9]

At the same time, standards and regulations have become the instrument of choice to maintain segregation by income or race. By stipulating minimum lot sizes (1 acre, for example) and the maximum number of units per lot (one, perhaps) a town can easily write out entire populations through its zoning ordinances without explicitly saying so. By virtue of the size of the parcel of land, the type of building that is allowable on it, and how it may be used, a zoning code can effectively lead to the construction of generous single-family homes unaffordable to anyone below a certain income range.[10] This reality is the basis of a federal consent ruling brought against Westchester County, New York, in 2009, for failure to comply with fair housing obligations that came with federal funding, which the county had received for decades. The county's suburban towns have less than 2 percent African-American residents, whereas for the county overall (which includes more urban settings such as Yonkers) that number is 13 percent. Despite generous federal incentives that were given with the court ruling, the county has stalled its construction of affordable, multi-family housing, arguing that this is federal overreach into local autonomy.[11] Standards can thus cut two ways: they can aim to advance equality and fairness, or be used precisely toward the opposite end. While the actions of Westchester County can easily be ruled to constitute deliberate discrimination, the June 2015 Supreme

Court ruling in *Texas Department of Housing and Community Affairs v. The Inclusive Communities Project* states that certain policy decisions, even if unintentional, create a "disparate impact" on discrimination in housing, and are therefore illegal under the Fair Housing Act.[12]

Historically, rather than being perceived as furthering social equality, the minimum standards written into zoning and building codes in the postwar period were often equated with a type of top-down standardization that stifled individual expression and choice. "Diversity" of design, use, and economic standing became the overarching goal, at least for cities, as advanced by Jane Jacobs and other critics, and was pitted against enforced "sameness."[13] A generally positively construed diversity remains a key term in housing policy debates today, with its relationship to economic and social inequality unresolved. That is: diversity is advanced in lieu of any substantive dialogue about inequality or affordability. A case in point is the "Making Room" initiative, launched in 2009 by the Citizens' Housing and Planning Council (CHPC). Its goal is to reform regulations in New York City today in order to enable the production of housing that would better match the reality of how today's households live. CHPC is focused in particular on those regulations tied to normative definitions such as "family" which limit the production of both housing for single adults or nontraditional larger households; they point to the fact that two parents and their children constitute only 17 percent of New York City's households. Another of CHPC's targets are regulations that prohibit a combination of commercial and residential uses, despite a rise in people working from home. As realistically minded as these efforts are, it is important to note that such initiatives tread precisely on the standards that have their origins in leveling the playing field of real estate development, advancing quality, and protecting those with little or no power to survive in the open market.[14]

1.3.3   Mixed Results

New forms of spatial organization linked to codes, regulations, and design guidelines, have often been linked to new models of real estate development. The housing built by the federal Public Works Administration (PWA)—a pilot program whose projects led to the institutionalization of public housing in 1937—was intrinsically connected to the modern housing movement inspired by European housing models. The Labor Housing Conference linked its advocacy for a non-commercial, non market–based housing program to forms of collective living that would follow a new, nontraditional aesthetic and provide amenities including swimming pools and other communal facilities [See HH: 1934].[15] Sixty years later, with the redevelopment of public housing through HOPE VI, the strategy of linking advocacy for a new form of housing—mixed-income and market-based—to a specific planning and design idea, has not been any different. The urban design and architectural paradigm articulated by the Congress of the New Urbanism was linked to the Department of Housing and Urban Development (HUD)'s initiative to promote a real-estate model that minimized, on the surface, direct public involvement in housing, and instead prioritized private financing, ownership, and management of mixed-income housing.[16]

The program was implemented differently in different cities. By 2013, HOPE VI had distributed 262 revitalization grants and 285 demolition-only grants throughout the country for an approximate total of $6.7 billion [See HH: 1994].[17] Chicago, the city with one of the most iconic collections of high-rise developments, was one of the cities to embrace HOPE VI most emphatically [See HH: 1947]. The city's "Plan for Transformation," launched in 2000, targeted a unit mix consisting of one-third public housing, one-third affordable housing, and one-third market-rate housing in new construction [See HH: 1954, 1962].[18]

Residents displaced by the redevelopment received vouchers to rent from private landlords elsewhere, and those who wished to return were asked to reapply.

As an example of how development and design ambitions worked together, the redevelopment goal of the ABLA Homes into Roosevelt Square on Chicago's Near-West Side was to create roughly 2,400 units on the 100-acre, 35-block area in five phases. Three- and six-family buildings were selected in reference to earlier Chicago building types, working in accordance with New Urbanist principles that emphasize the public realm of the street. As one of many architectural firms involved in the project writes: "Vintage architectural elements found in typical Chicago neighborhoods bring a historical flavor to this new community."[19]

Critiques of the role of New Urbanism in HOPE VI, many focusing on Chicago, have been multiple from its inception. Some contend its spatial determinism is no different than that of the modern movement.[20] Others decry its conjuring of an idea of "community" based not on people, but on place.[21] Still others highlight its indifference to the most vulnerable populations, populations that public housing was aimed at helping: since the housing vouchers provided are subject to budgetary curtailment, permanent, deeply-subsidized housing has undergone an overall net-reduction.[22] Evaluations of completed redevelopment projects consistently point out that the emphasis on the physical aspects of new development has been to the detriment of its social aspects, ignoring, among other things, the lasting influence of race upon the interaction of new residents while focusing exclusively on income [See 1.1.4, 1.2.3].[23] Another study has analyzed the central role of design, in particular the role of an "architecturally appealing and marketable product," in securing private funding, as well as in obscuring the true cost borne by the public sector.[24] Finally, the effects on the social mobility of low-income residents in this new mixed-income housing have been shown to be minimal, if existent at all.[25] The architecture—in this case, the form-based, aesthetic codes of New Urbanism—did not create inequality, but it did enable and was instrumental in facilitating acceptance of a new real estate model.

While HOPE VI was an effort to recast public housing specifically, two of its main tenets have become commonly accepted for all affordable housing development. First, the private sector—whether nonprofit or for-profit—has become the only acceptable lead actor in the field of affordable housing development. Second, affordable housing is not built to look "affordable" per se, but integrated with and indistinguishable from market-rate housing. Public housing is only mentioned if absolutely necessary, and is today generally subsumed under the more broadly acceptable term "affordable." These policies are based on a dual premise: that the stigma of low-income housing should be removed through design, and that low- or moderate-income households would benefit culturally and economically from the proximity of residents from higher economic strata. This design and development policy of invisibility is connected to a political strategy of invisibility: the subsidy necessary to make new housing affordable to certain income groups—whose income will never allow rents or mortgage payments high enough to pay for its construction—is hidden, and thus less open to political attack, by transferring it from households and budgets to tax credits or property tax abatements [See HH: 1986].

In many cities, two main strategies help to generate affordable housing by saddling onto market-rate development: density bonuses, which allow a developer to build more than zoning normally permits if the development includes affordable housing; and inclusionary zoning, which requires the inclusion of a certain percentage of affordable units in market-rate developments. In some high-priced cities, including Boston or San Francisco, inclusionary zoning is mandatory for buildings above a certain number of units.[26] In others, like New York City, it is incentivized through higher densities, subsidized through tax abatements, or both.[27] The practical problem with these strategies is that generating new income- and price-restricted housing is directly tied to the real-estate cycle: if the development of market-rate apartments stalls, development of below-market rate units will stop. The more principled problem is that the goals of private for-profit development—return on investment—are not reconcilable with the goals of affordable housing development—creating housing accessible to low-, moderate- and middle-income households. By definition, the latter cannot pay what would generate acceptable profits, at least not in high-priced cities, leading to what some have called a "Faustian pact" between the public and private sectors.[28]

In New York City, historically an exception both in terms of the excesses of its property market, and due to successive administrations' commitment to regulate housing, this balancing act has proven difficult. A recent debate exemplifies the contorted political negotiations around the issue of how to combat inequality in and through housing: whether new affordable housing developments subsidized by New York City should require contractors to pay prevailing wages. A key official argued against this requirement, which would have combatted income inequality through wages, calculating that it would result in a reduction of 17,000 affordable units being built.[29]

The city's policies of furthering mixed-income housing through density bonuses and inclusionary zoning have evolved over the years. City agencies renegotiate depending on site, subsidies, and variances granted, sometimes permitting the affordable units to be realized entirely off site, other times allowing for them to be concentrated in one part of a building, and in yet other instances demanding they be spread indistinguishably throughout the development.[30] For instance, in "The Toren," a highrise in downtown Brooklyn completed in 2012, designed by Skidmore Owings & Merrill for BFC Developers, all of the affordable apartments were confined to the five-story base of the building, while the tower was reserved for market-rate units.[31]

In the summer of 2014, a scandal erupted around a more egregious architectural variation of this mixed-income policy at One Riverside Park, a luxury condominium tower on the Upper West Side developed by Extell Developers and designed by Goldstein, Hill & West.[32] In exchange for a 25-year property tax abatement as well as a density bonus, the project was required to include 20 percent affordable apartments. It did so not within the building, but in an adjacent one, named Fifty Riverside Boulevard. The 291 residences of One Riverside Park have sunset views across the Hudson River, and the units include up to 7-bedroom duplex apartments with swimming pools located on private terraces. The 55 income-restricted apartments count no more than two bedrooms, are accessed from around the corner, and have more basic amenities, including bicycle storage. The creation of a "poor door" was first reported by a neighborhood blog in late 2013, and the newly coined term helped spur the story's international coverage.[33] Though from the street the two buildings are distinguishable, with the midrise affordable section clad in more stone and the high-rise luxury section in more glass, together they create a whole. And yet the difference between the amenities on the one side and those on the other are so extreme that public discomfort was immediate.

It was that very real and graspable architectural image of two separate entrances—not just personnel and service staff in the back, residents and guests in the front,

but the separation of residents of the same publicly subsidized deal—that revealed the contradictions of a society that continues to assert that its members are created equal. The separate doors were too similar an image to the "separate but equal" policies that segregated the public spaces of black and white Americans for many decades after the end of the Civil War. Residents without the resources to "choose" to live in One Riverside Place, if they fall within precise income eligibility criteria, can submit an application to a city-run lottery.[34] Over 88,000 households did so, and 55 were accepted.[35] That is 1 in 1,600. What originated in a policy of invisibility—hiding both the cost to the public sector and the stigma of low-income housing—imploded when these issues were suddenly visible in the form of two doors. In June of 2015, the zoning policy that allowed for the poor doors was rescinded.[36]

The policy debate, of course, is less about the look of housing, and much more about the underlying socioeconomic calculations. Those in favor of place-based arguments might say: This segregation-by-building is compensated for by the fact that the residents will enjoy the benefits of the Upper West Side—high-quality public schools, parks, employment, transit, and retail—all of which are the hallmarks of an inclusive society of equal opportunities.[37] Others will argue that the taxes collected on these units, had they been sold at market-rate, could have generated twice as many apartments in parts of the city with lower land prices, or alternately, through cash transfers that give recipients choices on the open market.[38] A further argument pits maximizing the number of units produced against better design, or more colloquially, "beauty" against "cost,"[39]—the old argument advanced when stripping down basic features and quality of construction in low-income housing, which returns the discussion back to a building's "look" on the basis of its cost, or, inversely, cost on the basis of its look [See HH: 1946,

1960, 1982]. The debate about the role of David Adjaye's non-standard exterior design in securing philanthropic funding for Broadway Housing Communities' supportive and low-income New York housing project Sugar Hill is a case in point.[40]

As a profession, architecture provides a service.[41] Whether the project in question is the HOPE VI-funded Roosevelt Square in Chicago, the 421a-tax-abatement facilitated One Riverside Park in New York, or the philanthropically enabled Sugar Hill in Harlem: architecture serves the interests of those who pay the fees. Therefore, for an architect who objects to the inequalities built into the profit-driven system that enabled all of the above-mentioned projects, the only unambiguous action available is to turn down those commissions. The movement within the profession to refuse to design prisons due to the violence of the incarceration system represents one instance of such an objection.[42] The increasingly common provocation that an architect can "subvert" the client's brief, or creatively maneuver loopholes to create public benefit, can by definition only go so far. The same is true of the belief that architectural strategies that reduce construction cost will increase affordability. Minimizing size through efficient floor plans, or rationalizing construction through industrialization—ideas recently advanced in the "Making Room" initiative—are traditional strategies in this vein [See HH: 1918, 1946]. These efforts can, of course, reduce construction cost, but they will not lead to increased affordability if they are not also accompanied by a *will* to reduce the price (and hence profit) at which the product is offered.

Participating in one of the many organizations advocating pro-bono work or socially relevant architecture is another option for socially oriented designers, but one that has also its limits. Initiatives devoted to this work, including the now-defunct Architecture for Humanity, The One Percent, or The Institute for Public Architecture, among others, are all premised on improving design for those with a social and non-profit mission. But the system's underlying structures of ownership or profit are rarely challenged, not least due to how the work of these organizations is largely funded: through tax-deductible donations by financial institutions or corporations; or through grants by foundations, by definition non-profit and tax-exempt entities that promote specific missions. An upside of the proliferation of non-governmental organizations, of course, is a variety of approaches, and the liberty to pursue different options at multiple scales. The downside is a duplication of decentralized efforts, increased difficulty to implement larger projects, and, often, a lack of long-term planning and accountability.

These kinds of non-profit entities emerged in the late 1960s, and two of the most important that remain to this day share the acronym CDC: community design centers and community development corporations. The first aimed at providing design services to constituencies that otherwise have little access to them, the second to promote equitable human and physical development in neighborhoods suffering from disinvestment. The first became increasingly affiliated with university programs for institutional backing. The second increasingly found themselves with a double mandate: attracting tax-incentivized investment for housing development on the one hand, while preventing displacement caused by the rising real estate values that result in their now improving neighborhoods on the other. Since CDCs frequently lack the expertise to take on development, they are prone to partner with larger for-profit developers. "Community" has thus often become a fig leaf for its purported opposite: corporate investment in affordable housing whose price restriction is limited.[43] Development models intended to produce housing beyond the market in perpetuity—through community land trusts (CLTs) or limited-equity cooperatives, for instance—even if they have succeeded quite successfully in the past, are being implemented and supported today only at small scales [See HH: 1932, 1957, 1969, 1975].[44]

Identifying a directly causal relationship between design and inequality is a dubious undertaking. And yet design remains one of the most effective ways to make socio-economic inequities viscerally and immediately intelligible. In recent history, these linkages between architecture and inequality have either been made manifest in a principally negative tone (for instance, in public housing), or via small, tactically positive responses (for example, through CLTs). What we seem to have forgotten is to look at the underlying structure, called real estate development, which has also been designed. Inequality, architecture, and real estate development are intimately connected, each unable to exist without the others. Over the years, this fraught comingling has allowed real estate development, perhaps the least questioned of the three actors, to achieve statistical, discursive, and artistic dominance.

This artful hegemony is designed. For designers to affect it, they must first apprehend it, recognizing their role in its perpetuation and coming to terms with the necessary, uncomfortable contradictions therein. In this recognition—working to reimagine the terms through which architecture both illuminates and engages with the world, in a proportionally scaled response to real estate development's own planetary machinations—architects will necessarily confront seemingly intractable challenges [See HH: 1937]. This intractability is present, once again, by design, since real estate has come not simply to artfully manage the architectural imagination; but rather to govern it—with all the enforcement measures that implies. The response therefore, within and without architecture, will always be principally political in nature.

1. This was encouraged among other things by the fact that certain welfare payments at the time targeted single-parent households only, incentivizing fathers to stay away. This is shown in several scenes of the 2011 documentary film *The Pruitt-Igoe Myth* by Chad Freidrichs. See Katherine G. Bristol, "The Pruitt-Igoe Myth," *Journal of Architectural Education* 44, no. 3 (1991): 163–171. The text provided the cue for the title of the afore-mentioned documentary. The most recent publication to take on the persistent idea of "failed architecture" is *Public Housing Myths: Perception, Reality, and Social Policy*, ed. Nicholas Dagen Bloom, Fritz Umbach, and Lawrence J. Vale (Ithaca/London: Cornell University Press, 2015) in particular D. Bradford Hunt, "MYTH #2. Modernist Architecture Failed Public Housing." A selection of essays dissecting the varied and multi-faceted history of public housing, including design policies, was edited by Joseph Heathcott on the occasion of its 75-year existence: *Journal of the American Planning Association* 78, no. 4 (Autumn 2012).

2. The idea of an "easy" explanation of as well as an "easy" solution for problems is borrowed from Jason Hackworth, "Progressive activism in a neoliberal context: the case of efforts to retain public housing in the United States," *Studies in Political Economy* 75 (2005): 46. Cited in James Hanlon, "Success by Design: HOPE VI, New Urbanism, and the Neoliberal Transformation of Public Housing in the United States," *Environment and Planning* Vol. 42, No. 1 (2010): 92.

3. See Oscar Newman, *Defensible Space: Crime Prevention through Urban Design* (New York: Collier, 1973).

4. In the case of New York's Lincoln Center in the early 1950s, only one-third of former residents found accommodation in public housing city-wide. This is just one example that illustrates the pervasive problem of displacement. Samuel Zipp, *Manhattan Projects: The Rise and Fall of Urban Renewal in Cold War New York* (Oxford/New York: Oxford University Press, 2010), 211.

5. For a history of this development, see Sharon Zukin, *Loft Living: Culture and Capital in Urban Change* (New Brunswick: Rutgers University Press, 2014 [1982]). For an anthropological perspective on the reuse of buildings, see, Michael Guggenheim, "Immutable Mobiles: Building Conversion as a problem of quasi-technologies," *Urban Assemblages: How Actor-Network Theory Changes Urban Studies*, eds. Ignacio Farías and Thomas Bender (London/New York: Routledge, 2010), 161–178.

6. Prime examples are the work of Venturi Scott Brown starting in the mid-1960s, and that of a wave of younger firms, founded around 2000, including London-based FAT (Fashion Architecture Taste).

7. For a discussion of the changed image and value of a Brutalist high-rise in London, see Fosco Lucarelli and Mariabruna Fabrizi, "The Trellick Tower: Rise and Fall of a Modern Monument," *San Rocco Magazine* #5 (Fall 2012) ['Scary Architects']. For a more general description of the changing status of privatized council housing see: Jenny Gross, "Once A Housing Project, Now Prime London Real Estate," *Wall Street Journal*, November 6, 2012.

8. A good summary of the gradual implementation of building codes in housing is given in the introduction to Richard Plunz, *A History of Housing in New York City* (New York, NY: Columbia University Press, 1992).

9. The requirements given here are exemplary and taken from New York City Department of Housing Preservation and Development's "New Construction Guidelines," which are applicable in all housing financed in part by the City of New York. Building and zoning codes are typically regulated at the local levels, but are additionally affected by state and federal guidelines, for instance those pertaining to accessibility. The International Building Code (IBC) is an effort to standardize guidelines across jurisdictions, but does not give a unified definition of "a bedroom" other than by referring to egress requirements.

10. This is the basis for the case study of municipalities in New Jersey discussed in Massey, et al, *Climbing Mt. Laurel*.

11. The slow and halting proceedings have been well covered in the *New York Times*. For a more detailed report, released by the group that filed the original law suit in 2006, see: "Cheating On Every Level. Anatomy of the Demise of a Civil Rights Consent Decree," Anti-Discrimination Center, April 17, 2014, May 6, 2014 [revised], http://www.antibiaslaw.com/sites/default/files/Cheating_On_Every_Level.pdf.

12. For more on this June 2015 ruling, see Supreme Court of the United States, *Texas Department Of Housing and Community Affairs et al. v. Inclusive Communities Project, Inc., et al.*, October 2014. http://www.supremecourt.gov/opinions/14pdf/13-1371_m64o.pdf.

13. Jane Jacobs, *The Death and Life of Great American Cities* (New York: Random House, 1961).

14. Reactions to Making Room and the resultant pilot project to reduce the minimum dwelling size have ranged from embracing a less consumer-oriented urban lifestyle, to framing the proposals as "austerity measures." See, for instance, Jan Hoffman, "Shrink to Fit: Living Large in Tiny Spaces," *New York Times*, September 21, 2012; Michael Sorkin, "Little Boxes," *The Nation*, July 29, 2014. For more on Making Room, see "Making Room," Citizens' Housing and Planning Council, accessed June 15, 2015, http://makingroomnyc. com. Report co-author Susanne Schindler, part of Team R8, was involved in Making Room's design explorations, cosponsored by CHPC and the Architectural League in 2012.

15. This is well laid-out in Gail Radford, *Modern Housing for America. Policy Struggles in the New Deal Era* (Chicago: University of Chicago Press, 1996).

16. For a comparison of the first and second iterations of urban renewal, focusing on Atlanta and Chicago, see Lawrence Vale, *Purging the Poorest. The Design-Politics of Twice-Cleared Communities* (Chicago: Chicago University Press, 2013).

17. Numbers cited in Amy T. Khare, "Putting People Back into Place-Based Public Policies," *Journal of Urban Affairs* 37, no. 1 (2015): 49.

18. Alex Schwartz, *Housing Policy in the United States*, 3rd ed. (New York: Routledge, 2014), 196.

19. "Roosevelt Square, Chicago, IL," Brook Architecture, Inc., accessed July 15, 2015, http:// brookarchitecture.com/gallery/roosevelt-square/. Progress did not proceed as projected however, market-rate buyers walked away, and an entirely new plan for Roosevelt Square was launched in 2014. An in-depth study of HOPE VI as implemented in Chicago is Larry Bennett, Janet L. Smith, and Patricia A White, eds., *Where Are Poor People to Live: Transforming Public Housing Communities* (Abingdon/New York: Routledge, 2015 [2006]). For an example of both the type of coverage of and continued violence and tensions between residents, see Chloe Riley, "Gun-Toting Gangbanger Video, Continued Violence Trouble Roosevelt Square," *DNA Info Chicago*, December 18, 2013, http://www.dnainfo. com/chicago/20131218/near-west-side/gun-toting-gangbanger-video-continued-violence-troubles-roosevelt-square; Chloe Riley, "Roosevelt Square: CHA Seeks New Plan for Mixed-Income Housing Complex," *DNA Info Chicago*, February 4, 2014, http://www. dnainfo.com/chicago/20140204/near-west-side/roosevelt-square-cha-seeks-new-plan-for-mixed-income-housing-complex.

20. David Harvey, "The New Urbanism and the Communitarian Trap," *Harvard Design Magazine* (Winter/Spring 1997): 2.

21. Peter Marcuse, "The New Urbanism: The Dangers so Far," *disP - The Planning Review* 36, no. 140 (2000): 4. Marcuse's argument is based on Vincent Scully's wording. Marcuse cites Duany and Plater Zybek: "Simply put, we wish to improve the world with design, plain old good design, that is. We believe that the physical structure of our envionrmnet can be managed and that controlling it is the key to solving numerous problems confronting government today—traffic congestion, pollution, financial depletion, social isolation, and yes, even crime. We believe that design can solve a host of problems and that the design of the physcial enviornment does influence behavior." Andres Duany and Elizabeth Plater-Zyberk, "The second coming of the American small town," *Plan Canada* 33 (1991): 9.

22. Public housing stock in the United States has decreased by about 253,000 units, a loss of 18 percent since its all-time high. Schwartz, *Housing Policy*, 194.

23. Amy T. Khare, Mark L. Joseph and Robert J. Chaskin, "The Enduring Significance of Race in Mixed-Income Developments," *Urban Affairs Review*, June 25, 2014, 1–30. This also reflects Ta-Nehisi Coates's phrasing of "changing the subject" to refer to liberal politicians' not speaking about race, but purely about income. See "The Case for Reparations," *The Atlantic*, June 2014, accessed August 25, 2015, http://www.theatlantic.com/magazine/ archive/2014/06/the-case-for-reparations/361631/."

24. Geographer James Hanlon analyzes the award-winning HOPE VI project Park DuValle in Louisville. Hanlon, "Success by design," 2010. A thoroughly positive evaluation, positing New Urbanism as the blending of Jane Jacobs and Ebenezer Howard, and emphasizing its origins in the urban crisis of the 1970s, is provided by Robert Fishman, "New Urbanism," *Planning Ideas that Matter: Livabiliy, Terriotriality, Governance, and Reflective Practice*, ed. Bishwapriya Sanyal, Lawrence J. Vale, and Christina D. Rosan (Cambridge, MA: MIT Press, 2012), 65–90.

25. There are extensive studies on these questions by geographers and political scientists. See the recent issue of HUD's *Cityscape: A Journal of Policy Development and Research* titled "Mixed Messages on Mixed Incomes," 13, no. 2 (2013). For a more journalistic reflection on the excessive restrictions placed on the public-housing residents of

mixed-income developments, see Maya Dumasova, "The Problem with Mixed-Income Housing," *Jacobin*, May 21, 2014.

26. "Inclusionary Housing Program," City and County of San Francisco, Mayor's Office of Housing & Community Development, accessed June 29, 2015, http://sf-moh.org/index.aspx?page=263; "Inclusionary Development Design Guidelines," Boston Redevelopment Authority, last updated July 2009, accessed June 29, 2015, http://www.bostonredevelopmentauthority.org/getattachment/8eebf160-301b-41ab-b4e1-9ce6674b1d28.

27. The most controversial of these is the 421a property tax abatement. A political stalemate in June 2015 at the New York State level pitted the extension of this program against the extension of the city's rent regulation and stabilization program. For a summary of the issues, see Editorial, "New York's Housing Emergency," *New York Times*, June 12, 2015.

28. Oliver Wainwright, "Poor doors are not the worst thing about social housing," *Guardian Arts and Design Blog*, July 30, 2014, http://www.theguardian.com/artanddesign/architecture-design-blog/2014/jul/30/poor-door-social-housing-apartheid.

29. Will Bredderman, "Deputy Mayor: Prevailing Wages Would Cost City 17,000 Affordable Apartments," *New York Observer*, June 1, 2015, accessed August 25, 2015, http://www.theatlantic.com/magazine/archive/2014/06/the-case-for-reparations/361631/.

30. For current guidelines, see New York City Department of City Planning, "Zoning Tools: Inclusionary Housing," accessed July 14, 2015, http://www.nyc.gov/html/dcp/html/zone/zh_inclu_housing.shtml. For an example of the ambiguity in formulating the regulations despite inclusionary zoning being mandatory in Boston, see Boston's "Interior Standards for Affordable Housing Units": "The design, quality and materials of the affordable housing units must be indistinguishable from the market rate units. This does not mean that the affordable must be identical to the market rate units, but instead the affordable units must not be noticeably different from the market rate units." Accessed June 29, 2015, http://www.bostonredevelopmentauthority.org/getattachment/8eebf160-301b-41ab-b4e1-9ce6674b1d28.

31. Juliette Spertus, "Luxury for All?" *Bauwelt* (October 2012): 26–29.

32. It is remarkable that the real-estate value and desirability of One Riverside Boulevard was not created by an architect whose name is well-known. See: Matt Chaban, "Goldstein, Hill & West: How New York's Most Anonymous Architects Have Taken Over the Skyline," *New York Observer*, October 16, 2012, accessed August 25, 2015, http://observer.com/2012/10/goldstein-hill-west-architects-new-york-city-skyline-shapers/.

33. West Sider, "New UWS Development could have separate Entrance for Poorer People," *West Side Rag*, August 12, 2013, accessed July 14, 2015, http://www.westsiderag.com/2013/08/12/new-uws-development-could-have-separate-entrance-for-poorer-people. For examples of international coverage, see Marc Pitzke, "Luxuswohnen in New York: Arme müssen durch die Hintertüre," *Spiegel Online*, October 30, 2014, http://www.spiegel.de/wirtschaft/poor-doors-new-yorks-luxusimmobilien-mit-tueren-fuer-arme-a-998732.html; or multiple entries on *The Guardian's* blog, by Owen Hatherley and others, comparing New York to the London context.

34. "Upper West Side 'Poor Door' Rentals Start At $833/Month," *Curbed*, February 18, 2015, accessed June 9, 2015, http://ny.curbed.com/tags/40-riverside-boulevard.

35. Mireya Navarro, "88,000 Applicants and Counting for 55 Units in 'Poor Door' Building," *New York Times*, April 20, 2015, accessed August 25, 2015, http://www.nytimes.com/2015/04/21/nyregion/poor-door-building-draws-88000-applicants-for-55-rental-units.html?_r=0.

36. Jana Kasperkic, "New York Bans 'Poor Doors' in Win for Low Income Tenants," *Guardian*," June 29, 2015, accessed July 4, 2015, http://www.theguardian.com/us-news/2015/jun/29/new-york-poor-door-low-income-tenants-rent.

37. See the multiple studies funded by the MacArthur Foundation's "How Housing Matters" program that seeks to quantify the benefits of well-located affordable housing: http://www.macfound.org/programs/how-housing-matters/.

38. The debate between in-kind and cash transfers is well-summarized in Edward Glaeser, "There Are Worse Things in Housing Policy than Poor Doors," Discussion 12: "The Dream Revisited: The Poor Door Debate," Furman Center, March 31, 2015, http://furman-center.org/research/iri/glaeser.

39. Rebecca Baird-Remba, "Balancing Cost and Beauty: Architects Talk Affordable Housing Design," *New York YIMBY*, May 1, 2015, accessed June 15, 2015, http://newyorkyimby.com/2015/05/balancing-cost-and-beauty-architects-talk-affordable-housing-design.html.

40. The conundrum of rallying "better" architecture for low-income housing, intended to be replicable, then dismissed on the basis of above-average cost, was last displayed in New York City by Sugar Hill. There and elsewhere the exceptional architect was selected in part to support the extensive fund-raising efforts, which drafted philanthropic money. For a more detailed discussion of the role of David Adjaye in this project, see: Susanne Schindler, "Architecture vs. Housing: The Case of Sugar Hill," *Urban Omnibus*, September 3, 2014, http://urbanomnibus.net/2014/09/architecture-vs-housing-the-case-of-sugar-hill/.

41. Reinier de Graaf, "Architecture is now a tool of capital, complicit in a purpose antithetical to its social mission," *Architectural Review* 24 (April 2015), http://www.architectural-review.com/essays/architecture-is-now-a-tool-of-capital-complicit-in-a-purpose-antithetical-to-its-social-mission/8681564.article.

42. See "About Us," Architects/Designers/Planners for Social Responsibility, accessed June 15, 2015, http://www.adpsr.org/home/about-us.

43. The research on the conflicting mandates on CDCs is extensive. See: Rob Rosenthal and Maria Foscarinis, "Community Development Corporations: challenges in supporting a right to housing," in eds. Rachel G. Bratt, Michael E. Stone, and Chester Hartman, *A Right to Housing: Foundation for a New Social Agenda* (Philadelphia: Temple University Press, 2006), 340–359; Justin Steil and James Connolly, "Can the Just City be Built from Below?: Brownfields, Planning, and Power in the South Bronx," in Peter Marcuse et al. eds., *Searching for the Just City: Debates in Urban Theory and Practice* (London/New York: Routledge, 2009): 172–193; James DeFilippis and Susan Saegert, eds. *The Community Development Reader* (New York: Routledge, 2012); Tom Angotti, *New York for Sale: Community Planning Confronts Global Real Estate* (Cambridge, MA: MIT Press, 2008).

44. For an overview of the legal and organizational challenges and opportunities of CLTs in the United States today, see the website of The National Community Land Trust Network, http://cltnetwork.org. For documents on the history and evolution of the model in the United States, see John Emmaeus Davis, ed., *The Community Land Trust Reader* (Cambridge, MA: Lincoln Institute of Land Policy, 2010); for a brief sketch of the connection to affordable housing, see Oksana Mironova, "The Value of Land: How Community Land Trusts Maintain Housing Affordability," *Urban Omnibus*, April 29, 2014, http://urbanomnibus.net/2014/04/the-value-of-land-how-community-land-trusts-maintain-housing-affordability/.

Part 2 Architecture

2.1 Real Estate Agency
Reinhold Martin

Simply put, real estate governs. This is different from saying that it—capital, real estate—"determines." But what is it to govern? It may seem self-evident that to govern one needs a governor, an agent or set of agents, an institution or set of institutions. "Real estate," or real estate development, may therefore seem an unlikely candidate for such a role. For though real estate is filled with agents, they typically figure as brokers, go-betweens; or, at the other end of the circuit, as "developers," oracles who discern and develop potential; and advisors or assistants who merely fulfill existing needs and desires.

But governing is an art; it derives from techniques, not agents. Inequality is one such technique. It is designed, built into the system. To say what we already know as plainly as possible: *Inequality in housing is an intentional consequence of the real estate system, rather than a historical accident.* Were there no inequality in income or wealth—and most housing in the current system is a form of wealth, or capital[1]—there would be no opportunity for profit and no incentive to speculate, and the system would collapse. From this perspective, the more inequality the better, up to the point when it is no longer possible to extract additional profit from lower income groups lest they revolt, and higher income groups must be content to extract profit from one another.

Even an economist like Joseph Stiglitz, who has done so much to call attention to increasingly intolerable levels of inequality worldwide, admits that it is nevertheless structural to the present system:

> *I, and as far as I know, most progressives—do not argue for full equality. We realize that that would weaken incentives. The question is, How seriously would incentives be weakened if we had a little bit less inequality?*[2]

Stiglitz has been credited with popularizing the figure of the "1%" who control the vast majority of the world's wealth, in defiance of whom Occupy Wall Street protesters exclaimed, in the fall of 2011, "We Are the 99%!" As Stiglitz put it in a widely read article published in *Vanity Fair* earlier that spring,

> *Americans have been watching protests against oppressive regimes that concentrate massive wealth in the hands of an elite few. Yet in our own democracy, 1 percent of the people take nearly a quarter of the nation's income—an inequality even the wealthy will come to regret.*[3]

The reference was to the uprisings then unfolding across the Arab world, but neither here nor in his subsequent book, *The Price of Inequality*, does Stiglitz explain just how much inequality is acceptable in the United States or anywhere else. Instead, he concentrates on explaining how it might be reduced without fundamentally changing the existing system.

While this may make practical sense, it conceals a constitutive ambiguity, whereby socioeconomic inequality is challenged as a matter of moral principle, and partially addressed at a social level, while being accepted at an economic level. This ambiguity cannot be readily resolved, since it is the means by which inequality governs. That is: economic inequality, whether measured by income or by accumulated wealth, governs by submitting citizens of the global, neoliberal marketplace to a calculus that guides the production and management of cities, suburbs, towns, villages, and buildings by projecting virtue at an abstract level while withholding concretely the possibility of genuine parity. As an art form capable of bearing complex and contradictory meanings, architecture often acts as a guarantor of such virtue while also securing its absence. For, contrary to what is normally assumed, the economic calculus is not solely quantitative. Think about the gap that separates moral outrage at inequality from the embarrassed recognition of its necessity under the current system—leading even outspoken critics to ask, with a hint of irony but also in earnest, for only "a little bit less."

2.1.1   Norms

This gap is maintained by qualitative factors, including architectural ones, that appeal to a sense of "home," or of social status, or of a natural order of things. Which means that architecture is more than just an artful overlay or disguise that covers up the unsavory equations driving real estate development spreadsheets. It is a prerequisite. Even in its crudest form, or in its most latent (as an "architecture without architects" designed and built, say, by real estate developers), architecture plays into every calculation, if only as the material form taken by any quantity of usable—and rentable, or saleable—space. It does not do so merely as what economists call an "externality," or an incalculable quality that contributes to value, as in the real-estate mantra, "location, location, location." Rather, inequality is drawn and built into every building that is conceived as exchangeable property. Look closely at any such house or apartment plan, and you will see it.

Stiglitz argues that "inequality is, to a very large extent, the result of government policies that shape and direct the forces of technology and markets and broader societal forces."[4] This is true. In the United States, a measured degree of economic inequality is a matter of government policy. But it is also true that "the forces of technology and markets and broader societal forces" shape government policy. Specific policies, such as those that encourage homeownership by offering tax deductions on mortgage interest, do help shape the real estate markets. However, such policies are themselves shaped by narratives that extoll intangible qualities derived from the arts of living and the arts of governing. Without these narratives, the basic unit that defines the current housing system—the household—would evoke nothing more than square footage, rather than the social norms and morays of "family," "hearth," and "home" that we know it does [See 1.1.3].

Just as they have governed in the recent past through the practice of racial redlining and restrictive covenants, or through today's "poor doors," housing markets continue to govern through those social codes by which households are legally and financially constituted. As before, such codes take the white, middle-class, heterosexual, patriarchal family as their tacit model. The difference is that today, they appeal more fervently than ever to the consumer's or investor's need for security. It is this need to mitigate the emotional and financial risks that permeate an environment in which housing is, for a broad swath of the class spectrum, a primary generator of wealth as well as a place where social norms, including the desire for belonging (to a family, to a community, to a nation) are enacted and reinforced. In certain metropolitan or suburban locales as well as in certain state and federal policies, social codes such as those pertaining to marriage have been loosened, but predominantly in a direction that domesticates sexual difference by binding it to reassuring images of house and home, or reinforces gender stereotypes. Something similar can be said for the misguided announcements of a "post-racial" society that ignore tensions between a multiracial (often suburban, or urban professional) middle class and a largely African-American and Latino/a (urban and suburban) underclass. Rather than resolve underlying conflicts, such displacements signal only the remixing—rather than the elimination—of racial categories and biases related to sexuality and gender with class differentials in the shifting, treacherous firmament on which today's inequality debates take place.

Mixed in this way with regulating social norms, inequality drives the system forward by creating scarcity and hence, as Stiglitz puts it, "incentive." It also creates tables, charts, and scales that correlate those norms with the reigning economic hierarchy. Entire populations—in the language of statistics, percentiles—are measured and managed governmentally according to where they are located on the inequality spectrum: patronage for the 1%, morality for the ambiguous "middle class," and austerity for the rest. A real, underlying heterogeneity with respect to social patterns like family structure dissolves into smooth numerical rankings. Such seemingly inexorable distributions belie an artfulness that thrives on a plurality of actors, authors, and agents—including architects—whose otherwise disparate activities in the ethical-moral and economic spheres are synchronized by the relevant techniques. Together, this plurality draws and redraws the field of operations such that certain actions seem reasonable while others do not. Through a back and forth movement between artfulness and calculus, socioeconomic equality is made to seem abstractly desirable but pragmatically impossible, thus ruling out its objective possibility from the start. The question then seems only to be: How much inequality can the system tolerate? In consequence, the system's operators as well as its constituents are bound by an artificially limited field of action, with limited concepts, limited tools, and a limited vocabulary at their disposal. Thus bound, they concede in advance.

2.1.2   New York by Gehry: A Case Study

The techniques by which inequality is harnessed, managed, and reproduced do not come naturally. They must be learned. A popular method involves the "case study," a staple of business schools since the 1920s. By way of illustration, in 1971 the Urban Land Institute (ULI), a multi-disciplinary real estate forum, began compiling case studies that "showcase innovative approaches and best practices in real estate and urban development," for use by practitioners as well as by business students (and students in the still-new graduate real estate development programs) [See 3.3].[5] One such ULI study, which dates from the fall of 2014, is devoted to 8 Spruce Street, a residential tower in lower Manhattan. Originally named Beekman Place, the building was rechristened New York by Gehry by the time it opened in 2011. The details given in the ULI case study are instructive, as much for what they reveal about the tower as for the techniques of real estate development—including the art of inequality, broadly construed—to which both the building and the report are dedicated.

Construction on the tower, which at the time was the tallest of its kind in the city, began in 2006. It is owned and operated by Forest City Ratner, the New York division of Forest City Enterprises, Inc., a major real estate developer. In October 2011, Occupy Wall Street protesters marched past the tower chanting "We Are the 99%!" The chants were not directed at the tower, which had begun leasing units that spring. Rather, they were directed at the real and metaphorical Wall Street located about six blocks further downtown, on which stands the New York Stock Exchange where, as it happens, shares in Forest City Enterprises are traded daily.

As the ULI case study confirms, in some ways New York by Gehry is unusual; in others it is not. When the project began, it was planned as a mixture of condominium and rental units designed to profit from the strong growth in the Financial District's heretofore-limited residential market (slowed by the September 11, 2001 attacks but picked up again several years later). The timing involved in bringing the building's 899 units to market had to balance market volatility with the scheduled phase-out of tax abatements available through the federal Liberty Bonds program, established in the wake of 9/11 to stimulate development in the area. With the federal subsidy soon to expire, the developers moved up the construction start date to comply. They also revised their pro forma midstream into one based solely on rental units on the assumption that the local condominium market was fast becoming saturated. In 2009, in the midst of the international financial crisis, but with federal subsidies still in place, Forest City Ratner halted construction and renegotiated work contracts with construction unions (some of whom who would later join the Occupy Wall Street protests), lowering construction costs by $25 million. The architect, too, paid a price, when Ratner renegotiated downward the deal to use Frank Gehry's name on the building and in its marketing materials. Still, Gehry must have been relieved when his clients decided not to shorten the tower mid-construction to half of the projected 76 stories, a solution under serious consideration at the time to limit the risks amplified by the crisis.[6]

Ratner's equity partner in the building was the National Electric Benefit Fund (NEBF), a pension fund for electrical workers, who were represented in the financing by National Real Estate Advisors (NREA). Of the $680 million in bonds issued to finance the project, slightly less than one-third, or $204 million, were tax free Liberty Bonds. In April 2008, the New York City Housing Development Corporation (HDC) announced: "The Beekman Tower [8 Spruce Street] Liberty Bond program generated approximately $6 million in fees that HDC will devote to financing affordable housing."[7] In midsummer 2011, as protesters planned the occupation of Zuccotti Park for the fall, the financing for 8 Spruce Street was restructured. A year and a half later, in December 2012, Ratner and NEBF sold 49 percent of their jointly held equity in the project to the Teachers Insurance and Annuity Association – College Retirement Equities Fund (TIAA-CREF)—a financial services organization that specializes in non-profit industries, including higher education—in a transaction that valued the property at $1.05 billion.[8] As of 2012, the building's owners took in a net annual income after debt service of approximately $25 million, roughly equal to the concessions made by the unions during construction.[9]

Officially, Frank Gehry designed 8 Spruce Street. Or rather, Gehry Partners LLP did, in collaboration with Swanke Hayden Connell Architects (who designed the brick-clad public school at its base), along with James Corner Field Operations, Piet Oudolf Gardens and Landscapes, WSP Cantor Seinuk, Philip Habib & Associates, and others. This group was responsible for the building's exterior form and for its interiors, which combine to give New York by Gehry what the property's website calls a "distinctive aesthetic" marked by "undulating waves of stainless steel that reflect the changing light."[10] But it is also possible to say that the building was designed by another set of forces, of which the name "Gehry" is just an expression. It would be reductive to call this set of forces "real estate," or even "capital." Let us be more precise and say what the Occupy Wall Street protesters intuited: that the building and others like it were designed by inequality. This, and not its idiosyncratic pedigree, is what makes New York by Gehry typical of the latest phase in architecture's long partnership with speculative real estate development.

The real-time dynamics that informed the decision to shift from a mixture of sales and rentals to a rental-only building during construction are visible inside. The exterior undulations combine with irregular massing to yield 350 unique unit plans, ranging from 500 to 2,500 square feet. Of these, there are (or were initially) 191 studio apartments, 504 one-bedrooms, 164 two-bedrooms, 23 three-bedrooms, 4 penthouses, and 13 terrace apartments. Although this mix favors single tenants or couples, the presence of a public school at the base suggested the possibility of a growing market for larger families. Hence, studio apartments were placed adjacent to one-bedrooms to allow them to be combined in the event that such a market emerged.[11] The unit plans themselves are nondescript, although the bulging façade allows for bay windows with expansive views at the upper floors. Ceilings are somewhat higher than the current norm, at nine feet. Beyond that, the units are compact and efficient, with the Gehry signature having been applied to the selection of interior finishes and appliances, as well as to the assorted amenities—game room, fitness center, "grilling terrace," etc.—scattered throughout the building. All apartments are equipped with central air conditioning rather than the more common (and less expensive) through-wall units.[12] In these and other respects, New York by Gehry combines a series of conventional calculations regarding location, square footage, finish, and amenity with the less calculable but no less consequential factor of what a Forest City Ratner vice president called "great architecture."[13]

As of summer 2014, the building was fully leased, with a typical studio apartment renting at $3,100 per month, a one-bedroom apartment at $4,500 per month, and a two-bedroom apartment at $7,100 per month. At the

10 ft   20 ft

Gehry Partners LLP, New York by Gehry, developed by Forest City Ratner Companies, New York, New York, completed in 2010. Partial plan, Floors 9–22 (studio and one-bedroom apartments). Drawn by Nabila Morales Pérez.

lower end, then, the annual housing cost of $37,200—taken as the maximum recommended one-third of gross income—sets entry-level income for the building at around $112,000 annually.[14] In 2014, the U.S. Census Bureau calculated mean household income nationally at $51,939, putting the lowest earners in the building at twice the national mean, somewhere in the top 20 percent nationwide.[15] At the upper end, and at the top of the building, the four penthouse units rented for around $25,000 per month, or $300,000 annually, suggesting a minimum household income of $900,000, which sits comfortably within the top 1 percent of earners against whom the Occupy Wall Street chants were directed. Calculated proportionately, the average rent in the building in 2014 was approximately $5,000 per month or $60,000 annually, suggesting a household income of about $180,000. That would put at least half of the residents in Gehry's New York (i.e., New York by Gehry) if not in "the 1%" then at least in the top 10 percent of earners nationwide.[15]

However, the architecture of inequality is not limited to calculations like those translated into stainless steel and concrete at the higher end of the real estate market by the Gehry team. It defines the multidimensional, transnational "Wall Street" addressed by the Occupy protests, where the market performance of New York by Gehry contributed to an overall portfolio against which shares in the developer's parent company, Forest City Enterprises, Inc., traded. In this respect, New York by Gehry was not only shaped by capital; *it is capital.* That includes the architecture, which factored into the development strategy and financing from the beginning. This is nothing special. While it may still be relatively unusual for a "star" architect to be involved so intimately with the commercial aspects of real estate development to the point of selling his or her name, the commercial and investment value of any building *always* includes its architectural characteristics, even if those are as mundane as ceiling heights, square footage, or finishes. And a building's owners, be they residents, developers, or shareholders, are increasingly positioned on the scales of relative wealth based on the value of that property, and of any other property they own, rather than what they earn from their labor.

This latter point is among the central insights of Thomas Piketty's influential *Capital in the Twenty-First Century*, which was published to international acclaim in 2013, shortly after New York by Gehry, and the world to which it belongs, came online. Strikingly, Piketty finds inequality of capital (or wealth) increasing much more rapidly than inequality of wages since the 1970s in Europe and the United States. He begins with what we know:

> [W]hat primarily characterizes the United States at the moment is a record level of inequality of income from labor (probably higher than in any other society at any time in the past, anywhere in the world, including societies in which skill disparities were extremely large) together with a level of inequality of wealth less extreme than the levels observed in traditional societies or in Europe in the period 1900–1910. It is therefore essential to understand the conditions under which these two logics could develop, while keeping in mind that they may complement one another in the century ahead and combine their effects. If this happens, the future could hold in store a new world of inequality more extreme than any that preceded it.[16]

At present rates what Piketty describes as "high inequality" in capital ownership, in which 10 percent of the population owns 70 percent of the wealth, becomes within about fifteen years, "very high inequality" in which the top 10 percent owns 90 percent of the wealth. However, this 10 percent is not necessarily the same 10 percent of wage earners represented by the tenants of New York by Gehry, since even in "very high inequality" of labor income, *that* 10 percent would command only 45 percent of the wages. The difference—between wealth due to capital and wealth due to wages—is what accounts for the much higher measure of "total inequality" projected by Piketty, in which 10 percent of the population accounts for a combined 60 percent of wages *and* capital.[17]

Conceived as a useful commodity, then, New York by Gehry attains prices and values that govern the relative upper end of the residential real estate market in large, wealthy cities like New York. Conceived as capital, however, New York by Gehry assimilates those prices and values into an investment designed to profit from the environment that both Piketty and Stiglitz describe, wherein an increasingly smaller proportion of the population controls an increasingly greater proportion of the wealth. As a diagram of wage inequality, then, New York by Gehry is par for the course; as a diagram of wealth inequality, it is exemplary.

2.1.3   Surveys and Indexes

Piketty also points out that in the United States, owning real estate constitutes the primary form of capital accumulation for about nine of the top 10 percent by wealth, where, it "accounts for half of total wealth and for some individuals more than three quarters."[18] Below that, the importance of real estate in determining household wealth is often still greater. While above, in the top 1 percent, its significance diminishes in relation to securities and other financial instruments, the importance of which is near total among the very largest fortunes. To the extent that its financial performance depends on high earners, while also contributing to the retirement portfolios of college professors who invest with TIAA-CREF, and to the performance of publicly traded shares in Forest City

Enterprises, New York by Gehry operates at both levels.

However, assuming that it is the primary residence for all 899 of the households it harbors, its residents occupy a slightly eccentric position relative to the norms enforced by national policies. According to the 2013 American Housing Survey, of the 115.8 million occupied housing units nationwide, only about 40 million were rentals, of which only 880,000 cost $2,500 per month or more. When the data are divided this way, the residents of New York by Gehry represent less than 0.1 percent of the general population. This is different than saying that they are in the top decile of income and are therefore among the nation's elites. Instead, it reminds us that the particular way of life represented by the building is quite unusual, and would be even more so if we factor in the relative scarcity of residential rental buildings with 50 or more units, which comprise about 3.5 million total units. Far more common are the country's 62.7 million owner-occupied detached houses.[19] This is no surprise, of course, since it reflects the widespread patterns of homeownership that extend well into the lower middle class. That the data exist in this particular form, however, is perhaps more telling.

As a technique for governing as well as a basis for extracting profit, inequality operates according to a fluid set of rules, categories, and procedures. The most visible of these (written into the word's mathematical connotations) is the act of counting and of measuring. In the contemporary United States, as elsewhere, although the individual level has been studied, the basic unit for generating data on economic inequality remains the household.[20] Commonly, these data are incorporated into comparative, macroeconomic quanta such as the Gini coefficient, which serve as synthetic indexes. The World Bank, for example, defines its quanta as follows: "[The] Gini index measures the extent to which the distribution of income or consumption expenditure among individuals or households within an economy deviates from a perfectly equal distribution." Measured this way, in 2010 (the most complete dataset as of this writing), the United States had a Gini index of .411, as compared to significantly lower (and therefore "less unequal") indexes in Tunisia (.358), the Slovak Republic (.273), Denmark (.269), and the United Kingdom (.380), among others.[21]

Although it obscures more granular differences, this tells us that the United States is among the most unequal of advanced economies. A closer look, however, tells us more about how such indexes work both to measure inequality *and* to reproduce it by providing one way of calculating the differences that make markets move. Gini metadata indicate that datasets were drawn from a variety of national sources, which have been correlated according to the "central concept of 'equivalized household disposable income,'" or, essentially, after-tax income adjusted for household size.[22] In the case of the United States, these data were translated from the Annual Social and Economic Supplement to the Current Population Survey, which is compiled jointly by the U.S. Census Bureau and the Department of Labor Statistics.[23] It is based on interviews with "a probability selected sample of about 60,000 selected households" that begins with an address and then sorts for eligibility to exclude vacant units, business, and other nonresidential addresses.[24] Telephone interviews are then conducted over a period of four months to determine and verify household data pertaining to occupancy, family makeup, employment, and income.[25]

In this way the survey, and hence the data, presupposes and utilizes the basic infrastructure of housing, including the postal system, the telephone system, and all of those other systems that combine in the delimitation and enclosure of the unit itself. Scaling up, the U.S. Current Population Survey essentially supplements data gathered via similar methods through the annual American Community Survey, which samples about 150,000 households. Most comprehensive of all is the full U.S. Census conducted every ten years, the most recent of which was also completed in 2010.[26]

From the other direction, data related to housing stock itself are compiled annually by the Department of Housing and Urban Development in collaboration with the U.S. Census Bureau in the American Housing Survey (AHS). In this case the object of study is the physical "housing unit" rather than the socioeconomic "household," with the aim being to "[ask] questions about the quality of housing in the United States."[27] The Census Bureau indicates that "policy analysts, program managers, budget analysts, and Congressional staff use AHS data to monitor supply and demand, as well as changes in housing conditions and costs, in order to assess housing needs."[28] Since the vast majority of public policy related to housing in the United States is market-based, it quickly becomes clear that the AHS is, in effect, a market survey that helps to shape, rather than merely measure, its object of study: the housing unit.[29] If this is not self-evident, the AHS website makes it so, when it adds euphemistically that "academic researchers and private organizations also use AHS data in efforts of specific interest and concern to their respective communities."[30] This is another way of illustrating how the AHS makes itself available to the real estate industry. The maps of inequality provided by the U.S. Census and the Gini index correlate with the market surveyed by the AHS. Together, these point to an important way that lives are governed where the housing system and the real estate system meet; where the basic commodity is the housing unit and where the basic unit of governance is the household.

Tied as it is to the housing unit, the household is a distinctly infrastructural category that presupposes an entire urban field. It also presupposes tangible architectural qualities, like the grouping of bedrooms, and intangible ones, like the feeling of "home." Government instruments like the AHS are used by real estate developers and investors to evaluate the market. But these instruments also measure and manage qualitative differences that appear at the intersection of households and housing units. From this perspective, they enable us to glimpse a statistical imagination in which populations are divided according to the wealth they possess, and that wealth, in turn, is determined by how they are housed. In a circular fashion, that wealth also limits the field of possible housing alternatives. In that sense, each house, each apartment, each bedroom, and each bathroom is an integer, a statistical unit by which the household it contains—we should really say, the household it produces and maintains—is situated on a spectrum of inequality that, in turn, governs the way we live.

2.1.4   The Household

The statistical unit of the household is therefore actually a set of intersecting material units, including humans, houses, bedrooms, bathrooms, cars, and cities. Let us call this set "architecture." Looking at it more closely enables us to grasp how the spectrum of inequality is maintained in a manner that reproduces certain norms and categories in order for the real estate system to do its work. In what follows, a series of cases show concretely how the principles and practices of real estate development govern the construction and inhabitation of new housing. Moving across the country, and up and down the inequality spectrum, they take a partial inventory of building types, markets, and financial models through which we can see more clearly the diverse ways in which housing options are defined by (but also as) capital. Even in the most disparate of contexts, the discourse of the household repeats architecturally, delineating the social unit by which wealth is measured.

On the opposite coast from New York by Gehry, but about ten miles from the offices of Gehry Partners LLP, sits Cloverdale 749, in Los Angeles, designed by Lorcan O'Herlihy Architects (LOHA). In June 2013, the website la.curbed.com described the building's six available condominium units, listing from about $749,000 to $999,000, as having "open-plan living spaces, Caesarstone countertops, under-cabinet LED lighting in kitchens, carpeting in the bedrooms, and completely separated walls to keep the noise down."[31] The website toplacondos.com added: "An experience of light, flow and true craftsmanship throughout interesting architectural spaces defines Cloverdale. Comfortably refined. Impeccably designed. Contemporary luxury with European style, paired with a warmth you simply don't find in modern condominium residences today . . . 749 Cloverdale is a new standard in condominium living."[32]

Floor plans compress bathrooms, utilities, and stairs (for duplexes) in a central core, maximizing the openness of the surrounding spaces, which are screened on either end with a glass and perforated, ventilating metal skin. Kitchens are galley type, with open islands. Balconies and stairs wrap the exterior, and parking on the urban site is underground.

Assuming a 20 percent down payment, the monthly mortgage of about $3,700 on the higher-end units puts the owners of these units somewhere close to the top 10 percent of earners, with a household income of at least $130,000. Assuming a mortgage paid in full (i.e. full ownership) but no other financial assets (which is unlikely), the owners would certainly be in the top 20 percent in terms of net wealth but probably much higher, according to available data that put the median wealth of that group at about $630,000.[33] For comparison, in 2012 *The New York Times* estimated the household income of the top 1 percent to start at around $380,000 but their net

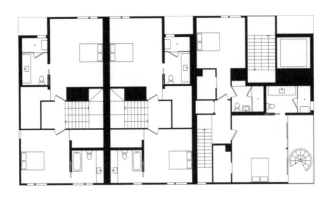

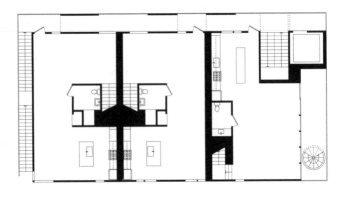

10 ft   20 ft

Lorcan O'Herlihy Architects, Cloverdale 749, developed by Richard Papalian and
P.J. Roxas-Chua, Los Angeles, California, completed in 2014. Third-floor plan (below),
Fourth-floor plan (above). Drawn by Nabila Morales Pérez.

wealth to be at least $8.4 million per household, based on federal data from 2007.[34] That puts the residents of Cloverdale 749 somewhat lower on the inequality spectrum than those of New York by Gehry, but probably still among the elites: the top 10 percent, or "upper class" who, according to Piketty, are on track to control 60 percent of income from labor and capital combined by 2030, before the first mortgages on the building likely come due.

Compare this slice of the top to that represented by Eden Prairie Woods, in Eden Prairie, Minnesota, a single family "home community" by Toll Brothers, with prices beginning around $650,000. According to its developers, this "exclusive development" is located in a town twice selected as among the "Top 3 Best Places to Live in America by Money Magazine" in 2011 and 2012 (having been voted #1 in 2010). Its main commodity, a single family house, which is also to be understood as an investment, is distinguished by "Traditional Minnesota home designs including two-story foyers and family rooms, secluded master suites, oak main staircases, secondary staircases, an exceptional list of standard features, hundreds of customizable options, and much more!"[35]

Houses at Eden Prairie Woods come in five models: Columbia II (3 bedrooms, 2½ baths, 3 car garage, 3,122 s.f. @ $647,995); Palmerton (3 bedrooms, 2 ½ baths, 3 car garage, 2,735 s.f. @ $670,995); Duke (4 bedrooms, 3½ baths, 3 car garage, 3,554 s.f. @ $689,995); Hopewell (4 bedrooms, 3 ½ baths, 3 car garage, 3,377 s.f. @ $694,995) and Stansbury (4 bedrooms, 4 ½ baths, 3 car garage, 4,235 s.f. @ $742,995). On average then, at about $689,000, considered as a capital investment for their owners (rather than just as exchangeable commodities for their builders), a fully paid house in Eden Prairie Woods would certainly put its owners among the top 20 percent and, combined with other assets and income, probably among the top 10 percent.

In this case, however, unit plans, which, as in the Cloverdale duplexes, separate the household into sleeping (i.e. bedrooms) on the second floor and "living" below, are dominated by amenities, including optional sundecks or sunrooms, and the ubiquitous three-car garage. Kitchens are in the center, as part of an exploded or dispersed core that typically includes pantry, powder room, and laundry, bisected by a passageway and adjoining stair. Houses are sited on a minimum of about one-third of an acre, and the entire development of 52 houses is surrounded by a wooded "conservation area."

Compare these formulas, again, to the more modest Pinhook Flats at Aksarben Village, in Omaha, Nebraska, "Where life comes in first."[36] Built on the grounds of a former harness racing track, Pinhook Flats featured, as of December 2012, studio, one, and two bedroom rental units from ranging from 481 to 1,081 square feet. A major developer of the mixed-use but predominantly residential complex made up mainly of four-story apartment buildings is the aptly named Alchemy Development. In March 2015, Alchemy announced the most recent planned addition to Aksarben Village, a 53-unit apartment building named Cue. Also in Aksarben Village, though developed separately, is The Broadmoor, where "style and architecture are a priority. Kitchens are designed for entertaining with granite islands and open floor plans. Need room for that 'small' shoe collection? Walk-in closets are standard in all bedrooms. Nine-foot ceilings and large decks add to the feeling of spaciousness. And when you need a little sanctuary, retreat to your own oval soaking tubs. No detail for stylish living has gone overlooked."[37] Unit plans are compact, with balconies, open kitchens, and windows along one wall. Like New York by Gehry, Cloverdale 749, and the houses at Eden Prairie Woods, housing here is named—distinctively.

As of mid-2015, a one-bedroom, one-bath apart-

10 ft   20 ft

Toll Brothers, Stansbury model, Eden Prairie Woods, Eden Prairie, Minnesota, approved 2001. First-floor plan (below), Second-floor plan (above). Drawn by Nabila Morales Pérez.

113

10 ft   20 ft

Broadmoor Development Company, Broadmoor Apartments, Aksarben Village, Omaha, Nebraska, announced in 2015. Typical unit plans, from left: Brandeis (studio), Flatiron (studio). Drawn by Nabila Morales Pérez.

10 ft   20 ft

Humphreys & Partners Architects, Pinhook Flats, developed by Alchemy Development Corp., Aksarben Village, Omaha, Nebraska, completed in 2012. Typical unit plans, clockwise from top left: Strike the Gold (studio), Unbridled (two-bedroom), Timeless Design (live/work one-bedroom). Drawn by Nabila Morales Pérez.

ment at Pinhook Flats rented for between $940 and $1,275 per month, while a two-bedroom, two-bath went for between $1,220 and $1,365.[38] That puts the one-bedroom units close to the middle of the household rent scale tabulated by the AHS.[39] And, assuming a household income of about $40,000, it puts the residents of Pinhook Flats' one-bedroom apartments in the lower half of the population by income, and possibly in the bottom 40 percent or what Piketty calls the "lower class;" those who are projected to control only 15 percent of the country's wealth by 2030.[40]

In typological and sociological contrast, Wind by Neo, a 41-story condominium tower, was opened in 2008 by Neo Epoch, "the progressive developer that pioneered lofts in the Miami downtown area with its previous Neo Lofts and Neo Vertika projects." Here, even rooms have distinctive names. According to miamicondolifestyle.com:

> *The kinetic nature of Wind by Neo provided the inspiration to create a completely different urban living environment with flexible spaces that are adaptable to each person's individual preferences. From Exo-Rooms—11-foot deep spaces which function as outdoor living areas—to the interior K-Rooms—kinetic residences with flexible indoor spaces—Wind by Neo is sure to meet the ever changing lifestyles of its occupants by offering maximum flexibility in a downtown living experience.*[41]

Between December 2014 and April 2015, nine units sold in Wind by Neo, from one to three bedrooms, at an average price of about $350,000.[42]

Assuming a fully paid mortgage and no additional capital, ownership of a unit in Wind by Neo probably puts residents somewhere in the fourth quintile, or the top 40 percent (in the middle of Piketty's "middle class") by wealth, exclusive of other income. Their life-

10 ft   20 ft

Revuelta Vega Leon Architects, Wind by Neo, developed by Neo Epoch I Corp. and Downtown River Village, Miami, Florida, completed in 2008. Typical floor plans, units K5 and K6. Drawn by Nabila Morales Pérez.

style is somewhat atypical, however. Of the 75.6 million owner-occupied units counted by the AHS, only about 744,000 were in buildings containing fifty or more units. Likewise for the floor plans, which maximize exterior exposure with a jagged profile that alternates balconies with bay windows. Apartments are arranged along a double-loaded corridor, with glazed exposures on one side of each unit, and an efficient service core tucked against the inner wall. Outward orientation reigns.

Contrast these outward-looking units to the inward-looking cells offered to investors in the Corrections Corporation of America (CCA), a publicly traded Real Estate Investment Trust (REIT) [See HH: 2015]. The CCA's publicity boasts an 85,000+ total bed capacity in 60+ operating facilities housing 70,000+ inmates in 600+ programs across the country.[43] Unit plans are unavailable. Founded in 1983, the CCA "designs, builds, manages, and operates prisons, jails, detention centers and residential reentry centers on behalf of the Federal Bureau of Prisons, Immigrations and Customs Enforcement, the United States Marshals Service, [and] many states and counties across the country."[44] As the "fifth largest corrections system in the nation, behind only the federal government and three states," the CCA enters into public-private partnerships in which the majority of its facilities are company-owned.[45] This yields profit that can be leveraged, which means that, like shares of Forest City Enterprises, Inc. (owners of New York by Gehry), shares of the CCA are traded on the New York Stock Exchange: prisons as capital.

Among the CCA's properties is the Adams County Correctional Facility in Natchez, Mississippi, with a capacity of 2,567 male inmates. The facility is accredited by the American Correctional Association (ACA), which means, according to the company, that it "must meet nearly 500 professional standards in all areas of operations, including security, food service, fire/safety, sanitation, maintenance, medical, education, recreation, visitation, mail and administration."[46] In May 2012, violence broke out at the Adams County Correctional Facility. One corrections officer was killed, and twenty-five employees were taken hostage by about 300 prisoners. A lawsuit filed by the officer's family against CCA alleged that "the facility was short staffed and underequipped," and therefore unprepared to deal with the violence.[47] The CCA's stock price declined slightly in the following month, to about $20 per share, but has since doubled, trading at about $40 a share in early 2015.[48] There is little point in locating the residents of the Adams County Correctional Facility on the inequality spectrum, other than to note that they are among the 1.5 million housed in prisons nationwide, a disproportionate number of whom are African American.[49]

Contrast this investment product, again, to Greenville Overlook, a luxury home community in Greenville, Delaware, developed by Toll Brothers, that replicates the company's strategy (which we have already encountered in Minnesota) in the Mid-Atlantic region. Greenville Overlook comprises eight house types, ranging from 2,900 to 4,900 square feet and priced from about $660,000. Here the model names read like a half-forgotten history textbook: The Westbrook, The Gettysburg, The Manor, The Lexington, The Savannah, The Colonial, The Traditional, The Heritage, with surnames like Columbia, Elkton, Waterford, Duke, Langley, Claridge, Stansbury, Malvern. All include "nine-foot first floor ceilings, walk-out or daylight basements, stunning 2-story foyers, and first-floor master bedroom suites," sprinkled with vaulted ceilings, double-turned staircases, kitchen islands, overlooks, Roman tubs, arches, and French doors.[50] Prospective buyers are invited to "design" their own homes by adding amenities like powder rooms, curved oak stairs, "designer" fireplaces, solaria,

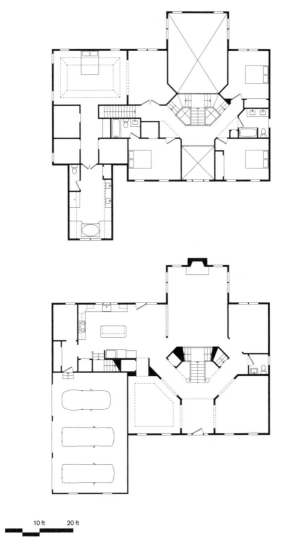

10 ft   20 ft

Toll Brothers, Langley model, Greenville Overlook, Wilmington, Delaware, begun in 2009.
First-floor plan (below), Second-floor plan (above). Drawn by Nabila Morales Pérez.

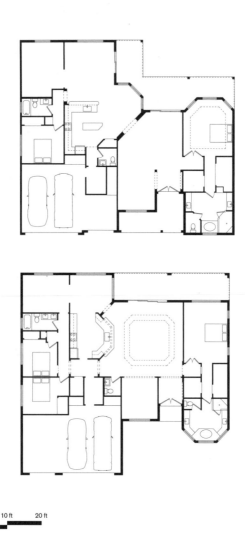

10 ft   20 ft

Levitt & Sons, Pinehurst (above), Doral (below), Summit Greens, Clermont, Florida, completed in 2006. Plans. Drawn by Nabila Morales Pérez.

and a "Luxurious Master Bath Package."[51] Toll Brothers illustrates the personalized "customer experience" in making what "may be one of the biggest and most important investments you'll ever make" with testimonials from homeowners, that attest to the knowledgability of the Greenville Sales Team.[52]

Compare this type of exclusivity to that which defines Summit Greens, a gated, "deed restricted over 55 community containing almost 800 homes and over 1,400 residents . . . governed by an elected board of directors of the homeowner's association," complete with an 18-hole golf course, residents clubs, and evening entertainment: "There is always something to do at Summit Greens."[53] Summit Greens was constructed between 2001 and 2006 by Levitt & Sons. Houses run in twelve models, from a 1,250 square-foot two-bedroom type (excluding garage) to the 2,400 square-foot three-bedroom Pinnacle series. Garages include space for golf carts, and actual floor plans reflect various upgrades.[54] Among the realtors representing Summit Greens properties is Susan H. of Keller William Realty LLC, a Wisconsin native who has lived in Summit Greens since 2003, "with a tremendous appreciation for Central Florida's enticing climate and attractions, along with her hard working ethics from the north." A "Certified Short Sale Specialist" (i.e. a specialist in selling homes with "underwater" mortgages), Susan "builds her client relationships through dedication, commitment, honesty, and good communication, while delivering the highest quality of service to all of her buyers and sellers and creating seamless and stress free transactions."[55] Except, of course, for those whose mortgages are underwater.

Differently supporting the growth of capital—including, in this case, human capital—and oriented toward a population with school-age children rather than to retirees, is Promontory Pointe, in Monument, Colorado, near Colorado Springs. Promontory Pointe is located in Lewis

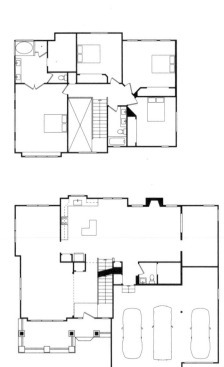

Classic Homes, Windsor, Promontory Pointe, Monument, Colorado, opened in 2011.
First-floor plan (below), Second-floor plan (above). Drawn by Nabila Morales Pérez.

Palmer School District 38, where "students post SAT and ACT scores well above the national average."[56] Developed by Classic Homes, a Colorado Springs based builder, Promontory opened with fifty lots in 2011, and continues to offer new build-to-order houses based on 19 floor plans, with prices ranging from approximately $310,000 to $400,000, as well as re-sales. Plans range from a two-bedroom, two-car garage ranch house (The Amber), to a six-bedroom, three-car garage duplex (The Sierra), available in three standard packages: Classic, Renaissance, and Carefree Living.[57] Based on average home prices of around $360,000 and an estimated monthly mortgage payment of around $1,700, their owners probably sit close to the national median, somewhere between the top 50 and top 40 percent of earners.[58] Equally important for their status as investors, however, these homeowners are emotional beings: one testimonial refers to the developers' agent as a "home counselor," who is described as "thorough, conscientious, detail oriented, amiable, hard working, flexible, and thoroughly committed to Customer Satisfaction on every level."[59] Local banks are listed as preferred lenders. This is "place-based" development at its most basic, most functional, and most ubiquitous.

The above cases offer merely a partial sample of the dominant types of large-scale real estate development in the United States. They exclude the practices of small builders, most of which replicate their logics, strategies, and housing types, at different price points, different scales, and with local variation. Nor do they include the range of alternative means for providing housing, from community land trusts to not-for-profit development to various governmentally incentivized public-private partnerships. As an example of the latter, then, consider Via Verde, a mixed-income affordable housing development, which has received considerable public attention for the alternative model that it appears to represent.[60]

Via Verde is a 171-unit mixed-use building in The Bronx, New York, developed by for-profit Jonathan Rose Companies and the not-for-profit Phipps Houses, and designed by Dattner Associates and Grimshaw Architects. Opened in 2012, the building comprises 151 rental units for low-income tenants, and 71 cooperative units for middle-income owners. As with New York by Gehry, a ULI case study locates the project in the housing system, as real estate. Via Verde began as a competition in 2006 sponsored jointly by the New York Department of Housing Preservation and Development (HPD), the New York City chapter of the American Institute of Architects, the New York State Energy Research and Development Authority, and Enterprise Community Partners, an affordable housing organization dedicated to supporting "public-private partnerships with financial institutions, governments, community organizations and other partners."[61] Via Verde was the result of one such partnership. The site in the south Bronx was owned by HPD, and the Rose/Phipps/Grimshaw/Dattner team was announced as the winning team in 2007. According to the Jonathan Rose Companies, their mission was "to repair and strengthen the fabric of cities, towns and villages, while preserving the land around them."[62] This, in support of "market-place strategies [that] combine a disciplined investment approach with innovative green solutions to produce superior, risk-adjusted returns."[63]

Therefore, like all of our other examples, Via Verde is capital. The development team acquired the site from HPD for $1, as subsidy for the low-income units, along with Low-Income Housing Tax Credits and other affordable housing financing from state and federal agencies [See 1.1.2]. The market-rate co-ops were also subsidized at the city and state level. Project costs were about 10 percent higher than typical, with an estimated 3 percent accounting for the added "green features."[64]

Units vary in size and configuration, with rentals running from 462 square-foot studio apartments to 1,089 square-foot three-bedroom units, and co-ops running from 664 square-foot one-bedroom units to 1,379 three-bedroom units. Sales prices for the co-ops have ranged from $78,894 to $192,750, or, at the highest end, roughly 80 percent of the median national home price in February 2012.[65] The rental units were intended to "be affordable for households earning 40 to 60 percent of the area median income (AMI)" for a thirty year term, after which the owners are permitted to "reposition" them in the market.[66] The median household income for The Bronx from 2009–2013 was $34,388.[67] Potential residents apply for admission and are chosen by lottery; rents are established relative to actual income. Via Verde has won at least a dozen awards for its combination of above-average design, affordable housing, "green living," and—we must add—profit. The ULI case study concludes that Via Verde "serves as a model for developments around the country, demonstrating that design innovation, urban revitalization, and healthy living are attainable development goals for affordable housing," while conceding that "one criticism of the development is how to replicate a project like Via Verde without the level of [public] financial support it received."[68] In other words, even with a mission of social and environmental sustainability, the laws of profit remain non-negotiable.

A Provisional Conclusion

These cases all show the means by which real estate development governs both the economic life and the imagination of housing in the United States. Though by no means exhaustive, they demonstrate how something as concrete as a house or apartment plan functions as an investment: sometimes, by correlating a certain lifestyle with a certain market; and sometimes, by helping to shape a particular type of "household" as the primary

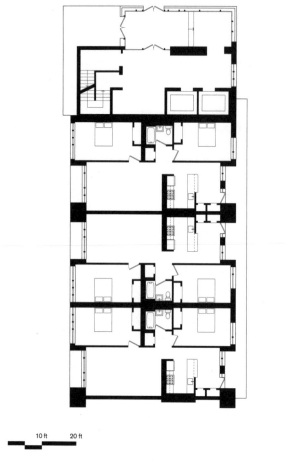

10 ft 20 ft

Dattner Associates and Grimshaw Architects, Via Verde, developed by Jonathan Rose and Phipps Houses, The Bronx, New York, opened in 2012. Partial plan, first floor (two-bedroom units). Drawn by Nabila Morales Pérez.

socioeconomic unit around which wealth is built. When we recall that wealth more than income is becoming the leading driver of economic inequality, we again see quite concretely the ways in which architecture, together with housing policy and economic policy, helps to produce inequality by producing and managing wealth, as real estate.

Architectural specifics, from floor plans to construction materials to styles to building names, also mix with social codes and regulating norms to shape the economics of inequality along racial and gender lines, with the household as their basic unit. If these lines are less visible in the above cases than the more directly economic disparities measured in unit prices and median income, it is worth noting that such metrics, too, can and have been cross-correlated. For example, the U.S. Census noted that from 2000 to 2011, where white households saw an average 3.5 percent increase in median net worth (mostly in the upper three fifths), black households on average saw their net worth *decrease* by 37.2 percent, most of which was experienced by the lowest and middle fifths of the economic spectrum.[69] To put these stark disparities differently: in 2011 the median net worth in the upper 20 percent of white households was around $750,000; in the upper 20 percent of black households it was around $225,000.[70] Although by no means an exclusive factor, real estate—as capital, or wealth—imparts a crucial dimension to the complex socioeconomic matrix witnessed by these numbers. It is reasonable to infer from them that, by and large, black households simply own less architecture than do white households while conversely, ownership of architecture—as real estate—correlates with socioeconomic status more generally.

Broadly construed, architecture is nevertheless much more than an abject piece of property. As a floor plan, an ambience, a collection of fixtures, a building type, a neighborhood, a name, *it is what makes real estate real.*

To study the architecture of housing in this way is therefore also to study the architecture of inequality that pervades American cities and American landscapes. It is not too much to say that, as a necessary component in the technique of governing that we have been describing—namely, the technique of governing through inequality—architecture also governs. It does so subtly and discreetly, less through monumental symbols or monolithic institutions than through the everyday practices by which houses and apartments are designed, built, bought, sold, and financed. Under these conditions, architecture is imagined first and foremost as an investment, the returns on which are by definition to be unevenly distributed. Thinking and making it otherwise remains a fundamental, unmet challenge for our times.

1. I use the term "capital" here in its narrower sense, as used by Thomas Piketty to denote wealth, or, as he puts it, "the sum total of nonhuman assets that can be owned and exchanged on some market." Piketty, *Capital in the Twenty-First Century*, trans. Arthur Goldhammer (Cambridge, MA: Harvard University Press, 2014), 46.
2. Joseph E. Stiglitz, *The Price of Inequality: How Today's Divided Society Endangers Our Future*, 2nd ed. (New York: Norton, 2012), 133.
3. Joseph E. Stiglitz, "Of the 1%, by the 1%, for the 1%," *Vanity Fair,* May 2011, http://www.vanityfair.com/news/2011/05/top-one-percent-201105.
4. Stiglitz, *The Price of Inequality*, 136.
5. Urban Land Institute, "ULI Case Studies: New York by Gehry at 8 Spruce Street" (November 2014), http://uli.org/publications/case-studies/.
6. Ibid., 3–4.
7. NYCHDC, "HDC Closes on a 904-Unit Frank Gehry Designed Tower in Lower Manhattan, Real Estate Rama," April 1, 2008, Available at http://newyork.realestaterama.com/2008/04/01/hdc-closes-on-a-904-unit-frank-gehry-designed-tower-in-lower-manhattan-ID0259.html, and cited in Urban Land Institute, "ULI Case Studies: New York by Gehry at 8 Spruce Street," 4.
8. Ibid., 5.
9. Ibid., 9.
10. "New York by Gehry," accessed August 8, 2015, http://www.newyorkbygehry.com/the-building.
11. Urban Land Institute, "ULI Case Studies: New York by Gehry at 8 Spruce Street," 7.
12. Ibid., 7.
13. Ibid., 5.
14. Ibid., 10.
15. Carmen DeNavas-Walt and Bernadette D. Proctor, "Income and Poverty in the United States: 2013," *U.S. Census Bureau* (September 2014), 5, https://www.census.gov/content/dam/Census/library/publications/2014/demo/p60-249.pdf.
16. Piketty, *Capital in the Twenty-First Century*, 265.
17. Piketty, *Capital in the Twenty-First Century*, tables 7.1–3, 247–249.
18. Piketty, *Capital in the Twenty-First Century*, 260.
19. "2013 American Housing Survey for the United States—Complete Set of Tables and Standard Errors," U.S. Census Bureau, accessed August 18, 2015, http://www2.census.gov/

programs-surveys/ahs/2013/AHS_2013_National_Tables_v1.2.xls.

20. For data on individuals, see Wojciech Kopczuk, Emmanuel Saez and Jae Song, "Earnings Inequality and Mobility in the United States: Evidence from Social Security Data Since 1937," *The Quarterly Journal of Economics* 125, no. 1 (2010): 91–128.

21. "GINI Index (World Bank estimate)," World Bank, accessed August 9, 2015, http://data.worldbank.org/indicator/SI.POV.GINI. Indices vary somewhat according to methods used and underlying data sources. Thus, according to the Organization for Economic Co-operation and Development (OECD) for the same year, the U.S. Gini index was .380, with those of most other countries proportionately lower as well. See "Income Distribution and Poverty," Organization for Economic Cooperation and Development, accessed August 9, 2015, http://stats.oecd.org/Index.aspx?DatasetCode=IDD.

22. "Income Distribution and Poverty," Organization for Economic Cooperation and Development, accessed August 9, 2015, http://stats.oecd.org/Index.aspx?DatasetCode=IDD.

23. "Metadata on OECD Income Distribution Database (IDD)," Organization for Economic Cooperation and Development, accessed August 9, 2015, http://www.oecd.org/social/soc/IDD-Metadata.pdf; See also "Current Population Survey: A Joint Effort Between the Bureau of Labor Statistics and the Census Bureau," U.S. Census Bureau, http://www.census.gov/cps/.

24. "Current Population Survey (CPS): Collecting Data," U.S. Census Bureau, accessed August 9, 2015, http://www.census.gov/cps/methodology/collecting.html.

25. Ibid. Methodologically, "household" is defined as follows: "A household consists of all the people who occupy a housing unit. A house, an apartment or other group of rooms, or a single room, is regarded as a housing unit when it is occupied or intended for occupancy as separate living quarters; that is, when the occupants do not live with any other persons in the structure and there is direct access from the outside or through a common hall. A household includes the related family members and all the unrelated people, if any, such as lodgers, foster children, wards, or employees who share the housing unit. A person living alone in a housing unit, or a group of unrelated people sharing a housing unit such as partners or roomers, is also counted as a household. The count of households excludes group quarters. There are two major categories of households, 'family' and 'nonfamily'."

26. "American Community Survey (ACS)," U.S. Census Bureau, accessed August 9, 2015, http://www.census.gov/acs/www/; "History: Decennial Census," accessed August 9, 2015, https://www.census.gov/history/www/programs/demographic/decennial_census.html.

27. "American Housing Survey (AHS): Methodology," U.S. Census Bureau, last revised April 3, 2015, http://www.census.gov/programs-surveys/ahs/about/methodology.html.

28. "American Housing Survey (AHS): About," U.S. Census Bureau, last revised February 11, 2014, http://www.census.gov/programs-surveys/ahs/about.html.

29. See Alex Schwartz, *Housing Policy in the United States: An Introduction*, 3rd ed. (New York: Routledge, 2015 [2006]) for an overview of the past and present of U.S. housing policy.

30. "American Housing Survey (AHS): About," U.S. Census Bureau, accessed August 9, 2015, http://www.census.gov/programs-surveys/ahs/about.html.

31. "5 Units Left in LOHA-Designed Condos in the Miracle Mile," *Curbed Los Angeles*, June 10, 2013, accessed August 9, 2015, http://la.curbed.com/archives/2013/06/5_units_left_in_lohadesigned_condos_in_the_miracle_mile.php.

32. "749 Cloverdale," *Top LA Condos*, accessed August 9, 2015, http://www.toplacondos.com/749-Cloverdale.

33. According to the U.S. Census, the median household net wealth of the top quintile (top 20 percent) was $630,754. Marina Vornovitsky, Alfred Gottschalck, and Adam Smith "Distribution of Household Wealth in the U.S.: 2000 to 2011," 12, accessed August 9, 2015, https://www.census.gov/people/wealth/files/Wealth%20distribution%202000%20to%202011.pdf.

34. Robert Gebeloff and Shaila Dewan, "Measuring the Top 1% by Wealth, Not Income," *New York Times*, January 17, 2012, accessed August 9, 2015, http://economix.blogs.nytimes.com/2012/01/17/measuring-the-top-1-by-wealth-not-income/?_r=0.

35. "Eden Prairie Woods," Toll Brothers, accessed August 9, 2015, https://www.tollbrothers.com/MN/Eden_Prairie_Woods.

36. "Pinhook Flats," Alchemy Development, accessed August 9, 2015, http://www.pinhook-flats.com.

37. "Aksarben Village by Broadmoor," accessed August 9, 2015, http://www.broadmoor.cc/apartments.aspx?cid=17.

38. "Aksarben Village," Robert Hancock & Co., accessed August 9, 2015, http://roberthan-cockco.com/pinhook-flats-at-aksarben-village/.

39. "American Housing Survey 2013," U.S. Census Bureau, Table C-10-RO, accessed August 9, 2015, http://www.census.gov/programs-surveys/ahs/data/2013/national-summary-report-and-tables---ahs-2013.html.

40. "What Percent Are You?" *New York Times*, January 14, 2012, http://www.nytimes.com/interactive/2012/01/15/business/one-percent-map.html.

41. "Wind by Neo Condos for Sale," *Miami Condo Lifestyle*, accessed August 9, 2015, http://www.miamicondolifestyle.com/wind-by-neo.php.

42. Ibid.

43. Corrections Corporation of America, accessed August 9, 2015, http://www.cca.com.

44. Ibid.

45. "Who We Are," Corrections Corporation of America, accessed August 9, 2015, http://www.cca.com/who-we-are.

46. "Quality Assurance," Corrections Corporation of America, accessed August 9, 2015, http://www.cca.com/security-operations/quality-assurance.

47. Iulia Filip, "Family Sues CCA for Death in Prison Riot," *Courthouse News Service*, May 10, 2013, https://www.courthousenews.com/2013/05/10/57518.htm.

48. "Corrections Corp of America," Dividend.com, accessed August 9, 2015, http://www.dividend.com/dividend-stocks/services/management-services/cxw-corrections-corp-of-amercia/; "Corrections Corporation of America (CXW)," accessed August 9, 2015, Yahoo! Finance, https://finance.yahoo.com/q/hp?s=CXW&a=04&b=1&c=2012&d=04&e=4&f=2015&g=d&z=66&y=0.

49. E. Ann Carson, "Prisoners in 2013," Bureau of Justice Statistics, U.S. Department of Justice (September 30, 2014), http://www.bjs.gov/content/pub/pdf/p13.pdf.

50. "Greenville Overlook," Toll Brothers, accessed August 9, 2015, https://www.tollbrothers.com/DE/Greenville_Overlook and "Greenville Overlook: Home Designs," Toll Brothers, accessed August 9, 2015, https://www.tollbrothers.com/DE/Greenville_Overlook#home-designs.

51. "Greenville Overlook: The Duke," Toll Brothers Design Your Own Home, accessed August 9, 2015, https://security.tollbrothers.ml-scp.com/FloorPlan/Details/30933?com=1446.

52. "Greenville Overlook: Customer Experience," Toll Brothers, accessed August 9, 2015, https://www.tollbrothers.com/DE/Greenville_Overlook#customer_experience.

53. "Summit Greens Community," Keller Williams Realty, LLC, accessed August 9, 2015, http://summitgreensflhomes.com/summit.html.

54. Ibid.

55. "About Susan," Keller Williams Realty, LLC, accessed August 9, 2015, http://summit-greensflhomes.com/susan.html.

56. "Promontory Pointe," Classic Homes, accessed August 9, 2015, http://www.classichomes.com/index.cfm?id=83F84B1D-A1BA-4250-A9A521C706F408F4.

57. "The Renaissance Package," Classic Homes, accessed August 9, 2015, http://classichomes.com/index.cfm?id=0aafcc84-d749-9173-478b1eed4b19a2ce.

58. Vornovitsky, Gottschalck, and Smith, "Distribution of Household Wealth in the U.S.: 2000 to 2011," 12.

59. "Classic New Home Buyer Reviews," Classic Homes, accessed August 9, 2015, http://classichomes.com/index.cfm?id=79dd9035-0db2-47cc-99ea0205300d39c4.

60. See, for example, Michael Kimmelman, "In a Bronx Complex, Doing Good Mixes With Looking Good," *New York Times*, September 26, 2011, http://www.nytimes.com/2011/09/26/arts/design/via-verde-in-south-bronx-rewrites-low-income-housing-rules.html; and Anne-Marie Lubenau, "On the Road with the Rudy Bruner Award: Via Verde – Bronx, NY," Metropolis, April 11, 2013, http://www.metropolismag.com/Point-of-View/April-2013/On-the-Road-with-the-Rudy-Bruner-Award-Via-Verde-Bronx-NY/.

61. Urban Land Institute, "ULI Case Studies: Via Verde," (January 2014), accessed August 9, 2015, http://uli.org/case-study/uli-case-studies-via-verde/; and "Strategic Plan," Enterprise Community Partners, Inc., accessed August 9, 2015, http://www.enterprisecommunity.org/strategic-planhttp://www.enterprisecommunity.com/about/mission-and-strategic-plan.

62. "Mission: To Repair the Fabric of Communities," Jonathan Rose Companies, accessed August 9, 2015, http://www.rosecompanies.com/about-us/mission-to-repair-the-fabric-of-communities.

63. "Rose Investments," Jonathan Rose Companies, accessed August 9, 2015, http://www.rosecompanies.com/investments.

64. Urban Land Institute, "ULI Case Studies: Via Verde," 4–5.
65. "Median and Average Sales Prices of New Homes Sold in United States," U.S. Census Bureau, accessed August 9, 2015, https://www.census.gov/construction/nrs/pdf/uspricemon.pdf.
66. Urban Land Institute, "ULI Case Studies: Via Verde," 7.
67. "State & County QuickFacts: Bronx County, New York," U.S. Census Bureau, accessed August 9, 2015, http://quickfacts.census.gov/qfd/states/36/36005.html.
68. Urban Land Institute, "ULI Case Studies: Via Verde," 9.
69. Vornovitsky, Gottschalck, and Smith, "Distribution of Household Wealth in the U.S.: 2000 to 2011," 3–4.
70. Ibid., 16.

Part 3 Tools

Contracts
Manuel Shvartzberg Carrió

Real estate is embedded within legal arrangements. It is both determined by and productive of them. In what follows, the reader will find a brief history of real estate's relation to the law. This history is necessarily episodic, because the law itself is composed of multiple dimensions—pieces of an ever-shifting puzzle that range from politics and philosophy to media and finance. It is also episodic because legal frameworks diverge according to different units of sovereignty; here, we focus only on the Anglo-American tradition of Common Law (as opposed to Civil Law), and only on certain legal actors.

Real estate historically mediates agreements and disputes over land—a form of power struggle that has become codified through the law. The central object of contention is not just land *per se*, but the very ontology of land—its status as something that can be variously possessed by an individual, traded, speculated upon, or held together by different political arrangements. Real estate thus has to be framed alongside legal-philosophical discourses of the individual's right to private property, and, more fundamentally, the modern conception of individuality as a naturalized condition. Property, personhood, and market economics together form the historical-conceptual milieu out of which the field of real estate emerges.

This field engages diverse agents and actors; the law provides them with force and stability through specific legal instruments such as writs, deeds, statutes, professional accreditations, and, as discussed here, contracts. Contracts are agreements between individuals and other entities, and are thereby the vehicles by which the law's proper subjects (including entrepreneurs, tenants, corporations, or debtors) are recognized and produced. In turn, legal instruments and actors mediate the expansion of the market economy across space and time, requiring the invention of new legal, political, and financial forms, such as the management of the future via speculative arrangements of credit, debt, duty, and desire.

3.1.1
INVENTING
PRIVATE
PROPERTY:
AUTONOMY
AND SELF-
REALIZATION

Private property is, substantially, a modern invention. It was not until the sixteenth century that landed property began to operate as an individual's exclusive right, whether to be used or to be sold. At least three main reasons account for this change: 1) the rise of the modern administrative state in lieu of the monarchical one, 2) the development of a philosophical doctrine of individual natural rights, 3) the legal shift from a notion of property tied to customary obligations to a merely transactional one in the context of a growing market economy.

Prior to the modern state, landed property was bound up with the political and social institutions of monarchical sovereignty. In this arrangement, the lords who guarded the land administered all its relationships, including the lives and livelihoods of those who lived on it. The landlord-tenant relation was one of extreme inequality, but also of paternalistic guardianship—land was not a commodity but the source of subsistence for a stratified community.[1] Property was thus tied to customary practices that discharged various social functions—duties and obligations of moral, economic, and legal nature. Rather than being individually owned and disposed of, properties often bore a multiplicity of rights by a variety of non-exclusive users.

Centuries of struggle, however, traced a shift in the locus of power: from the singular figure of the monarch, sovereignty was gradually dispersed among the many bodies of proto-modern societies, such as courts and state legislatures. Originally instruments of a powerful, land-holding elite, these institutions were reformed in large part to guarantee the individual property rights of an emerging bourgeoisie.[2] To this day, property signifies rights *in* or *to* things, not the things themselves. The task of the state is to enforce these rights as stipulated by law.[3] Private property, as opposed to public property (managed by the state) and common property (for non-exclusive uses), means the right to lawfully exclude others from an individual's use of or benefit from something. As such, it reifies modern notions of individual autonomy and self-realization defined against others. This legal-philosophical framework, originating in the sixteenth century and enshrined in

135

liberal thought over the next four centuries, is a primary vector of modernity and capitalism.

With the slow naturalization of the autonomous individual, property came to be increasingly confused with things themselves (rather than understood as rights in or to things), and also became more fungible within a growing market economy: disposable, saleable, and transferable by persons and firms acting to make a profit.[4]

3.1.2
EQUITY AS
FAIRNESS: A
SUBSTANTIVE
VIEW OF
CONTRACTS

Throughout the eighteenth century, contracts—agreements or promises between parties—became the chief vehicle for the commercial exchange of property. This contrasted with older modes of codifying transfers and arrangements, whether those of familial inheritance, mixed tenure relations rooted in customs, or the endowments (grants) of colonial expansion.

However, the law was slow to engage a merely transactional view of private commercial exchanges. Throughout the pre-modern era, it was mostly a substantive principle of justice that governed the courts' determinations of contractual claims.[5] In the British American colonies, which unevenly adopted English law, judges ruled on disputes over exchange according to what was considered equitable (just) in a customary sense. Usually, judges would rule so that the disputed exchange could be resolved based on what was equitable in a universal sense—for instance, if goods had not been delivered as agreed, the judge would rule that they should be. The persistence of an equitable conception of contracts was related to the fact that the rulings assumed a personal character to the exchanges, whether these took place in the literal face-to-face of local markets or through the figuration of a personalized merchants' custom in international trades. At both levels, the courts understood contracts as instruments to secure the terms of transfer over specific *goods and services*; they were not expected to secure a transfer of *value* itself, such as with claims over an expected future return, or a bet on a particular land deal.

In this "title" theory of contract (pursuant to the transfer of rights over things as borne in legal titles), values were framed as being universally objective either through their customary definitions or through their equity in terms of fairness. The intention was to limit unequal (unfair) exchanges, preempting usurious or malicious gain at the expense of others.[6] In cases where bargains were deemed to be unfair, the courts would routinely intervene to ensure the equity of the exchange—in effect, equalizing the contracting parties' sides of the bargain. The amalgamation of cases articulated by Common Law, upon which judges based their rulings, were used to argue for limitations on contractual obligations whenever these were found to be in contradiction with equitable custom.

3.1.3
EQUITY AS
NATURAL
PROPERTY
RIGHT: THE
CASE OF THE
MORTGAGE

As early as the sixteenth century, however, a different kind of sovereignty rooted in the "natural property" of the individual self, and which thus could never be expunged, had been posed as an alternative legal-philosophical framework for governing land and social relations.[7] This development occurred very unevenly throughout the early modern period, both geographically and also in terms of the legal practices employed to manage it. The history of the mortgage, as a contract regulating the financing of interests in land, illustrates this ambiguity.[8]

Originally, mortgages were a type of promise (or "security") given by the borrower to the lender, which declared the borrower's willingness to forfeit the land, all at once and in one instance, if he could not repay the full amount at the specified date when the debt was due (hence the word "mortgage", which literally meant "dead pledge"). However, as the landowning gentry and judges acquired autonomy, the mortgage's debt was dispersed over time rather than being due on a specific date. As long as the full price was eventually paid, even years later, creditors and judges allowed the mortgagor to keep (a part of) the title to the property while he was paying—what was called "equity of redemption." This extension of the payment over time thus affected the development of land as a financial product, extending its status beyond that of a substantive commodity and toward a fungible one. When mortgagees wanted to recuperate their stake in the land due to a non-paying mortgagor, they had to get a judicial writ to foreclose the property, forcing the borrower to sell and pay off the debt. The proceeds of the sale over and above the debt, however, went to the original owner, a remainder that was said to be his "equity" in the land. Thus by the late eighteenth century, a shift in the conception of justice can be seen in the development of mortgages: from equity as a principle of substantive fairness (referring to an absolute, universal measure of justice), to equity as a stake in capital (referring to the relative value of a financial interest).[9]

If customary practices were giving way to more formally privatized contractual relations, the increasing autonomy of individuals with respect to their sovereign was echoed in the way land itself was understood and used. Previously, under feudal conditions, land had been understood in terms of its capacity to sustain the peasant families (and their lords) living from it. Soil fertility, measured in the specific amount of seeding required to feed a number of families, was giving way to an abstract quality that could be compared quantitatively across vastly different contexts: the notion of geometric area and the practice of measurement (surveying) mediated a transition from the subsistence economy to the development of speculative agricultural and real estate markets. Land was becoming less important for how it could specifically sustain a particular community, and more important for how it could produce value for an anonymous market—either agriculturally (disembedding socio-ecological relationships) or in itself as a universalized territorial commodity that could be sold in the land market.[10] This shift thus made land abstract in the sense of being understood (or represented) as equal to other lands which were comparable to it only by reference to an external signifier, the price of a unit area, in a "universal" sphere, the market.[11]

3.1.4
THE WILL
THEORY OF
CONTRACT:
PROCEDURE
TAKES
COMMAND

As commodities were increasingly produced for the market, and labor sold for wages, the rise of liberal philosophy and political economy helped to configure how, and by whom, these things were to be exchanged. Toward the end of the eighteenth century, the equitable theory of contract was being displaced by a "will" theory in which the value of things being exchanged was no longer understood as being objective, as it had under substantive principles of law.[12] Rather, exchanges were increasingly viewed as occurring between sovereign individuals (namely, entrepreneurs and merchants) who competitively determined, on their own, the value of their exchanges. Individuals' subjective judgments of value were now understood and accepted as being objectively unequal: rooted in arbitrary and relative individual desires.[13] The courts began deferring to the particular terms of the contract arranged between individuals, thus neutralizing the extent of the authority and use of the Common Law tradition. Judges only ruled on the lawfulness of an exchange in cases where fraud was clearly involved. The contract became a vehicle by which individuals could "contract out" of normative straitjackets, pitting rules of commercial usage against the rule of Common Law. "Equity," understood as fairness, was no longer a variable in judicial rulings: the contract was now sovereign, and "absolute fairness" was fragmented into the unique, localized, and incommensurable nature of each particular exchange.[14]

The causes for this shift from a substantive to a procedural view of the contract are simultaneously technical and philosophical. Judges recognized the diversity and complexity of commercial customs, but could not rule on them both for practical reasons (they lacked the specific know-how to decide on the technical aspects of increasingly heterogeneous and sophisticated bargains), and for ideological reasons (they preferred not to interfere with the growth of business). However, seeing the contract as an intrinsically unknowable meeting of desiring wills—the black box of commercial customs—could itself be articulated as a universal law by construing each particular commercial contract as a disaggregated chapter of universality itself. The merchants' particularism was thus elevated to the universal: justice deferred to the exceptionalism of the merchant classes as the ostensibly natural agent of social progress.[15]

The radical subjectivism of contracts between private individuals, understood as the simple expression of a "meeting of minds" that cannot be predetermined, became the objective basis upon which a formalistic view of the law was constructed. This impersonal quality enabled the development of bigger businesses and larger markets to be established, as contracts could now allow for limitations in warranties and speculation in future values—things that the customary, substantive, or "equitable" view of the law had explicitly sought to discourage.

3.1.5
CONTRACTS AND
SPECULATION:
HEDGING RISKS
The will theory of contract developed within and mediated the expansion of the market economy in the nineteenth century, particularly as it enabled the growth of commercial speculation. This techno-philosophical development had two components: on one hand, the will theory articulated the contract as an instrument for the formalization of individuals; these were no longer subject to an external standard of fairness or value, but were considered formally equal in their being "naturally unequal."[16] On the other hand, this natural inequality correlated the unknowability of wills and capacities to the unknowability (and thus fluctuation) of prices—differentials that formed the basis for speculative business operations and profits, now increasingly celebrated rather than shamed. As the market economy model extended in both quality (with different kinds of goods and services being traded) and quantity (over larger expanses of space and time) judges began to rule on contractual claims according to their implicit consequences, such as claims over the expected prices of stocks. What had been unthinkable within the doctrine of equity as fairness was becoming normalized: a functional view of the contract as demanded by commercial and transactional imperatives, that would ensure the discharge of the contracts' terms regardless of their "equitable" merits. The increasingly influential merchants posed their own interests, which were intrinsically incommensurable from each other—i.e., having no universal measure—as the new standard of justice.[17]

In the late eighteenth century, there had been a marked increase in market speculation tied to state securities, commodities trade, the building industry, and real estate, which the courts were now willing to enforce as long as the "wills" of the contracting parties could be established. The court would not assess the validity of a bargain, it would only certify that the parties had freely agreed to enter into contract—that there had been a "meeting of the minds." This transactional and naturalistic view of contracts sanctioned individual price and performance speculation, thus allowing the inclusion of speculative claims over the future (on the basis of the market) to enter into the legal sphere. For the first time, claims over losses of expected future profits could be reclaimed in the courts as liquidated damages.[18]

The contract was thus becoming a hedge, by both parties, over a risky and sometimes unknowable bet, rather than the mere transfer of a property title.[19] The hedge made use of the contract to limit liabilities (i.e., explicitly excluding Common Law warranties) to ratify the particularities of the speculative exchange. Since price differentials (profits) may arise from asymmetries in information, contracts were drawn to establish the validity of these asymmetries by construing them as factual differences in opinion and merit, thus preempting charges of unfairness or exploitation of one party over another. Following the doctrine of *caveat emptor* ("buyer beware"), the parties individually assumed the risks of competitive speculation by explicitly excluding the protections of Common Law through their particular contract terms. Contracts over real estate, with their inherently speculative logic, played a key role in institutionalizing differentials of opinion and information as the basis of competitive profit making.[20]

3.1.6
LEGAL AGENTS
AND MARKETS:
THE SUBJECT
AS INVESTOR

Throughout the nineteenth century a variety of legal actors came into existence, each responding to, or interjecting, a particular way in which the law represented and accounted for the development of the market economy. Individual entrepreneurs increasingly operated as firms of partners who professionalized the procurement of goods and services. As capital accumulated around certain trades or familial groups, organized as syndicates and trusts, their productive activities shifted to the management of their inheritances, investments, and rents. Further accentuating the division between a managerial and an owning class, corporations allowed investors to focus on financial expansion without the risk of personal liability, generating a completely new kind of natural-artificial "person" in the eyes of the law.[21] In effect, contracts, and the legal battles they aroused, created such agents.

As the market economy expanded both quantitatively and qualitatively, business operations scaled up and labor markets disembedded the relation of the worker to both master and place. Employment contracts (becoming more common around the 1830s) were set up to limit the liability of employers, and to legitimate the (higher) risks taken by employees in the form of competitive, privately negotiated, wages—signalling (higher) rewards.[22] This commodification and professionalization of labor therefore individualized both risks and returns, while enabling the development of more competitive and larger industries without due regard to local customs, traditions or social protections.[23] The growth of markets was supported by legal-contractual theory and practice in both the forms of partnership business owners could now establish, as well as in the availability of an unhinged and incentivized workforce. The courts rationalized the growth of businesses and markets as proof of the existence of a natural, autonomous and universal sphere of commercial custom that accrued enough weight and consistency as to displace the older traditions of Common Law itself. As we have seen, this sphere was construed as universal both extensively in terms of pertaining to all places of the "civilized world," and intensively as emanating from a universal "natural reason."[24] The physical correlates of the natural reason of commerce were the "objective" ever-extending markets and commodities, factories, and business operations that configured them. Legal conflicts could therefore now be determined by reference to the inherent laws of this new realm, the rational-universal market, in which the individual speculator was king.[25]

However, in this formally universalized world, the radical limitation of liability offered by the particularization of contracts created a problem. While businesses used contracts to insure themselves against risky dealings and legal attacks, expanded markets and industries required standardized products and predictable outcomes. Industrialization and

142

mass production generated a need for minimal levels of warranty—generally of kind rather than quality—which the courts were inclined to enforce.[26] For this reason, further legal entities were born that could displace these liabilities away from individuals and into other kinds of legal "persons". Trusts and corporations responded to this need by increasingly separating the management of the business from the actual owners, and limiting the liability of the business to the organization itself rather than its constituent owners and investors.[27]

The limitation of liability and growth of absentee ownership has continued from the late nineteenth all the way to the twenty-first century. In real estate, this is perhaps best illustrated by the dramatic expansion, in recent years, of Real Estate Investment Trusts (REITs)—corporations that own and manage real estate [See HH: 2015]. Investors can speculate with REITs as equity, by buying and selling shares in REITs, rather than speculating on the "real" real estate. This secondary-market speculation, also referred to as "securitization," allows for the further abstraction of real estate itself, making it more fungible, competitive, speculative—and thus, potentially profitable—to investors worldwide. The historical functions of the contract, as a device for transferring ownership, limiting risk, and reifying universal rationality and subjective self-realization, can now take place in seconds through securities speculation in the global financial markets.

The extended pervasiveness and speed of speculative-contractual property transactions marks another shift in the conception of property itself—beyond an enforceable claim over rights to things, property above all signifies an enforceable claim to a revenue.[28] But as real estate becomes an increasingly large part of the apparatus for accumulating and privatizing global wealth, its legal enforcement is not (exclusively) limited to the organizational and coercive framework of the sovereign nation-state; rather, its very logics become self-enforced (naturalized) through procedure and repetition. Enforcement is achieved by presenting a seemingly unquestionable consensus around vexing problems: like the modes of subjectivity enshrined by academic curricula; the best

143

practices promoted by global financial institutions; or the formalization of the architectural imagination to the tune of the real estate industry. The legal subject has become the speculator in the market; there is, allegedly, no outside—the contract has been drawn, other modes of being and interaction, foreclosed.

Many thanks to Columbia University Professor Elizabeth Blackmar for her continued support and advice on the questions opened by this short text.

1. Andro Linklater, *Owning the Earth: the Transforming History of Land Ownership* (New York: Bloomsbury, 2013), 30.
2. On the juridical, philosophical and techno-political dimensions and evolution of sovereignty, in Europe, from the early Modern period, see: Michel Foucault, "Society Must Be Defended," *Lectures at the Collège De France, 1975–76* (New York: Picador, 2003), and *Security, Territory, Population: Lectures at the Collège De France, 1977–78* (New York: Picador, 2007). Foucault theorized a large paradigmatic shift in the history of government: the transformation of power, evolving since the middle ages, from "sovereignty"—an external, transcendental, and self-serving rule of law chiefly dedicated to maintaining territorial power—to "governmentality"; a form of power emerging roughly around the middle of the eighteenth century which is integrally bound with the population; governed and governing by and for itself through not only laws, but also "tactics" that are at once internal and external to the state:

    "By this word 'governmentality' I mean three things. First, by 'governmentality' I understand the ensemble formed by institutions, procedures, analyses and reflections, calculations, and tactics that allow the exercise of this very specific, albeit very complex, power that has the population as its target, political economy as its major form of knowledge, and apparatuses of security as its essential technical instrument. Second, by 'governmentality' I understand the tendency, the line of force, that for a long time, and throughout the West, has constantly led towards the pre-eminence over all other types of power—sovereignty, discipline, and so on—of the type of power that we can call 'government' and which has led to the development of a series of specific governmental apparatuses (*appareils*) on the one hand, and, on the other to the development of a series of knowledges (*savoirs*). Finally, by 'governmentality' I think we should understand the process, or rather, the result of the process by which the state of justice of the Middle Ages became the administrative state in the fifteenth and sixteenth centuries and was gradually 'governmentalized.'" Foucault, *Security, Territory, Population*, 108.
3. "[T]o have property is to have a right in the sense of an enforceable claim to some use or benefit of something, whether it is a right to a share in some common resource or an individual right in some particular things. What distinguishes property from mere momentary possession is that property is a claim that will be enforced by society or the state, by custom or convention or law." C. B. Macpherson, "The Meaning of Property," in *Property, Mainstream and Critical Positions.* (Toronto: University of Toronto Press, 1978), 3.
4. "The more freely the market operated, the more this was so. It appeared to be the things themselves, not just rights in them, that were exchanged in the market. In fact the difference was not that things rather than rights in things were exchanged, but that previously unsaleable rights in things were now saleable; or, to put it differently, that limited and not always saleable rights *in* things were being replaced by virtually unlimited and saleable rights *to* things." Macpherson, *Property*, 7–8.
5. See Chapter VI "The Triumph of Contract," in Morton J. Horwitz, *The Transformation of American Law, 1780–1860* (Cambridge, MA: Harvard University Press, 1977), 160. Much of the account on contract law provided here is derived from this text.
6. "[T]he concept of customary prices [rooted in the medieval just price theory of value] formed the necessary foundation for a legal system which awarded contract damages according to measures of fairness independent of the terms agreed to by the contracting parties. By the end of the eighteenth century, however, the development of extensive markets undermined this system of customary prices and radically transformed the

role of contract in an increasingly commercial society." Horwitz, *The Transformation of American Law*, 173.

7. "From the sixteenth and seventeenth centuries on, more and more of the land and resources in settled countries was becoming private property, and private property was becoming an individual right unlimited in amount, unconditional on the performance of social functions, and freely transferable, as it substantially remains to the present day." Macpherson, *Property*, 10.

8. See Linklater, *Owning the Earth*, in particular Chapter 3 "The Rights of Private Property," 39.

9. Ibid., 33–35.

10. See Karl Polanyi, *The Great Transformation* (Boston: Beacon Press, 1957).

11. "[I]n every country where the concept of individually owned landed property has taken hold, one unmistakable indicator of its arrival has been provided by a change in the way land is measured....In a localized, peasant economy where the earth was valued primarily for its ability to support people, measurements that varied according to the fertility of soil provided the most useful indication of what a farmer needed to know. Around the world, the amount of seed that had to be sown to feed a family from the harvest provided a basic, and perhaps primeval, unit of measurement of the earth....
But in a market involving buyers with no local knowledge, an objective, unchanging quality such as area allowed strangers to compare the value of different commodities, Thus one unmistakable indicator that a true market in land had developed was the appearance of exact, invariable measurements in place of local, organic units." Linklater *Owning the Earth*, 32–33.

12. "The development of extensive markets at the turn of the [nineteenth] century contributed to a substantial erosion of belief in theories of objective value and just price. Markets for future delivery of goods were difficult to explain within a theory of exchange based on giving and receiving equivalents in value. Futures contracts for fungible commodities could only be understood in terms of a fluctuating conception of expected value radically different from the static notion that lay behind contracts for specific goods; a regime of markets and speculation was simply incompatible with a socially imposed standard of value. The rise of a modern law of contract, then, was an outgrowth of an essentially procommercial attack on the theory of objective value which lay at the foundation of the eighteenth century's equitable idea of contract." Horwitz, *The Transformation of American Law*, 180–181.

13. "Between 1790 and 1850 the overwhelming emphasis in legal and economic thought was on the random and fluctuating nature of value that had been introduced by a market economy....the overwhelming message of Verplanck and all other legal writers and judges before mid-century was that price could not provide a social measure of value because it radically fluctuated due to "the speculation, the tastes, wants, or caprices of purchasers." Ibid., 198.

14. "If value is subjective, nineteenth century contracts theorists reasoned, the function of exchange is to maximize the conflicting and otherwise incommensurable desires of individuals. The role of contract law was not to assure the equity of agreements but simply to enforce only those willed transactions that parties to a contract believed to be to their mutual advantage. The result was a major tendency toward submerging the dominant equitable theory of contract in a conception of contractual obligation based exclusively on express bargains." Ibid., 181.

15. "Thus, contract, reflecting the 'self-legislative instinct of society,' could legitimately abrogate all preexisting common law duties. 'Considered as emanating from . . . courts, it is a system of paternal, regulating, construing, preservative legislation, which does not aim to restrain or control, but only systematizes, harmonizes, and combines the enterprises and inventions which men voluntarily undertake.' For one of the 'chief excellencies' of this 'system of political economy' is that it 'leaves men to make their own arrangements, and contents itself with regulating them.' Under the influence of the contractarian theory and its laissez-faire underpinnings, common law judges after 1830 began to allow private agreements to suspend long-standing customary duties." Ibid., 203–204.

16. "[Gulian C.] Verplanck's *Essay* [1825] represents an important stage in the process of adapting contract law to the realities of a market economy. Verplanck saw that if value is solely determined by the clash of subjective desire, there can be no objective measure of the fairness of a bargain. Since only 'facts' are objective, fairness can never be measured in terms of substantive equality. The law can only assure that each party to a bargain is given 'full knowledge of all material facts.' Significantly, Verplanck defined 'material facts'

145

so as not to include 'peculiar advantages of skill, shrewdness, and experience, regarding which . . . no one has a right to call upon us to abandon. Here, justice permits us to use our superiority freely.' 'All know what a wide difference exists among men in these points, and whatever advantage may result from that inequality, is silently conceded in the very fact of making a bargain. It is a superiority on one side – an inferiority on the other, perhaps very great, but they are allowed. This must be so; the business of life could not go on were it otherwise.' Thus, while he refused in theory to separate law and morality, Verplanck confined fraud to a range sufficiently narrow to permit the contract system to reinforce existing social and economic inequalities." Gulian C. Verplanck, *An Essay on the Doctrine of Contracts: Being an Inquiry How Contracts Are Affected in Laws and Morals, By Concealment, Error, or Inadequate Price* (New York: G. & C. Carvill, 1825), cited and discussed in Horwitz, *The Transformation of American Law*, 182–183.

17. "[I]n a society in which value came to be regarded as entirely subjective and in which the only basis for assigning value was the concurrence of arbitrary individual desire, principles of substantive justice were inevitably seen as entailing an "arbitrary and uncertain" standard of value. Substantive justice, according to the earlier view, existed in order to prevent men from using the legal system in order to exploit each other. But where things have no "intrinsic value," there can be no substantive measure of exploitation and the parties are, by definition, equal. Modern contract law was thus born staunchly proclaiming that all men are equal because all measures of inequality are illusory." Horwitz, *The Transformation of American Law*, 161.

18. This is not to say that speculations over the future value of investments were not a feature of pre-eighteenth century markets (in fact, market speculation has been traced to, at least, the thirteenth century, such as with the development of Genovese contracts of "comanda" for long-distance trade), but rather that contracts were not an essential legal-bureaucratic vehicle for the establishment of regional, national, and international market economies until the late eighteenth century. Until then, merchants had relied on a variety of customs, documents, and instruments to stabilize, hedge, or attempt to fix the risks associated with bad investments and the potential of a party's failure to perform as agreed. These (juridically) non-enforceable instruments and practices included private forms of mercantile arbitration, the use of bills of exchange, bonds, and sealed agreements to govern business dealings—instruments that were rarely considered worthy evidence in cases of contractual breach by pre-eighteenth century courts, but which were able to exert pressure in the realms of banking and the market. See Ibid., 172.

19. "[T]he moment at which courts focus on expectation damages rather than restitution or specific performance to give a remedy for nondelivery is precisely the time at which contract law begins to separate itself from property. It is at this point that contract begins to be understood not as transferring the title of particular property, but as creating an expected return. Contract then becomes an instrument for protecting against changes in supply and price in a market economy. The first recognition of expectation damages appeared after 1790 in both England and America in cases involving speculation in stock. . . . Between 1799 and 1810 a number of English cases applied the rule of expectation damages for failure to deliver stock on a rising market. In America the transformation occurred a decade earlier, in response to an active "futures" market for speculation in state securities which rapidly developed after the Revolutionary War in anticipation of the assumption of state debts by the new national government. The earliest cases allowing expectation damages on contracts of stock speculation appeared in South Carolina, Virginia, and Pennsylvania." Ibid., 174.

20. "The underlying logic of the attack on a substantive doctrine of consideration came to fruition in America with the great New York case of *Seymour v. Delancey* (1824), in which a sharply divided High Court of Errors reversed a decision of Chancellor Kent, who had refused to specifically enforce a land contract on the ground of gross inadequacy of consideration between the parties. 'Every member of this Court,' the majority opinion noted, 'must be well aware how much property is held by contract; that purchases are constantly made upon speculation; that the value of real estate is fluctuating.' The result was that there 'exists an honest difference of opinion in regard to any bargain, as to its being a beneficial one, or not.' The court held that only where the inadequacy of price was itself evidence of fraud would it interfere with the execution of private contracts." Ibid., 179–180.

21. On the history of corporate "personhood", see Joshua Barkan, *Corporate Sovereignty: Law and Governance under Capitalism* (Minneapolis: University of Minnesota Press, 2013), Chapter 3, "Personhood."

22. "[C]ontractarian ideology above all expressed a market conception of legal relations. Wages were the carefully calibrated instrument by which supposedly equal parties would bargain to arrive at the proper "mix" of risk and wages. In such a world the old ideal of legal relations shaped by a normative standard of substantive justice could scarcely coexist. Since the only measure of justice was the parties' own agreement, all preexisting legal duties were inevitably subordinated to the contract relation." Horwitz, *The Transformation of American Law*, 209.

23. "The doctrine of "assumption of risk" in workmen's injury cases expressed the triumph of the contractarian ideology more completely than any other nineteenth century legal creation. It arose in an economywhich already had all but eradicated traces of an earlier model of normative relations between master and servants. And without the practice of enforcing preexisting moral duties, judges and jurists could no longer ascribe any purpose to legal obligations that were superior to the expressed "will" of the parties. As contract ideology thus emasculated all prior conceptions of substantive justice, equal bargaining power inevitably became established as the inarticulate major premise of all legal and economic analysis. The circle was completed; the law had come simply to ratify those forms of inequality that the market system produced." Ibid., 210.

24. "Since the authority of commercial custom could not easily be absorbed into the traditional category of ancient usage, Mansfield instead emphasized its universal character and its correspondence with the dictates of natural reason. It was, Mansfield frequently reiterated, not the law of any one country but of the entire civilized world. Proof of particular commercial customs, therefore, served only as evidence of universal mercantile custom that already had ripened into a rule of law." Ibid., 189–90. "Once the subjective theory of contract had performed the function of enabling judges and jurists to destroy the connection between contract law and a conception of objective value, they felt free once again to revive an objective theory of contract and to reintroduce its intellectual companion, a conception of general mercantile custom." Ibid., 196.

25. "Courts, in essence, were developing a series of new doctrines designed to apply to large impersonal business dealings between commercially sophisticated insiders which, we have seen, were rapidly replacing the face-to-face transaction as the dominant mode of trade." Ibid., 200.

26. "Once contractual obligation was founded entirely on an arbitrary 'meeting of minds,' it endowed the parties with a complete power to remake law. To the extent that it was seriously followed it made every contract a unique event depending only on the momentary intention of the parties. National markets, however, required uniformity and standardization, which inevitably entailed a sacrifice, at least in theory, of the individual's power to contract. The emergence of the objective theory, then, is another measure of the influence of commercial interests in the shaping of American law. No longer finding it necessary to enter into battle against eighteenth century just price doctrines, they could devote their energies to establishing in the second half of the nineteenth century a system of objective rules necessary to assure legal certainty and predictability. And having destroyed most substantive grounds for evaluating the justice of exchange, they could elaborate a legal ideology of formalism, of which Williston was a leading exemplar, that could not only disguise gross disparities of bargaining power under a facade of neutral and formal rules of contract law but could also enforce commercial customs under the comforting technical rubric of 'contract interpretation'." Ibid., 200–201.

27. Thorstein Bunde Veblen, *Absentee Ownership. Business Enterprise in Recent Times: The Case of America* 3rd ed. (New Brunswick: Transaction Publications, 2009 [1926]). See also: Adolf A. Berle, and Gardiner C. Means, *The Modern Corporation & Private Property* (New York: Macmillan, 1932).

28. "[F]rom about the beginning of the twentieth century the preponderant nature of property has been changing again, and property is again beginning to be seen as a right to something; now, more often than not, a right to a revenue rather than a right to a specific material thing….[T]he rise of the corporation as the dominant form of business enterprise has meant that the dominant form of property is the expectation of revenue. The market value of a modern corporation consists not of its plant and stocks of materials but of its presumed ability to produce a revenue for itself and its shareholders by its organization of skills and its manipulation of the market. Its value as a property is its ability to produce a revenue. The property its shareholders have is the right to a revenue from that ability." Macpherson, *Property*, 8.

Textbooks
Erik Carver, editor, with contributions by
Alissa Anderson, Cezar Nicolescu,
Pollyanna Rhee, Susanne Schindler, and
Manuel Shvartzberg Carrió

What follows are reviews of five real estate text-books. With backgrounds in architecture, urban design, and the humanities, members of the *House Housing* research teams read these texts to appraise real estate as a discourse with unique contours and unexpected topologies of knowledge. Like aspiring developers, we studied these books to learn the theory and practice of real estate.

Unlike other sources, such as econometric or ethnographic histories, textbooks are active, qualitative interfaces between a discipline and a profession. Textbooks perform disciplinarity—their very existence lays claim to an exclusive terrain of knowledge. The professional textbook then erects upon this ground an edifice of institutional codes. The textbook is both a catalog of norms and the map of a system. The resulting artifact works to both socialize inductees and legitimize real estate as a field. Thus, we can understand its fundamental assumptions by following repetitions, anomalies, and omissions in the texts.

We selected a representative sample of textbooks assigned in introductory courses in major North American real-estate programs today. The schools assigning each text are noted below. These texts reflect the major divisions by which syllabi have constructed real estate as a discipline: development, finance, law, and urban economics. A member of the research team reviewed each text, paying special attention to concepts and actors deployed. The reviews were then edited for consistency and legibility. This exercise helped us to understand the ways in which real estate discourse constructs contingent relationships between theoretical assumptions and practical coordinates. No simple nexus between space and capital, it rather orchestrates a complex, interdisciplinary set of agents and instruments. These agents inhabit a risky but manageable world of rational actors, marginal governments, and instrumental architects. To function, this world requires creative organizers, experienced professionals, and sources of judgment: it requires *developers*.

3.2.1   *Real Estate Transactions, Finance, and Development*

6th ed. (Newark, NJ: LexisNexis, 2009 [1993]), 891 pages, $159.00

George Lefcoe, Professor of Law USC; BA Dartmouth 1959, LL.B Yale Law 1962

Assigned at: NYU Stern, UPenn Wharton

Read by *Pollyana Rhee*

George Lefcoe's *Real Estate Transactions, Finance, and Development* illustrates the relationships structuring real-estate transactions of all scales. With constant reference to legal cases and codes, the first half of the book maps the actors, documents, and scenarios involved in buying and selling property. The second half extends this frame to include the unique financial and political environments of property development.

CLARIFY
RELATIONSHIPS
AND RISKS

As these broad objectives imply, the book addresses aspiring real estate lawyers, attorneys in related fields, and students planning to invest in or develop real estate.[1] Above all else, by clarifying the relationships between parties to real estate transactions, it instructs readers on how to anticipate and manage risk. Focusing on the economic relationships between buyers and sellers who do not necessarily know each other, Lefcoe considers who should be involved in a transaction and why, who is trustworthy, and what roles they should play. He emphasizes the operation of a procedural apparatus—centered on paperwork—that identifies each party, formalizes their relationships, and assembles the necessary modes of documentation for every transaction. Yet few contracts "anticipate every risk and contingency."[2] Potential risks include fraud and negligence, which may be attended to by a written contract countering "the fogginess and inherent bias of memory" by memorializing "the results of the parties' negotiations" and providing "confirmation and evidence" of an agreement.[3]

AVOID
CONFLICTS

A corollary of the text's focus on transactions is its emphasis on interested actors. Though interests motivate actors to complete transactions in reliable ways, they also lead to conflicts. For example, in buying or selling land, determining the value of a property often requires a land inspector to examine it for defects. In this way, the text's foregrounding of roles extends to the putative object of exchange—land itself. Land inspectors typically come to prospective buyers recommended by real estate brokers. Because brokers make commissions on sales, they are thus subject to competing interests.[4] They desire a careful inspector who will maintain their reputations by catching "undisclosed flaws," but they also want a reliable inspector who will not "kill the deal."

The book describes financial institutions, buyers and sellers, brokers, architects, and contractors in terms that strip down their responsibilities to those of instrumental functions, supplemented by notes on their roles as defined by law or by professional organizations. For example, architects "translate the owner's objectives into buildable plans and construction documents, [and] assist owners in obtaining bids and negotiating with contractors."[5]

BUY ACCESS
LAWFULLY

For Lefcoe, the contract between a buyer and seller is also a model for describing larger social, political, and ecological worlds, from neighbors to local governments to zoning ordinances and environmental regulations.[6] To the degree that the notion of public good appears, it is a public in need of redemption by development. Ostensibly political acts, such as campaign contributions—"buy[ing] access lawfully"—are simply links in a chain of operational transactions. One just has to avoid crossing into illegality.[7]

DELINEATE
THE SOCIAL

Social relations form the center of this text, driven by the question of how to get one's money's worth in a landscape where personal relationships are unclear. Trust and authenticity are useful insofar as they alleviate the economic anxieties of buying or renting a home, entering a partnership, or developing a property. Yet, the right of a seller not to disclose "psychologically tainted" property is emblematic of a structural divide between the personal and social.[8] No amount of clarification or documentation will cure these anxieties.

TURN RAW LAND INTO A USEFUL PRODUCT

Mortgage lenders and developers have different roles than sellers.[9] Here descriptions move from transactional relations to the norms of development. One of the main assumptions about land is that it is raw, and a developer shapes "raw...or previously developed, but derelict or underutilized sites, into a useful product much like a manufacturer might mold plastic or carve wood into furniture."[10]

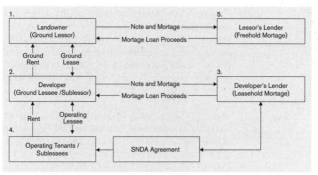

Key Players in Ground Lease Development, Lefcoe, p. 729.

ORCHESTRATE PROFESSIONALS IMAGINATIVELY TO REALIZE PROJECTS

The chapters on development portray the developer as someone who uses a "fertile imagination" to mix the components that allow the project to come to fruition.[11] The skill of a commercial real estate developer is "not necessarily [that of] architects or contractors, engineers or financiers," but instead the bringing of these specialties together to serve those who need space to carry on their businesses. Further chapters cover how to choose an entity for real estate investment in order to formalize a relationship between developers and investors to share risks and rewards together.[12] Developers may not "draw up blueprints or erect steel or pour concrete, but they cause these things to happen."[13]

3rd ed. (Washington, D.C.: Urban Land Institute, 2012 [1992]),
404 pages, $99.95

Richard Peiser, Professor of Real Estate Development,
Harvard Graduate School of Design; BA Yale University 1970,
MBA Harvard Business School 1973, PhD Land Economy,
University of Cambridge 1980

David Hamilton, Principal, Qroe Preservation Development LLC; BA
Middlebury 1995; M.Arch Harvard Graduate School of Design 2000

Assigned at: Harvard Business School, UCLA Luskin School of
Public Affairs

Read by *Alissa Anderson*

Peiser and Hamilton's *Professional Real Estate Development* advises aspiring developers on building the reputations necessary for success. The first two chapters show how real estate development processes and organizations work. The following five chapters cover project types: subdivision, multifamily residential, office, industrial, and retail. The final chapter looks backward to provide a history of the industry, including recent crises, and looks forward to appraise current trends.

TILT THE ODDS

The book begins with the question, "What is a Developer?" It answers this question with a language of mastery and equipoise: the developer is a flexible visionary, a prepared improviser, is creative yet rigorous; a detail-oriented generalist who coordinates human "inputs."[14] Developers build the very "fabric of our civilization," yet are faced with complexity unknown thirty years ago, ranging from local politics to global competition, securitization, and new technologies.[15]

The developer takes on the risks of real estate and reaps the rewards. Due to the inherent contingencies of real estate, a successful project—one yielding profits for the developer and lenders—can never be guaranteed. A good developer is one who can tilt the odds towards success. A record of success facilitates access to capital. A failed project does not really fail unless it hinders this access.[16]

The text's main purpose is to walk beginning developers through five major activities: 1) identifying fruitful development opportunities by reading local conditions and trends; 2) acting on opportunities at the right time by synchronizing project schedules to real estate cycles; 3) raising capital by convincing banks and other lenders of the project's soundness; 4) minimizing risk by lowering one's personal financial stake in the project; and 5) completing the project efficiently—"within the window of time for which the market is favorable"—by managing it meticulously.[17]

BUILD RECORDS WITH KNOWLEDGE AND CREATIVITY

Peiser and Hamilton recommend the close replication of existing practices as a sound formula for success. Developers should cultivate, through market studies, a shrewd awareness of conditions and trends, as well as a well-defined set of customers. They should furthermore gain intimate familiarity with legal and financial mechanisms, which can affect a project's speed. The authors laud creativity, defined as pragmatic and reactive rather than disruptive. Young developers need to proceed with special caution until they can build their records, and early deals "should not set a new precedent" or challenge political and financial norms.[18]

ADAPT TO CYCLES

Beginning with the first chapter, and throughout the text, the real estate cycle looms as a force animating development and demanding constant attention. Cycles register and coordinate forces diverse in scope and origin, including federal interest rates, large-scale employment and migration trends, and localized lags between supply and demand for space.[19] Following real estate researcher Glenn Mueller, the book describes a cycle as a composition in four parts: recovery, expansion, hypersupply, and recession.

PROVIDE PRODUCTS TO TENANTS

The developer improves and trades real estate products. The product type is like the architect's building type, yet is not formal. Instead, it straddles use and ownership: single-family products, rental products, residential products, industrial products, and so on. Chapter 3 shows that while "raw" land is not a product, a subdivided parcel of land decidedly is. The architect becomes necessary only well into the product design process, following data collection and the generation of a detailed development concept. Here the architect functions primarily to control costs of construction and operation.

Sometimes the architect has another key role. While successful products generating net profits are a major component of development work, they are not its ultimate aim: "It is the tenant that makes the property valuable, not the building itself."[20] Chapters 4 to 7 provide extensive design guidelines for product types, detailing selected aspects: site, parking, exterior, interior, and "privacy and security." Architects appear in these pages as specialists in attracting and maintaining the right type of tenant.

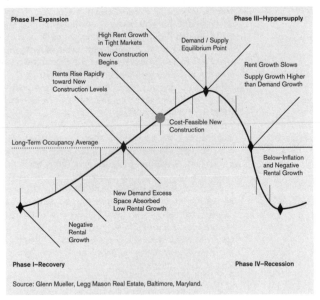

Phase II—Expansion

Phase III—Hyppersupply

High Rent Growth in Tight Markets

New Construction Begins

Demand / Supply Equilibrium Point

Rent Growth Slows

Supply Growth Higher than Demand Growth

Rents Rise Rapidly toward New Construction Levels

Cost-Feasible New Construction

Long-Term Occupancy Average

Below-Inflation and Negative Rental Growth

New Demand Excess Space Absorbed Low Rental Growth

Negative Rental Growth

Phase I—Recovery

Phase IV—Recession

Source: Glenn Mueller, Legg Mason Real Estate, Baltimore, Maryland.

Physical Real Estate Cycle Characteristics, Peiser, p. 16.

GET CULTURE   Peiser and Hamilton divide the development world into three groups of actors: The first is "building professionals," in turn subdivided into (a) surveyors, planners, engineers, architects, and designers; (b) specialized consultants, contractors, and tradespeople; (c) tenants and customers. The second group of "professionals" is comprised of legal and financial actors: attorneys, bankers and investors, and government officials.[21] The final, unnamed category consists of citizens' groups, homeowners' associations, and community organizations. This group of non-professionals, sometimes referred to simply as "community," has become an oppositional force in recent times [See HH: 1994, 1997]. A good developer, however, is able to partner with the community by learning its interests.[22]

While communities tend to desire the status quo, developers want to replicate the popular, as found for example in market studies.[23] Development thus becomes the repeated reconciliation of community and market, mediated by culture. Creativity here takes on an additional purpose, beyond avoiding contingencies and deferring structural conditions: it is through creativity that development becomes an art.

3.2.3   *Principles of Corporate Finance*

11th ed. (New York: McGraw-Hill Irwin 2014 [1980]), 976 pages, $305.67

Richard A. Brealey, Emeritus Professor of Finance, London Business School; MA in Philosophy, Politics, Economics Oxford

Stewart C. Myers, Professor of Finance, MIT Sloan School of Management; BA Williams 1962; MBA Stanford 1964, Ph.D. 1967

Franklin Allen, Professor of Finance and Economics, UPenn Wharton; BA East Anglia 1977, MA Economics 1979; PhD Economics Oxford 1980

Assigned at: MIT Center for Real Estate, UPenn Wharton, Yale Economics

Read by *Manuel Shvartzberg Carrió*

Brealey, Myers, and Allen's *Principles of Corporate Finance* instructs managers in the use of financial theory to accumulate and retain wealth. Their book communicates general financial principles via examples, including real estate case studies that explain economic rents, hedging strategies, and the nature of financial crises.

The book's three initial sections define value and risk, show how to calculate them, and explain their use in investment decisions. Sections 4 through 8 discuss how to raise money through debt and equity. Describing the use of options to modulate risk and value, the text goes on to explore the implications of contracts and global conditions for risk management. Sections 9 and 10 cover the diagnosis, planning, and restructuring of corporations. The typical chapter begins with an overview; features examples, articles from financial publications, and guidance on how to use Excel spreadsheets; and concludes with problem sets and brief case studies.

VALUE
SHAREHOLDERS

This book upholds shareholder value as the key to corporate finance. Corporations serve as agents of the shareholder, who could be an individual, firm, or mutual fund. The task of the corporation is to maximize share values.[24] Value maximization is an ahistorical human drive, the expression of innate competitiveness.[25]

EXPLOIT
INEFFICIENCIES

Competitive advantages ensure economic rents, or "profits that more than cover the cost of capital."[26] According to the efficient markets hypothesis, transparency and freedom from regulation will, in the long run, eliminate economic rents by encouraging competitive equilibrium. Given this dynamic, financial management works to increase value by maximizing more or less temporary competitive advantages using mathematical techniques. Tacit in this formulation, yet clear in the examples, is the fact that to the degree that it is scarce and unique, land also earns economic rents. Property in the form of land can bring opportunities for leveraging asymmetrical access (i.e. unavailable to non-owners). For example, in deciding whether to open a department store on a parcel of land, an investor is making "two bets—one on real estate prices and another on the firm's ability to run a successful department store." Depending on real estate projections, the owner may be better off either renting out the real estate or selling the land and renting it back for the store.[27]

THINK OF
REAL ESTATE
AS AN ASSET

In Brealey, Myers, and Allen's text, real estate, while a tangible commodity linked to a plot of land, appears as one of many kinds of assets. It is thus described relationally: like gold and oil, it has extensive markets and is easy to price. Like banks and utilities, it has high abandonment value—used properties are easy to sell.[28]

156

Due to its ease of trading, the real estate sector relies on debt financing, which is taxed at a lower rate.[29]

DISTRIBUTE OWNERSHIP AND RISK WITH SECURITIES

Real estate can also be traded as market securities, which are claims on real assets. Entities such as real estate investment trusts (REITs) assemble portfolios that include real-estate securities. [See HH: 2015] For any given portfolio, analysts estimate returns on investment by researching the performance of similar portfolios, a technique which, the efficient-markets hypothesis holds, will provide fair, "fundamental" valuations. Many of these securities offerings lump together diverse properties in order to minimize overall risk. But other products select for specific types of properties—grouped, for example, by use and size—creating particular risk and value profiles often used by investors to shape larger portfolios.

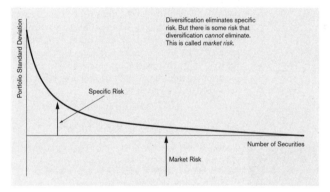

Specific Risk and Market Risk, Brealey, Myers, and Allen, p. 170.

Financial actors trade not only claims on real assets, but also their risks, which can take on value in the form of derivatives. Sophisticated analysis of the values of specific groups of assets and derivatives can give one a competitive advantage through means such as arbitrage, the risk-free exploitation of loopholes in the market.

BEWARE OF MARKET DISTORTIONS

However, there is a potentially fatal anomaly in the efficient-markets hypothesis: bubbles. Sometimes, instead of being dictated by "fundamentals," speculative frenzies drive up asset prices to levels unjustified by profit outlooks, as when the Japanese bubble of the late 1980s caused "the few hundred acres of land under the Emperor's Palace in Tokyo ... [to be] worth as much as all the land in Canada or California."[30] While bubbles can be "exhilarating" for financial managers, they also pose "ethical challenges" and legal hazards [See HH: 2011].[31]

The authors' main theory of bubbles is that artificial distortions cause the rational self-interest of financial agents to diverge from that of the shareholders they are supposed to represent. The global financial crisis of 2007–09, for example, grew out of such conflicts of interest: banks, investors, rating agencies, government corporations, and consumers all speculated as if there were no risk. The authors attribute blame for this on the US government's backing of mortgage risks. This market intervention distorted incentives and thus created an "agency and incentive problem," where different parties felt they could safely "out-fool" each other in pursuit of profits.[32] The second possible reason for bubbles is the possibility that markets are not efficient.[33] An implication of this view would be that we as financial actors are, in the end, irrational.

3.2.4   *Urban Economics and Real Estate Markets*

(Englewood Cliffs, NJ: Prentice Hall, 1995), 378 pages, $112.80

Denise DiPasquale, President, City Research, formerly Visiting Assistant Professor at John F. Kennedy School of Government, Harvard; BA Carnegie Mellon; PhD MIT

William Wheaton, Professor of Economics, MIT; BA Princeton 1968; PhD University of Pennsylvania 1972

Assigned at: MIT Center for Real Estate, UPenn Wharton

Read by *Cezar Nicolescu*

DiPasquale and Wheaton's *Urban Economics and Real Estate Markets* use mathematical formulas to describe urban growth and programming. Beginning with the question "What is real estate?" the first section of their book models the relationship between capital and real estate properties in terms of supply and demand. The next two sections consider land in terms of micro and macroeconomics. The final section assesses questions of regulation and the public good.

The authors make assumptions that land markets are efficient due to the fact that tenants are mobile, and that density reflects land value. At the same time, changes in transportation technology drive spatial changes by spurring industrial and residential diffusion, followed by office and retail spaces.

ANTICIPATE EQUILIBRIUM

The book's "comparative static" equilibrium model anchors its macroeconomic model in a description of the real estate market as a web of four interlinked supply-and-demand relationships. In the asset market, rents and construction prices rise together, as do construction prices and construction activity. In the property market, construction activity and building stock are also directly related; while rents and building stock, on the other hand, vary inversely (housing shortages mean higher rents). As the economy expands, it exerts a centrifugal pressure on this equilibrium, with all values increasing in some measure.[34]

Changes in a particular quadrant of the graph will produce ripple effects. Lower interest rates, risks, or taxes will cause investors to move funds into real estate, rotating the rent-price (or asset valuation) curve counter-clockwise, raising prices. This will then increase construction activity and building stock, lowering rents. Conversely, increasing interest rates or adding onerous regulations will shift the construction-price (or asset construction) curve left so as to reduce construction activity, thus raising prices and rents and lowering stock.[35]

UNDERSTAND LAND MARKETS TO PREDICT VALUE

The authors explain land value in such disparate urban areas as New York City, Phoenix, and Tokyo in terms of a unified theory of land markets. In doing so, they extend political economist David Ricardo's 1817 model, which held that demand for land is elastic and produces relative value, while supply is inelastic and establishes overall value. This predicts that land prices will increase closer to employment centers. Furthermore, different residential groups will segregate themselves naturally due to unique

159

sets of preferences and incomes. When it comes to variations among cities, the book notes the need to account for the variables of climate, region, and history. However, the three factors of city size, expected growth, and construction costs account for 76 percent of housing price variation.[36]

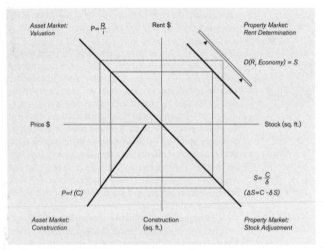

Static Equilibrium Model, DiPasquale and Wheaton, p. 12.

ACCOUNT FOR
TECHNOLOGY

Technology acts to transform the intensity of these relationships over time. The authors explain postwar patterns of manufacturing and distribution decentralization in terms of new transportation, production, and storage technologies.[37] Similarly, residential real estate has continuously suburbanized, though technology's influence on home prices remains mostly implicit in this text.[38] The dispersal of office and retail clusters, on the other hand, derives from residential suburbanization, as stores relocate to chase commuters and offices move to lower-rent areas where they can pay lower wages.[39]

Commuter transportation systems are characterized as barriers to the fully decentralized city. Though perfect sprawl would be "logically consistent and economically rational," this ideal is unrealizable in practice; real highways and rail systems necessarily channel commuters in ways that produce and reinforce concentrations.[40]

VALUE
HISTORIES

In addition to the equilibrium model, other kinds of images, such as line graphs and maps of regional intensities, populate this book. In the line graphs we can read a story of change over time. They convey the change of such values as the relationship between price and density, legible within the epoch in which the equilibrium model is relevant. These historical values provide evidence with which models are built and tested.[41]

However, the book also acknowledges a sense of historical rupture, one that leaves a legacy that does not conform to economic logic. Bounding this logic in time is the transition to a new, post-industrial economy. This rupture rises to visibility in some of the book's case study maps of the Boston region. While earlier industrial patterns do not fit contemporary models, they persist in two modes: as recalcitrant, sub-optimal building stock, and as neighborhoods with historic values defended by residents.[42]

FACTOR IN
PLEASURE

This historic value is sometimes quantified, becoming one of the various, heterogeneous components of "hedonic value." Economists adopted hedonic value from utilitarianism as a way to describe the complex factors entering into the price of a building. These include quantitative factors like a unit's square footage, features like second bathrooms; they also include expert assessment of more subjective values, like "the general quality of the neighborhood."[43]

3rd ed. (Philadelphia, PA: Linneman Associates, 2011 [2003]), 498 pages, $135.00

Peter Linneman, principal, Linneman Associates, former founding chair, UPenn Wharton, Real Estate Development Department; BA Economics, Ashland University 1973, MA Economics 1976; PhD Economics University of Chicago 1977.

Assigned at: Columbia Business School, UPenn Wharton

Read by *Susanne Schindler*

Peter Linneman's *Real Estate Finance & Investments*, in teaching the reader how to become a real estate developer, emphasizes the importance of judgment. Though it introduces techniques like modeling; key metrics like discounted cash flow and net present value; and legal structures, like bankruptcy and real estate investment trusts, these in themselves are not sufficient for success. A great developer learns by experience.

The book addresses readers as if they were students unfamiliar with basic financial concepts like value and rates of return. The first two chapters describe real estate's particular risks and opportunities and outline a typology of real estate properties. Chapters 3 through 7 teach lease and market analysis. After describing how to appraise particular developments and real estate companies, the book takes us on a tour of debt and equity instruments in chapters 11 through 18. Going on to consider decision making and cycles, it concludes in chapter 21 with a discussion of ethics. Appendices provide a primer on finance fundamentals, case studies, exams, and a guide to Argus financial software.

MANAGE RISK
TO CREATE
VALUE

For Linneman, the key relationship in real estate is between value, risk, and opportunity. Done efficiently, development is handsomely profitable "true value creation;" it renders the final product, or building, "more valuable than the ingredients."[44] But sophistication in the field means patiently learning to manage risk while exploiting opportunities in order to create value. Performance is possible to forecast; one must balance desired rates of return with allowable risk via pro forma analysis and financial modeling of the market.

A key metric for Linneman is choosing the capitalization rate, or "cap rate," of a property, which is its net present value divided by the projected annual net operating income, and accordingly is a formula indicating the relationship of risk to return. "8 cap" means income is 8 percent of value. Cap rates allow a developer to estimate the "value creation potential" of a property. For a building with a given income, "building to a 10," but selling "to an 8," means a 20 percent profit margin. He is not shy about stating expectations: "[G]ross profit margins . . . are typically 15-25 percent."[45]

But one should pursue financing only after due diligence verifies basic assumptions concerning an investment. This kind of careful knowledge is worlds away from Wall Street. Instead, one learns the business "from the ground up, one day at a time."[46] Linneman finds Manhattan as unsuitable for a development as it is for a "dairy farmer," directing students to "unsexy" but promising locales like Chester, Virginia.[47]

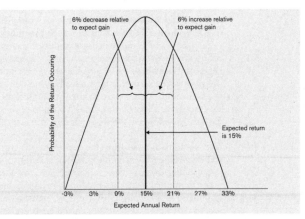

Probability Distribution for Expected Returns on a Sample Investment, Linneman, p. 8.

BUILD REPUTATION

Ethics is important because a good reputation is necessary for long-term success in the business. For this reason, the development world oscillates between bounded community and impersonal market. The developer should know the territory, hear the talk of the town, and give people more or less what they are used to. The goal is to reap a profit on sound investments, not to change the world.

LEAD THE DESIGN PROCESS

Developers should direct the design process, gathering knowledge from the existing production: "Get in your car ... and visit competitive properties." Architects need to be led: while they "can design what you need, they rarely know what you need." Too often architects and developers sacrifice profitability for good design and costly features. However, a good designer will optimize layout and design in a way that enhances success.[48]

WATCH OUT FOR POLITICIANS

In Linneman's world, politicians are self-interested obstructionists who abuse their power to distort the market. We don't hear about the government's role in urban or regional planning and related infrastructure investments, as a source of subsidies for development, or as the place where land-use decisions are decided through a democratic process. The economy grows naturally, except when harmed by government action.[49] The 2009 stimulus program, for example, is predicted to merely depress private-sector spending.[50]

Instead of genuine considerations of the public good, narrow political concerns drive legislation. Thus, the IRS bases deductions like the depreciation for new carpet not on empirical studies, but on Congress' need to collect taxes in a way that "gets them reelected." Linneman translates this into the language of developers: "Reelection is their pro forma!"[51]

RESPECT THE EXISTING

For Linneman, mentoring the reader means inculcating a respect for existing conditions. Rather than questioning existing types and processes, we learn how to replicate our everyday spectrum of built products: malls, warehouses, offices, housing, and hotels. Idealism and ethics are always circumscribed by the exigencies of personal utility in the face of 5 to 7-year project timelines. In development, the real is the rational.

164

1. George Lefcoe, *Real Estate Transactions, Finance, and Development*, 6th ed. (Newark, NJ: LexisNexis, 2009), 1.
2. Ibid., 64.
3. Ibid., 63.
4. Ibid., 105.
5. Ibid., 530.
6. Ibid., 797–798.
7. Ibid., 799.
8. Ibid., 113–114.
9. Ibid., 412.
10. Ibid., 495–496.
11. Ibid.
12. Ibid., 661.
13. Ibid., 495.
14. Richard Peiser and David Hamilton, *Professional Real Estate Development*, 3rd ed. (Washington D.C.: Urban Land Institute, 2012), 3.
15. Ibid., ix.
16. Ibid., 7.
17. Ibid., 15.
18. Ibid., 29.
19. Ibid., 15.
20. Ibid., 9, 14.
21. Ibid., 3.
22. Ibid., 6.
23. Ibid., 56–57.
24. Richard A. Brealey, Stewart C. Myers, and Franklin Allen, *Principles of Corporate Finance*, 10th ed. (New York: McGraw-Hill/Irwin, 2011), 9–12.
25. Ibid., 11–12. The authors find rhetoric, but not practice, around shareholder value to be culturally variable.
26. Ibid., 273.
27. Ibid., 269–271.
28. Ibid., 273.
29. Ibid., 440. Compare this to firms in pharmaceuticals and advertising, which use equity financing.
30. Ibid., 871.
31. Ibid., 334.
32. Ibid., 329.
33. Ibid., 321.
34. Denise DiPasquale and William C. Wheaton, *Urban Economics and Real Estate Markets* (Upper Saddle River: Prentice Hall, 1995), 7–10.
35. Ibid., 13–18.
36. Ibid., 49–57.
37. Ibid., 92, 102–103.
38. Ibid., 65, for example.
39. Ibid., 103–108, 122, 124–125, 140–143.
40. Ibid., 108. Another barrier to the achievement of full decentralization is the need for workers of "different wage rates," living in "different types of housing at various density levels."
41. Ibid., 13, Figure 1.3 for example.
42. Ibid., 83, 84. Figures 4.19, 4.10
43. Ibid., 67–68.
44. Peter Linneman, *Real Estate Finance and Investments*, 3rd ed. (Philadelphia: Linneman Associates, 2011), 160.
45. Ibid., 161.
46. Ibid., 163.
47. Ibid., 162.
48. Ibid., 174.
49. Ibid., 237.
50. Ibid., 389.
51. Ibid., 53.

Schools
Pollyanna Rhee

Real estate, according to Stephen Malpezzi of the University of Wisconsin School of Business, constitutes "roughly 70 percent of the world's tangible capital stock, and one of the largest elements of consumption."[1] But within academic institutions, he argues, real estate programs have historically found themselves occupying a tenuous position between different departments and schools. Though strongly tied to the profession, no official body accredits degrees in real estate or mandates the real estate curriculum in the United States, nor is there a uniform regulatory body for licensing.[2] The question arises: Is real estate development a practice? A discipline? A field?[3]

The timeline below, based in large part on an interview with Jesse Keenan, Research Director of The Center for Urban Real Estate at Columbia University in February 2015, presents a series of excerpts from publications by academics and professionals regarding the state and status of the evolving field of real estate development in the United States, contextualized with significant events, such as founding dates of real estate degree programs and relevant legislative acts. These impressions cover almost a century and highlight debates over not only the nature of the field, but the legitimacy of its existence within research institutions at all. While academics consider their relationship to other disciplines, they also keep in mind their ties to the real estate profession, which encompasses a workforce that ranges from individual brokers, to large-scale developers, to economists.

The selections aim to highlight the connections between research institutions and trade groups, beginning with a focus on land economics early in the twentieth century. From there we can trace a trajectory: from land grant universities, to financial analysis of real estate in business schools especially after World War II, to real estate development in architecture schools as part of urban design and planning programs. Taken as a whole, these various perspectives reveal conceptions of real estate as both plots of land open for development and intangible assets of exchange.

1881   Wharton School founded at University of Pennsylvania, offers first real estate course in 1905.[4]

1892   Richard Ely teaches "Landed Property and the Rent of the Land" at the University of Wisconsin, considered to be the first college-level real estate course.[5]

1903   Richard M. Hurd publishes what some consider the first important book in the modern age of real estate, *Principals of City Land Values*.[6]

1908   Establishment of National Association of Real Estate Exchanges, which becomes the largest trade organization for real estate brokers with 120 founding members, in Chicago.[7] In 1910 the NAREE founds the *National Estate Journal*. In 1916 they adopt the term "realtor" to identify professionals who are members of the association.

1920   Richard Ely founds the Institute for Research in Land Economics at the University of Wisconsin before moving it to Northwestern University in 1925.[8]

1920s   Ely's "Land Economics Series" includes: Ernest M. Fisher, *Principles of Real Estate*; Fly and Edward W. Morehouse, *Elements of Land Economics*; Fredrick A. Babcock, *The Appraisal of Real Estate*. Series continues into 1930s.

REAL ESTATE EDUCATION

1927   Arthur Mertzke, director of education and research for the National Association of Real Estate Boards: *"Real estate today is no longer one of the occupations in which one can be successful without a fair degree of special training. Even a long and costly experience does not teach a man all that he must know to conduct his business soundly and successfully . . . 52 universities and colleges now offer courses.[9] . . . Even though we discount some of the work now being done as superficial, the building of the permanent structure of professional real estate education, erected on the solid foundations of the new science of Land Economics, can no longer be questioned."[10]*

1932   Office of Education for US Department of Interior survey indicates 62 colleges and universities offer one or more courses in real estate. By 1936 this number rises to 73.[11]

1933   Homer Hoyt publishes *One Hundred Years of Land Values in Chicago*. Later Hoyt joins the Federal Housing Administration (FHA).[12]

1934   FHA mortgage insurance program begins. This and other forms of federal aid transform real estate financing and make older real estate textbooks inadequate. [See HH: 1939]

1936   Urban Land Institute founded.[13]

REAL ESTATE EDUCATION

1938   Richard Ely, Northwestern University, in his autobiography: *"Throughout all recorded history, the relation of the people to land has been an important factor in civilization. Land is the original source of wealth; the earth is utilized to supply us with food, clothing, shelter, recreation, and culture. The field of land economics reaches the end of the earth and to the minutest detail of economic interest."*[14]

DEVELOPMENTS IN THE FIELD

1945   Increased enrollment in business schools after World War II. This leads to strong demand for faculty as well as an interest in rectifying perceived weaknesses in American business education.[15] University of Florida develops a separate real estate division within its business school.

REAL ESTATE EDUCATION

1946   Daniel D. Gage, University of Oregon: *"Actually [real estate] represents not a new vocation but a reallocation of functions previously performed by other occupational groups on a part-time basis....Naturally the pioneer sponsors of courses in realty were confronted with the problem of securing competent instructors and textbooks. In the earlier period it was felt that real estate was pretty much legal in nature, therefore courses hinged about problems of conveyance...A sec-*

ond phase of the course was added, that of brokerage practice, and a practical real estate broker or operator augmented the legal theory with business practice. Prior to 1920 the instruction for the most part was either non-academic or juristic."[16]

DEVELOPMENTS IN THE FIELD

1950s
Architecture schools at University of Michigan, University of Southern California, and Cornell begin training urban planners and architects jointly in studios that are co-taught by an architect, a city planner, and an economist.[17] While Arthur Weimer is head of the department, Indiana University produces the largest number of real estate doctorates and faculty in the U.S.

1954
Through its Program in Economic Development and Administration, the Ford Foundation begins a project to reform business education in the United States. James E. Howell, a Ford consultant, believes that business programs enroll too many under-qualified students with faculties dominated by individuals who resist economic analysis and other social-science methods. These reports also recommended that courses in "minor" fields including real estate be reduced.[18]

REAL ESTATE EDUCATION

1956
Art Weimer, dean of the Indiana University School of Business: *"Typically, courses in real estate are taught either from the point of view of land economics or from the standpoint of the real estate business itself. It is contended here that a more appropriate approach to the teaching of real estate courses is that of the business manager or administrator."*[19]

DEVELOPMENTS IN THE FIELD

1960s
Universities including University of Texas, University of Pennsylvania, Penn State, University of Illinois, and UCLA begin offering doctoral programs with a concentration in real estate in their business schools.

REAL ESTATE EDUCATION

1961
Richard Ratcliff, University of Wisconsin: *"It is the thesis of this essay that urban land economics as a sub-*

169

ject field (with 'real estate' as an ill-defined mutation) was well defined at its origin in the early post WWI era; that it has become substantially dismembered and has lost identity, if not status in academic circles; that our institutions of higher learning are failing to meet a social need for trained professional analysts properly prepared to deal with urban problems; and that the time has come to constitute this subject in a form like unto its original concept and to consolidate and integrate, on our campuses, the processes and facilities which are essential to sound training and productive research into the economic problems of urban land." [20]

DEVELOPMENTS IN THE FIELD

1964

Academic organizations and journals devoted to real estate start to formally develop by 1964. The American Real Estate and Urban Economics Association (AREUEA) is founded at the meeting of the Allied Social Science Association (ASSA) as part of an articulated need for more information in the fields of real estate development, planning, and economics. To date, the ASSA acts as the academic organization for real estate faculty.[21] Meetings of the ASSA included gatherings for the American Economic Association, American Marketing Association, and other groups. AREUEA sponsors the journal *Real Estate Economics*. Before this time, some faculty had attended conventions of the National Association of Real Estate Boards, later National Association of Realtors.[22]

REAL ESTATE EDUCATION

1967

David T. Rowlands, University of Pennsylvania: *"Identification of real estate as a distinct discipline would contribute mightily to acceptance as one of the more worthwhile fields of functional specialization. Sharper delineation of the discipline than is customarily made is needed, particularly in distinguishing it from the fields of regional science and city planning."* [23]

DEVELOPMENTS IN THE FIELD

1970s

In the 1970s (and into the 1980s), universities including University of Georgia, Georgia State University, University of Florida, University of North Carolina, and University of California, Berkeley begin offering doctorates to students whose projects had real estate focus areas.[24]

1972   Texas A&M University establishes the Masters of Real Estate Development (MRED) Degree in its Mays Business School.

REAL ESTATE EDUCATION

1976   James A. Graaskamp, University of Wisconsin: *"Since the objectives of the administrative process are frequently established by major events and value judgments beyond the control of business, it is necessary to sensitize the student to the correct interpretation of the broad social constraints of the business enterprise as well as the best administrative techniques of objective and/or problem solving administration. . . . [P]lanning schools teach that the developers are Philistines, while business schools have tended to . . . the effect that public planners are naïve, fascist, and without techniques to plan. . . . Real estate as a special application of a cash cycle enterprise is returning to legitimacy as field of interest appropriate to the School of Business. However, real estate enterprise manufactures the physical terrarium of our society over time and such enterprise, public or private, is the ultimate client for all physical and environmental designers. Perhaps a contemporary real estate program could have its home base in either a School of Physical Design or a School of Business Administration, so long as it was permitted to be inductive, multidisciplinary, and problem solving."* [25]

1976   Jerome Dasso, University of Oregon: *"Real estate education desperately needs a clear image and strong leadership to become firmly established as a field of study at the university level. This is true of real estate education in the broad sense (which includes law, architecture, engineering, planning, and business) as well as the more narrow sense of business and professional real estate education. . . . Real estate, real estate administration, or the real estate process, just do not project a clear image. If a clear image can be developed, business and professional education in real estate should enjoy a promising future. Perhaps the present crop of real estate professors can develop*

171

the necessary image as part of their task of providing leadership in real estate education."[26]

1980   Jerome Dasso, University of Oregon: "*Today's real estate problems are multidisciplinary. No one program, whether at the community college, the trade organization, or university level, can satisfy all the needs for real estate education in our society. Further, even at the university level, consistency or alignment of courses in real estate (introduction, finance investment, appraisal, law, housing, marketing and administration) with other related and respected disciplines is extremely difficult if not impossible.*"

Lynn Woodward, Wichita State University: "*Two new directions have been noted in the recent literature on real estate education. A multidisciplinary approach is advocated by James Graaskamp (Wisconsin) while a second approach, advocated by Jerome Dasso (Oregon) is an extension of the financial management framework and the land economics or administrative approaches stressed by the authors in the past. More than anything the two approaches appear to represent close academic relationships with other specialized disciplines. At Wisconsin the relationship is with landscape architecture and civil and environmental engineering. At Oregon, a strong finance department relationship exists. Thus, as with the land economics and administrative approaches, the real estate educational emphasis stressed depends on the lead professor's orientation, the strengths of the institution, and the organizational placement of the real estate program. These two approaches therefore illustrate once again that specialized areas, including economics, urban affairs, regional science, and the physical design disciplines, have joined important areas of business administration to provide differing definitions of real estate.*"[27]

DEVELOPMENTS IN THE FIELD

1983   MIT begins offering the MRED through its architecture school.

1985   Founding of the American Real Estate Society (ARES).[28] Journals sponsored by the ARES include *Journal of Real Estate Research, Journal of Real Es-*

tate Portfolio Management, Journal of Real Estate Literature, Journal of Real Estate Practice and Education, Journal of Real Estate Strategy.

Columbia University establishes Mater of Science in Real Estate Development at its Graduate School of Architecture, Planning, and Preservation.

1990s More REIT papers appear. Over 100 REITs make their initial public offerings (IPOs).[29]

1993 University of San Diego establishes the Masters of Science in Real Estate (MSRE) program in its School of Business Administration.

REAL ESTATE EDUCATION

1996 Joseph D. Albert, James Madison University: *"Real estate academics are in many ways unique in the scholarly community. Probably more so than any other discipline, real estate is populated with individuals who, were it not for the lure of the academy, would have engaged in entrepreneurial activities. Many of [these individuals] have practiced what we have preached on some scale even if it were only a small investment property. We have, it seems, a need to be involved in a practical way in the discipline. It is precisely this entrepreneurial propensity and practical inclination that shapes the research interests of most of us towards a problem-solving, project-based orientation rather than broad policy issues.... Most real estate academics [in the 1980s] were housed in departments of finance, not economics departments, and had an academic background more grounded in finance than in urban economics. Indeed, the most uniquely real estate course taught by most of us was the appraisal of real property, a course the content of which is drawn primarily from the fundamentals of valuation theory that are found in the financial management and investment areas of the finance discipline.... While we did not deny or ignore the importance of spatial economics in our discipline, we did not view ourselves as* urban *or* housing *economists. But neither did we see ourselves as 'traditional finance' faculty. We were a group in search of an intellectual home that would represent the reality of what we taught and what we were."*[30]

1996 Stephen E. Roulac, Roulac Global and University of Ulster, Northern Ireland: *"By the 1980s real estate had overcome its earlier second-class status to assume an important, primary role in society and the political economy. Real estate classes of universities often attracted record enrollments. Real estate was a primary career choice for many and a favored investment for pensions funds. Real estate securitization represented both a significant individual investment vehicle and also a major contributor to the profits of Wall Street investment firms. . . . Real estate in the early 1980s was robust, dynamic, significant. . . . Over the last decade or so . . . real estate has sunk into an apparent malaise. . . . Declining enrollments in university real estate courses are stark testimony to real estate's less than favored status."*[31]

 "Unfortunately, the real estate discipline currently lacks coherence and consensus about what the essence of real estate is and what the operative paradigms are for comprehending and making order of the discipline."[32]

1996 Roy T. Black, Neil G. Carn, Julian Diaz III, and Joseph S. Rabianski, all of Georgia State University: *"[The] field of real property exists today because an academic group has chosen to study the significant amount of human energy expended in producing and extending the artificial environment. The focus on human activity is fateful, for it places real property among the applied disciplines and dictates its purpose. . . . A field does not need a generally accepted, unifying theory to be an academic discipline."*[33]

2002 James R. Webb, Cleveland State University, and Halbert C. Smith, University of Florida: *"Virtually all real estate research is done at universities. Some professional organizations claim to do some research, but it is mostly just data gathering and no statistical tests or hypotheses tested. A very few professional organizations fund academic research in their area."*[34]

DEVELOPMENTS IN THE FIELD

2002 About 25 different professional real estate organizations exist in the United States "dedicated to virtually every area of the profession and all property types."[35]

REAL ESTATE EDUCATION

2002   Stephen E. Roulac, Roulac Global and University of Ulster: *"The evolution of the property discipline embraces multiple perspectives of licensing, professional designations, university-based education, adult continuing education, applied 'how to' courses, theoretical research, applied research, multi-faceted application of theory and learning as well as multiple public interest concerns. The contemporary orientation of the discipline is reflected in the different paradigms employed for considering property, including economics, finance, geography, engineering, highest and best use, city planning, brokerage, legal, corporate decisions, the consumer transaction, and multi-disciplinary approach."*[36]

DEVELOPMENTS IN THE FIELD

2002   Approximately 200 universities offer real estate classes "usually as an area of specialization in the finance department of a College of Business," or in planning or urban economics.[37]

2004   Clemson University establishes the MRED program in the College of Architecture, Arts, and Humanities.

2005   Woodbury University founds its Masters of Science in Architecture (MSArch) in Real Estate Development in the School of Architecture.

2005   Georgetown University establishes a Masters of Professional Studies in Real Estate in its School of Continuing Studies.

REAL ESTATE EDUCATION

2009   Stephen Malpezzi, University of Wisconsin: *"Real estate as such is not a* discipline. *There is no* theory *of real estate, but real estate is an important field of study."*[38]

DEVELOPMENTS IN THE FIELD

2011   Tulane University founds MSRED focusing on Sustainable Real Estate Development in its School of Architecture.

2012	American University founds MSRED and Certificate program in its Kogod School of Business.
2013	University of Arizona founds MRED program in its College of Architecture, Planning, and Landscape Architecture.
2014	George Washington University establishes MBA and graduate certificate in "Walkable Urban Real Estate" in its School of Business.

REAL ESTATE EDUCATION

2014   Jesse Keenan, Columbia University: *"So if real estate development is both an art and a science (more specifically, social science), how does one try to understand the discipline and how do you communicate this understanding for the advancement of a profession? . . . . [W]e have endeavored to build a historic narrative and theoretical foundation for advancing an autonomous discipline of real estate development separate and apart from the academies of urban planning and real estate financial management often found in business schools. In contrast, real estate development is the confluence of an intricate composition and operation of design, finance, and law."*[39]

1. "About the James A. Graaskamp Center for Real Estate," Wisconsin School of Business, accessed April 15, 2015, https://bus.wisc.edu/centers/james-a-graaskamp-center-for-real-estate/about%20the%20graaskamp%20center.
2. Jesse Keenan, Research Director, Center for Urban Real Estate (CURE), Graduate School of Architecture, Planning, and Preservation, Columbia University, interview with the author, February 23, 2015.
3. Given the lack of a professional accrediting organization and the porous boundaries of real estate education, a comprehensive list of real estate programs in the United States may be impossible to compile given the variety of departmental homes and degree granting programs that offer an emphasis on real estate education.
4. *Journal of Property Management* (Spring 1946): 176.
5. Richard Ely, known as a founder of land economics and founder of the American Economic Association, taught at the University of Wisconsin, Madison for three decades starting in 1892.
6. Richard M. Hurd, *Principles of City Land Values* (New York: The Record and Guide, 1903). Hurd served as a mortgage officer and was president of the Lawyers' Mortgage Insurance Company rather than an academic.
7. The organization changed its name to the National Association of Real Estate Boards in 1916, then changed it to National Association of REALTORS in 1974. National Association of REALTORS, "Field Guide to the History of the National Association of REALTORS," accessed August 25, 2015, http://www.realtor.org/field-guides/field-guide-to-the-history-of-the-national-association-of-realtors.
8. According to Marc Weiss, the Institute was "an outgrowth of teaching and research on

'Landed Property and the Rent of Land' that Ely had been conducting for nearly two decades and was the "organization most responsible for studying economic aspects of housing policy in the 1920s. Through his tenure, Ely established relationships with government officials, civic associations, and trade organizations. Ely also edited the Land Economics Series of textbooks co-sponsored by the Institute, the National Association of Real Estate Boards, and the United YMCA Schools. Marc A. Weiss, "Richard T. Ely and the Contribution of Economic Research to National Housing Policy, 1920–1940," *Urban Studies* 26 (1989): 115–126.

9. These universities included New York University, University of Wisconsin, Ohio State University, University of Michigan, University of Pennsylvania, and Indiana University.

10. Programs and courses in real estate are housed in a combination of business schools, economics departments, and urban planning. To a large extent, academic real estate was a limited endeavor in the 1930s and 1940s. Individuals known for their scholarly work, such as Hurd, Ely, Richard Ratcliff, Henry Hoagland, and Homer Hoyt worked in government and the private sector as well as in universities.

11. *Journal of Property Management*, 176.

12. Homer Hoyt, *One Hundred Years of Land Values in Chicago: The Relationship of the Growth of Chicago to the Rise in its Land Values, 1830–1930* (Chicago: University of Chicago Press, 1933). This book stemmed from Hoyt's dissertation in economics at the University of Chicago. Throughout the 1930s textbooks by Ely, Earnest Fisher, Arthur Weimer, and Hoyt help establish the shape of the field.

13. "About ULI," Urban Land Institute, accessed July 15, 2015, http://uli.org/about-uli/.

14. Richard T. Ely, *Ground Under Our Feet: An Autobiography* (New York: Macmillan Co., 1938), 234.

15. Specific to real estate, in California after the war "some of the leading real estate people .... pondered the question of how to raise the educational level and technical ability of the many individuals in the real estate industry." With the support of the state legislature, the University of California developed real estate education and research programs at Berkeley and Los Angeles. "Real Estate Research Program," *Real Estate Bulletin* (September-October 1960): 457.

16. Daniel Gage received a PhD in economics from the University of Michigan and taught at the University of Oregon. Daniel D. Gage, "Status of Collegiate Real Estate Training," *Journal of Property Management* (Spring 1946): 175–184.

17. George Beal, "The Place of Planning in the Architectural Curriculum," *Journal of Architectural Education* 12, no. 1 (1956): 19.

18. In 1954 the Ford Foundation provided $35 million over 12 years to reform business education in the United States. James Howell taught economics at Stanford after receiving a PhD at Yale. The Carnegie Corporation also sponsored studies on business programs. Scott Kohler, "Program to Strengthen Business Education: Ford Foundation, 1954," Center for Strategic Philanthropy and Civil Society, Duke University, 2007, accessed August 25, 2015, https://cspcs.sanford.duke.edu/sites/default/files/descriptive/program_ to_strengthen_business_education.pdf."

19. Arthur Weimer, "The Teaching of Real Estate and Business Administration," *Land Economics* (February 1956), 92–94; James R. Webb and Halbert C. Smith, "United States," in *Real Estate Education Throughout the World: Past, Present and Future*, Karl-Werner Schulte, ed. (New York: Springer Science+Business Media, 2002), 324.

20. Richard Ratcliff, *Real Estate Analysis* (New York: McGraw Hill, 1961). Ratcliff taught at the University of Wisconsin and is credited with transforming Richard Ely's program in land economics into a formal department, now the Department of Real Estate and Urban Land Economics.

21. Patric H. Hendershott, Thomas G. Thibodeau, and Halbert C. Smith, "Evolution of the American Real Estate and Urban Economics Association," *Real Estate Economics* 37, no. 4 (2009): 559–560.

22. The NAREB and NAR have an Education Committee but real estate faculty at these meetings usually did not discuss academic topics, but rather realtor education and training.

23. David Rowlands taught at the University of Pennsylvania. David T. Rowlands, "Some Reflections on Real Estate and Urban Economics," *Proceedings*, American Real Estate and Urban Economics Association, Vol. II (1967): 5–11.

24. Jesse Keenan, Research Director, Center for Urban Real Estate (CURE), Graduate School of Architecture, Planning, and Preservation, Columbia University, interview with the author, February 23, 2015.

25. James A. Graaskamp, "Redefining the Role of the University Education in Real Estate and Urban Land Economics," *The Real Estate Appraiser* (March–April 1976): 23–6.

26. Jerome Dasso, "Real Estate Education at the University Level," *Recent Perspectives in Urban Land Economics* (September 1976): 177–178.

27. Jerome Dasso and Lynn Woodward, "Real Estate Education: Past, Present, and Future—The Search for a Discipline," *Real Estate Economics* 8, no. 4 (December 1980): 404–416.

28. Webb and Smith note that AREUEA meetings tend to emphasize housing issues while ARES emphasize real estate and finance issues, Webb and Smith, "United States," 321. Collectively the journals produced by these two organizations constitute most of the peer reviewed academic research in real estate. Ibid., "United States," 322.

29. The article was S. Titman and A. Warga, "Risk and the Performance of Real Estate Investment Trusts: A Multiple Index Approach," *AREUEA Journal* 14, no. 3 (1986): 414–431. Hendershott, Thibodeau, and Smith, "Evolution of the American Real Estate and Urban Economics Association," 29. In their study of the contents of AREUEA journals since the 1970s, the authors note that the 1990s marked a shift away from articles on housing and urban articles towards commercial real estate. Some of this can be credited toward the creation of journals focused on housing, but also reflected an increased in commercial real estate research in the 1990s. Ibid., 27–28.

30. Joseph D. Albert, "A Retrospective on the Intellectual Environment Surrounding the Establishment of the American Real Estate Society," *Journal of Real Estate Research* 12, no. 2 (1996): 123.

31. Roulac, "State of the Discipline," 111–112.

32. Ibid., 114.

33. Roy T. Black, Neil G. Carn, Julian Diaz III, and Joseph S. Rabianski, "The Role of the American Real Estate Society in Defining and Promulgating the Study of Real Property," *Journal of Real Estate Research* 12, no. 2 (1996): 185.

34. Webb and Smith, "United States," 321–322. Professional organizations that sponsor journals include the *Appraisal Journal* from the Appraisal Institute and *Real Estate Issues* from the Counselors of Real Estate.

35. Webb and Smith, "United States," 319–320. Webb and Smith's list of organizations include the Appraisal Institute, Association of Foreign Investors in U.S. Real Estate, Counselors of Real Estate, International Association of Corporate Real Estate Executives, International Council of Shopping Centers, Mortgage Bankers' Council, National Association of Industrial and Office Properties, National Association of Real Estate Investment Managers, National Association of REALTORS, Urban Land Institute.

36. Roulac, a real estate consultant, adds that "[t]o be effective in property involvements one must simultaneously be and provide the perspectives of: historian, behaviorist, global citizen, urban planner, geographer, business strategist, futurist, political economist, information specialist." Stephen E. Roulac, "Requisite Knowledge for Effective Property Involvements in the Global Context," in *Real Estate Education Throughout the World: Past, Present and Future,* Karl-Werner Schulte, ed. (New York: Springer Science+Business Media, 2002), 11–12.

37. Courses in the curriculum in these departments within universities generally consist of real estate finance, real estate investment, and valuation with other courses in economics and urban planning. In addition to universities, community colleges also offer courses in real estate "aimed at training/licensing so a person can quickly go into real estate." Webb and Smith, "United States," 320–321. Many of these are represented in this timeline.

38. Stephen Malpezzi, "The Wisconsin Program in Real Estate and Urban Land Economics: A Century of Tradition and Innovation," Department of Real Estate and Urban Land Economics, University of Wisconsin, 2009, accessed August 25, 2015, https://bus.wisc. edu/centers/james-a-graaskamp-center-for-real-estate/about%20the%20graaskamp%20 center/-/media/ef20196ae0394932888b49030d093787.ashx.

39. Jesse M. Keenan, "The Art & Science of Real Estate Development," *Volume* 42 (2014): 15.

Renderings
Sonya Ursell

It is often said that rendering is the most effective mode of two-dimensional representation to communicate three-dimensional design to non-designers.[1] Simply put, rendering is the layperson's architectural representation, charged with expressing the designers' intent in a compelling and convincing way. The lifestyle accessories that renderings frequently employ—balloons, kayaks, and bicyclists, to name but a few—have led to ubiquitous criticism in the architectural press.[2] Rather than critique the end product, here we examine how and why these images are made as a way to better understand the priorities of their clients when communicating with their intended audience.

The following renderings are a sampling from the broad range of imagery that accompanies the design and development process of residential projects in the United States today.[3] Interviews were conducted with those directly involved in the image-making process, seeking to understand how, for what purpose, and for whom housing is visualized—from the software used, to the labor required, to the ownership rights of the image; whether for testing designs, seeking approval by civic review boards, or marketing the product to potential buyers. Studying the priorities driving renderings' production begs questions about the closed feedback loops inherent to the process. If contemporary criticism faults the similarities between renderings, it is because changing these patterns of representation risks the very viability of the projects they are meant to promote. Beyond the rendering, however, identifying these processes in the built forms they help to generate allows us to see real estate development in architecture in ways that have otherwise proven elusive. And with this visibility, the feedback loops begin to open up.

PROJECT	702 North The Strand (Oceanside, CA); residential
OFFICE	Lucas Art Works (New Kensington, PA)
TYPE	Rendering and Visualization
SIZE	2 employees
IMAGE BY	Lucas Art Works, 2007
CLIENT	Robert Sachs, developer
PROCESS	Several perspective views are presented to the client for feedback and adjustments before the rendering is drawn; minor cosmetic changes are made afterward in Photoshop
PURPOSE	Community approval, approval with California Coastal Commission. Image supplemented with site analysis and photographs, architectural plans and elevations, summary of relevant development criteria
TIME FRAME	30 days
SOFTWARE	3D model (SketchUp), 2D rendering (pen/ink and watercolor), post-processing (Photoshop)
FEE	$900; price varies based on project and client (first-time vs. returning)
OWNERSHIP	Lucas Art Works owns the image but the architect owns the design; image cannot be sold by Lucas Art Works to others

David Lucas describes his rendering style as the "fine arts approach," drafting with pen and ink and applying watercolor by hand. For him, the difference between his approach and a more photorealistic one is that photorealistic renderings risk giving the client a false sense of reality that produces expectations that may not be met. Watercolors, on the other hand, maintain a certain level of ambiguity that does not produce the same expectations. Furthermore, photorealistic images may suggest that the project is already completed, removing a sense of ownership or individuality from a potential buyer who wishes to build a project to their own specifications.[4]

PROJECT	600 Harrison Avenue (Boston, MA); residential, retail
OFFICE	Utile, Inc. (Boston, MA)
TYPE	Architecture and Planning
SIZE	36 employees
IMAGE BY	Utile, Inc., 2013–2014
CLIENT	Utile, Inc., architect
PROCESS	Multiple rounds of revisions through design and rendering process
PURPOSE	Approval with Boston Redevelopment Authority, Boston Landmarks Commission, marketable image for Utile, Inc., also circulates in online press. Image supplemented with site analysis and photographs, proposed site plan-elevations-sections including surroundings, summary of relevant development criteria[5]
TIME FRAME	1 week
SOFTWARE	Software: 3D model (SketchUp, Rhinoceros), 2D rendering (Kerkythea, Maxwell), post-processing (Photoshop)
FEE	Approximately $3400
OWNERSHIP	Images are owned by Utile, Inc. but clients can use them as part of media related to project

For Michael LeBlanc, the design principal of the project, "the biggest role that the renderings play… is in the approvals process." The style of the rendering depends on the party sought for approval; in some cases, abstraction is preferable to photorealism because it requires the viewer to impose their own vision onto the project. Renderings produced for 600 Harrison Avenue for the Boston Landmarks Commission required that particular attention be given to addressing the materiality and scale of the surrounding context; ultimately, these "constraints" became opportunities that motivated some of the overall design decisions.[6]

PROJECT	La Central (New York, NY); residential, retail, community amenities
OFFICE	FXFOWLE Architects (New York, NY)
TYPE	Architecture and Planning
SIZE	132 employees[7]
IMAGE BY	BezierCG, 2013
CLIENT	FXFOWLE, architect
PROCESS	Art direction by FXFOWLE consisting of 3-4 rounds of revisions
PURPOSE	Submission to an RFP by NYC Department of Housing Preservation & Development, image also circulates in online press. Image supplemented with site analysis and photographs, proposed site plan-typical floor plans-elevations[8]
TIME FRAME	1 week
SOFTWARE	3D model (Rhinoceros, model and views provided by FXFOWLE), 2D rendering (3DS Max), post-processing (Photoshop)
FEE	Not available
OWNERSHIP	Not available

One of the challenges of rendering such a large-scale project is choosing views that capture all of the important elements of the proposal. Aerial views were chosen to illustrate the landscaped elements of the roof, whereas street views incorporate the community amenities—such as the YMCA—that will be part of La Central. Input from these community groups influenced various architectural and landscape elements of the project and these elements can certainly be seen in the project's renderings, but ultimately FXFOWLE acted as the sole art director for the exterior rendering shown here.[9]

PROJECT	TerraSol (Salt Lake City, UT); residential
OFFICE	Bowen Studios (Salt Lake City, UT)
TYPE	Rendering and Visualization
SIZE	10 employees
IMAGE BY	Bowen Studios, 2011
CLIENT	Garbett Homes, developer
PROCESS	Multiple rounds of revisions to develop overarching rendering style for project
PURPOSE	Marketing material (online, print). Image supplemented with site-unit plans and exterior perspectives
TIME FRAME	1–2 weeks to develop style (including collaboration with client); once style is established, renderings can be completed (independently) in 6 hours
SOFTWARE	3D model (SketchUp, Revit, AutoCAD), 2D rendering (3DS Max), minimal post-processing (Photoshop)
FEE	Approximately $1500 for the first image, $800 for others in similar style
OWNERSHIP	Image is owned by the client but Bowen Studios can use it for its own marketing; Bowen Studios requests credit only in newspaper or magazine articles

Founder Brent Bowen often works with developers to create marketable images of large residential developments. These images are intended to sell the unit to potential buyers after it has passed the civic approval process. While images for approval usually address the project's relationship to its surroundings, marketing images aim to create drama and desirability. For these reasons, small artistic liberties are taken when rendering the project, such as including furniture or slightly shifting a wall in order to achieve a more strategic view. These minor changes and additions do not affect the overall design but also do not necessarily reflect a truthful spatial experience.[10]

PROJECT	Pacific & Broadway (San Diego, CA); residential, retail
OFFICE	Kohn Pedersen Fox (KPF) (six global offices, project produced in New York, NY)
TYPE	Architecture and Planning
SIZE	650 employees[11]
IMAGE BY	DBOX, 2012
CLIENT	KPF, architect
PROCESS	Almost daily interaction between KPF and DBOX
PURPOSE	Approval process by Civic San Diego, marketing for project. Image supplemented with drawing package (approximately 50–70 architectural drawings) submitted at each phase of permitting process
TIME FRAME	Not available
SOFTWARE	Not available
FEE	Not available
OWNERSHIP	DBOX and KPF are joint authors (creators) but ownership ultimately belongs to KPF; depends on contract with image-maker

Richard Nemeth, principal at KPF, says that renderings should represent an aesthetically appealing building and encourage community groups and associations to accept the proposal. These groups can pose significant challenges to the project if the rendering does not address their concerns. Yet renderings are not treated so differently from more verifiable representation; Nemeth says that the architect is ultimately bound legally to make the building resemble the renderings produced. For this reason, marketing images do not differ substantially, if at all, from the more speculative renderings produced during the design and approval process.[12]

This approach:

business ethics;
transparency,

compliance, best
practices, highest best
use

1. In the foreword to a publication by the New York Society of Renderers, Alan Ritchie writes that "[a] rendering, unlike an architectural drawing, is a representation of an un-built project that can be shared and appreciated by all." Alan Ritchie, Foreword to *NYSR Portfolio of Architectural & Interior Rendering*, vol. 5 (New York: New York Society of Renderers Inc., 2004–2005), 1. Or, as in the foreword to *CLOG: Rendering*, "[t]ypically a perspectival image that can be understood without any knowledge of architectural drawing conventions, the rendering derives power from its accessibility to a wide audience ..." Foreword to *CLOG: Rendering* (2012, 2nd ed.): 5.

2. See, for example, Tess Hofmann, "Riffing on renderings: Architects unpack the pretty pictures," *The Real Deal*, February 6, 2015, accessed May 26, 2015, http://therealdeal.com/blog/2015/02/06/riffing-on-renderings-architects-unpack-the-pretty-pictures/. See also the blog "Rendering Redux: A Humorous Weekly Investigation Into Architectural Image Making," architizer.com.

3. I refer here only to the renderings that are widely circulated and easily accessible to the public via the internet, signage, and other marketing material. Renderings are certainly used for design development within architecture offices, but do not reach the same level of finish as distributed renderings.

4. David Lucas (founder, Lucas Art Works), in discussion with the author, April 2015.

5. "Information Requirements for BCDC Presentation," Boston Redevelopment Authority, accessed June 24, 2015, http://www.bostonredevelopmentauthority.org/planning/urban-design/boston-civic-design-commission. See also: "Review and Application Information, Instructions and Fees," Boston Landmarks Commission, accessed June 24, 2015, http://www.cityofboston.gov/landmarks/process.asp.

6. Michael LeBlanc (principal, Utile, Inc.), in discussion with the author, April 2015.

7. "FXFOWLE Architects," DesignIntelligence, accessed June 24, 2015, http://www.di.net/almanac/firms/fxfowle-architects/.

8. It is interesting to note that the Bronxchester RFP specifies that "[p]erspective drawings/renderings are optional; however, they must not replace required drawings. Color renderings and/or elevations are appreciated but not required." In other words, renderings are used to supplement, but not replace, more precise drawings of the project. "Bronxchester Request for Proposals," NYC Housing Preservation & Development, accessed June 24, 2015, http://www1.nyc.gov/site/hpd/developers/rfp-rfq-rfo-archives/Bronxchester-RFP.page.

9. Thomas Reeves (designer, FXFOWLE Architects), in discussion with the author, April 2015.

10. Brent Bowen (founder, Bowen Studios), in discussion with the author, June 2015.

11. "Kohn Pedersen Fox," DesignIntelligence, accessed June 24, 2015, http://www.di.net/almanac/firms/kohn-pedersen-fox/.

12. Richard Nemeth (principal, Kohn Pedersen Fox), in discussion with the author, May 2015.

Terms
Cezar Nicolescu

Disciplines are separated by languages that embed specific assumptions into their respective discourses. A brief, necessarily incomplete comparison of some key terms allowed us to expose the differences and similarities between the fields of real estate development and architecture. The operating vocabularies of these fields share terminology that, more often than providing agreement between the two disciplines, reveal dissonance.

Definitions were taken from four field-specific dictionaries. Real estate definitions are provided by Jack P. Friedman, Jack C. Harris, and J. Bruce Lindeman, *Dictionary of Real Estate Terms*, 8th ed. (Hauppauge: Barron's Educational Series, 2013 [1984]), and the online *Glossary of Commercial Real Estate Terms* published by the Realtors' Commercial Alliance. The first of these two sources is more academically oriented, while the second provides definitions for current professional practice. Definitions within architecture are represented by Cyril M. Harris, *Dictionary of Architecture and Construction*, 4th ed. (New York: McGraw-Hill, 2006 [1975]) and Robert Cowan, *The Dictionary of Urbanism* (Tisbury: Streetwise Press, 2005). The inclusion of a dictionary for urbanism allowed access to a vocabulary more likely to intersect with real estate at a larger, planning-oriented scale. The sources were selected on the basis of their recent publication dates to ensure active definitions. With the exception of *The Dictionary of Urbanism*, published in the United Kingdom, the terminology reflects American usage.

The juxtaposition of terms from different fields reveals often similar, sometimes different, and occasionally incompatible meanings—for example, related to the conflicting notions of "equity." The comparisons also reveal omissions of terms we had assumed were central. For example, "design" is missing in real estate dictionaries, which is surprising given that multiple possible notions of the term—from the development of financial modeling to creative problem solving—are fundamental to its practice.

Affordable

Affordable

Housing Affordability Index: An indicator of the proportion of the population that can afford to buy the average home sold during the current period. The intent is to measure the ability of area residents to buy homes in the area. A typical index compares median income to the income required by lenders for a loan large enough to buy a median-priced home.

Affordable housing: A general term applied to public- and private-sector efforts to help low- and moderate-income people purchase homes.

Architect

Architect

Architecture: The manner in which a building is constructed, including the layout, floor plan, style and appearance, materials used, and building technology used.

Affordable

Affordable

Affordable Housing: Housing
for rent set within the reach of
households with low incomes,
and/or housing for sale on a
shared ownership basis (predominantly provided by local
authorities and housing associations or trusts, or low cost
market housing). One US definition specifies affordable
as meaning available at a
mortgage payment or rental
of no more than 25 percent of
the starting salary of a local
elementary school teacher. The
term often conveys little when
it is used (as it often is) without
relating it to an income level.
The income level at which affordability becomes an issue depends
on local circumstances. Sir Peter
Hall (2001) reported that the
highly prosperous ski resort
and conference town, Aspen,
Colorado, decided that it needed
to build affordable housing for
doctors and lawyers. Providing
affordable housing is often set as
a planning obligation.

Architect
1. A person trained and experienced in the design of buildings and the coordination and
supervision of all aspects of the
construction of buildings.
2. A designation reserved, usually by law, for a person or organization professionally qualified

Architect
A person who designs buildings
and supervises their construction.

Architecture: The profession of
designing buildings. The style of
buildings. The design of the built
environment.

Client
The one who engages a broker,
lawyer, accountant, appraiser,
etc.

Client

and duly licensed to perform
architectural services, including
analysis of project requirements,
creation and development of
the project design, preparation
of drawings, specifications,
and bidding requirements,
and general administration of
the construction contract. An
architect usually renders services that require the application
of art, science, and the aesthetics
of design to the construction of
buildings, including their components and appurtenances and
the spaces around them, taking
into account the safeguarding
of life, health, property, and public
welfare; often includes consul-
tation, evaluation, planning, the
provision of preliminary studies,
designs, and construction documents; and may also include
construction management, and
the administration of construction documents.

Client
Owner:
1. The architect's client and
party to the owner-architect
agreement.
2. One who has the legal right or
title to a piece of property.

Client
A person who commissions
professional services. In relation
to architecture, Andres Duany
(2003) suggests, clients—as
distinct from patrons—"are not
so much sophisticated as savvy.
By making themselves available for contact with architects
during the design process, they
acquire a modicum of sophistication." Duany comments: "The
resulting buildings can be quite
good and sometimes excellent.

Common

Common area: Areas of a property that are used by all owners or tenants.

Common elements: In a condominium, those portions of the property not owned individually by unit owners but in which an indivisible interest is held by all unit owners. Generally includes the grounds, parking areas, recreational facilities, and external structure of the building.

Common

Common area: For lease purposes, the areas of a building (and its site) that are available for the nonexclusive use of all its tenants, such as lobbies, corridors, and parking lots. (Real Estate Information Standards)

Community

Community associations: General name for any organization of property owners to oversee some common interest.

Community

Clients underwrite most of the decent houses in America. Sometimes, an individual within government will rise to the level of a client."

Common
A large plot of grassy, fenced-in, publicly owned land, generally at or near the center of a village or town; in earlier eras, once shared by the townspeople as a pasture.

Common
A piece of land that belongs to local people collectively, and which is open for public use.

Community
A group of people having common rights, privileges, or interests, or living in the same place under the same laws and regulations.

Community
A grouping of people with common interests. The DETR (1998) defined community as "any group of individuals with a common bond above the family unit and below the first level of municipal administration. It is primarily those people living or working in a defined area... in general the people intended to benefit from regeneration and local services." The New Economics Foundation (2000) describes community as "a web of relationships defined by a significant level of mutual care and commitment."

Cost

Cost Approach: A method of appraising property based on the depreciated reproduction or replacement cost (new) of improvements, plus the market value of the site.

Cost Estimating: In construction, the act of predicting the total costs of labor, materials, capital, and professional fees required to construct a proposed project.

Cost

The actual dollar amount paid for a property or the amount needed to build or improve it at a specified time in the future.

Creative

Creative Financing: Any financing arrangement other than a traditional mortgage from a third-party lending institution. Creative financing devices include: loans from the seller, balloon payment loans, wrap-around mortgages, assumption of mortgage, sale-leasebacks, land contracts, alternative mortgage instruments.

Creative

Design

Design

Cost

Cost of construction: The sum of all direct and indirect costs of construction; generally categorized as equipment costs, job overhead costs, operating overhead costs, material costs, plant costs, and profit.

Cost

Cost Effectiveness Analysis: Comparing the costs of alternative ways of producing the same or similar outputs of a regeneration program without giving them monetary value.

Creative

Creative

Creative Class: Defined by Richard Florida (2002) as including people in science and engineering, architecture and design, education, arts music and entertainment, whose economic function is to create new ideas, new technology, and/or new creative content. Around this core, the creative class also includes a broader group of creative professionals in business and finance, law, health care, and related fields. These people engage in complex problem-solving that involves a great deal of independent judgment and requires high levels of education or human capital.

Design

To compose a plan for a building.

Design

An outline or sketch or plan of the form or structure of something to be constructed or carried out; instructions, particularly in the form

Development

Developer: One who transforms raw land to improved property by use of labor, capital, and entrepreneur efforts.

Development: The process of adding improvements on or to a parcel of land. Such improvements may include drainage, utilities, subdividing, access, buildings, and any combination of these elements. Also the project where such improvements are being made.

Development

Efficency

Efficiency Ratio: The proportion of a building's area that is leasable space.

Efficiency Unit or Apartment: a small dwelling unit, often consisting of a single room, within a multifamily structure. In most cases, kitchen and bath facilities are not complete.

Efficency

A measure of the capacity or effectiveness of space to produce the desired results with a minimum expenditure of time, money, energy, and materials.

Ethics

Principles by which one treats colleagues, clients, and the public in a fair, just, and truthful manner. Adherence to such standards is considered one of the requisites for recognition as a profession.

Ethics

of drawings, for making an object,
a building, or a development.

Development
1. A tract of previously undevel-
oped land which is subdivided
for housing and provided with
all necessary utilities, such as
roads, water, electricity, sewers,
etc.
2. A large-scale housing project.
3. Any man-made change to
improved or unimproved real
estate, including but not limited
to dredging, excavation or drill-
ing operations, filling, or paving
located within an area of special
flood hazard.

Development
Statutorily defined under the
[UK] Town and Country Planning Act 1990 as "the carrying
out of building, engineering,
mining, or the making of any
material change in the use of any
building or other land. ... "

Efficency
Area Efficiency: The ratio of the
net usable floor area (or the net
rentable area) to the gross floor
area.

Efficiency
The relationship between output
and input; the ratio of output to
input.

Ethics
Professional practice: The practice of one of the environmental
design professions in which
services are rendered within the
framework of recognized professional ethics and standards and
applicable legal requirements.

Ethics

Equity
The interest or value that the
owner has in real estate over and
above the liens against it.

Equity
Equity Lease: A type of joint
venture arrangement in
which an owner enters into a
contract with a user who agrees
to occupy a space and pay rent
as a tenant, but at the same time,
receives a share of the ownership benefits such as periodic
cash flows, interest and cost recovery deductions, and perhaps
a share of the sales proceeds.

Equity Yield Rate: The return
on the portion of an investment
financed by equity capital.

Family
A household consisting of two
or more related people.

Familial status: Characteristics
determined by a person's household type, such as marriage and
existing or prospective children.
Referred to in the Federal Fair
Housing Law and Fair Credit
Reporting Act; prohibits denying
rights to people younger than
age 18 who live with a parent or
legal guardian. Pregnant women
are specifically covered.

Family
Multifamily Housing:
Housing units that accommo-
date more than one family or
household.

Government

Government
Government Incentives: Conces-
sion given or measures taken
by local or regional government
to attract firms or investment
dollars to a given locality for the
purposes of promoting economic

Equity

The value of an owner's interest in property, computed by subtracting the amount of outstanding mortgages or liens from the total value of the property.

Equity

1. Fairness in access to resources; impartiality.
2. Money and resources provided by those who share in a property development's risk and profit.
3. A capital stake in a property.

Family

In urban planning, one or more persons occupying a single living unit.

Family

Government

GOVT: On drawings, abbr. for "government."

Government

Urban Governance: The methods by which an urban area is governed and administered by local government and a variety of other agencies.

growth and encouraging development.

House
In real estate usage, a residential structure containing a single dwelling unit.

House

Household
One or more persons inhabiting a housing unit as their principal residence.

Household
A housing unit or residence at a given location that is occupied by one or more persons (that is, a social unit comprised of one or more individuals living together in the same dwelling or place).

Housing
Structures intended for residential use.

Housing Starts: an estimate of the number of dwelling units on which construction has begun in a stated period. The number of housing starts each month is an important indicator of economic activity.

Housing
Housing demand: The total number of housing units demanded in a given market, defined as occupied household units divided by one minus the vacancy allowance for that market (where demand is affected by the rate at which new households are being added to the market, allowing for a normal level of vacancy).

Investment
1. Purchasing an asset, lending one's money, or contributing to a venture in hopes of receiving

Investment
Investing: Limiting current consumption in favor of future consumption.

House
1. A building or dwelling for human residence.
2. A theater, as a legitimate house.
3. (Colloq.) The auditorium in a theater; the audience space.

House
A dwelling, sometimes particularly as distinct from a flat.

Household
All persons, including family members and any unrelated persons, who occupy a dwelling unit.

Household
Defined in the UK census as one person living alone, or a group of people (who may or may not be related) living at the same address with common housekeeping, sharing either a living room or a sitting room, or at least one meal a day.

Housing
1. A notch or groove cut in one wood member, usually to receive another wood member, as in a housed joint; also called a trench.
2. A shelter or dwelling place, or a collection of such places.
3. A niche for a statue.

Housing
Residential accommodation.

Housing Mix: The range of housing in an area or a development in terms of such factors as its type, size, affordability, accessibility, and tenure.

Investment

Investment
Investment property:
Owner-occupied or rented land or buildings.

DICTIONARY OF REAL ESTATE TERMS	GLOSSARY OF COMMERCIAL REAL ESTATE
a return of the funds invested and a return on investment from those funds. 2. An asset purchased for the purpose of preserving and increasing wealth.	*Investment value*: The value to a specific investor, based on that investor's requirements, tax rate, or financing.
Model (See Simulate) *Simulate*: Artificially replicate the behavior of a system for purposes of analysis. The simulation may be less complex than the actual system, allowing the analyst to focus on certain variables that are of interest.	Model *Cash Flow Model*: The framework used to determine the cash flow from operations and the cash proceeds from sale.
Private *Private Sector*: All economic activity other than that of government.	Private
Project	Project

Model
A pattern of an item to be reproduced, often in quantity.

Model
A simplified representation of reality. This may be in the form of a theory, a set of mathematical or statistical formulae, or a scaled-down, three-dimensional, physical structure (in wood, card, or polystyrene for example). Physical models can help people to understand urban form (and can also be a means of deception). Mathematical models enable calculations to be made about what is likely to happen in a range of different circumstance (and can be used to create a spurious sense of objectivity). Other models are expressions, in words, of ideas.

Private
Private Area: The area, whether within or outside a building, which is reserved for the exclusive use of a single family.

Private
Privatism: The tendency for people to live their lives in private rather than in public, making less use of public space and being less involved in community organizations.

Project
1. A construction undertaking, composed of one or more buildings and the site improvements,

Project
1. A defined task; a set of activities carried out to fulfil a defined aim; and individual element in a

Property
The rights that one individual
has in lands or goods to the ex-
clusion of all others; right gained
from the ownership of wealth.

Property
Property Market: The supply and
demand for ownership interests
in property.

Public
Public Sector: The portion of the
economy run by various levels of
government.

Public

planned and executed in a fixed
time period.
2. The total construction designed by the architect, of which
the work performed under the
contract documents may be the
whole or a part.

regeneration scheme.
2. (U.S.) A public housing development. The equivalent in
England and Wales is "estate"
and in Scotland "scheme."

Property
Any asset, real or personal.
An ownership interest.

Property
Buildings, land, and infrastructure.

Public
Public Space: 1. An area within
a building to which there is free
access by the public, such as a
foyer or lobby.
2. In some codes, an area or
piece of land legally designated
for public use.

Public
Public Interest: That which
will be to the collective benefit
of society or of the inhabitants
of a particular place. Both politicians and some professionals
(town planners, for example)
choose to see themselves as
having a role in defining the
public interest.

Public sphere: The sociologist
Jürgen Habermas' concept of
the place where people talk
about life. It is a sphere which
"mediates between society and
state, and in which the public
organizes itself as the bearer
of public opinion" (Habermas,
1962). He sees its growth in
eighteenth-century England
with the development of a new
urban culture which flourished
in, among other places, the
coffee houses.

Real Estate
1. In Law, land, and everything more or less attached to it. Ownership below to the center of the earth and above to the heavens. Distinguished from personal property. Same as realty.
2. In Business, the activities concerned with ownership and use transfers of the physical property. Ex. *The following are engaged in real estate business activities: accountants, appraisers, attorneys, etc.*

Real Estate
Real Estate Fluctuations: Short-term variations in real estate prices or rents (usually lasting anywhere from one day to a few months), caused by natural hazards (such as tornadoes, hurricanes, floods, earthquakes, and wildfires), or boosts or shocks to the local economy (such as the entry or exit of major employers).

Real estate trends: Long-term movements or tendencies in the demand for commercial real estate (which can typically last for years or decades), usually tied to macroeconomic or business cycles.

Return
Return of Investment: Portion of the receipts from an investment that represents recovery of the amount invested.

Return
Rate of Return: The percentage return on each dollar invested. Also known as yield.

Risk
1. Uncertainty or variability. The possibility that returns from an investment will be greater or less than forecast. Diversification of investments provides some protection against risk.
2. The possibility of a loss. Insurance can offer protection against certain risks.

Risk
The probability that actual cash flows from an investment will vary from the forecasted cash flows.

Risk-Free Rate: The interest

Real Estate
Property in the form of land and all its appurtenances, such as buildings erected on it.

Real Estate
Immovable property such as land, buildings, ownership rights, businesses and lease-holds.

Return
The continuation of a molding, projection, member, or cornice, or the like, in a different direction, usually at a right angle. For example, see cornice return.

Return

Risk
Risk Management: In the building industry, the systemized practice of avoiding potential risks, such as culpability and liability or legal entanglements.

Risk
1. The possibility of an undesired outcome.
2. The possibility of an unexpected outcome. Where this second definition is being used (as in the world of property development), the possibility of an undesired outcome is referred to as "downside risk."

rate on the safest investments,
such as federal and government
obligations.

Site
A plot of land prepared for or
underlying a structure or
development. The location
of a property.

Site Plan: A document which
describes how a parcel of land
is to be improved.

Site
Site Analysis: The identification and evaluation of a site or
sites to satisfy a given use or
objective.

Value
Valuation:
1. Estimated worth or price.
2. The act of estimating the
worth of a thing.

Value
Add value: Fourth stage of
four-stage transaction management process pertaining to a
transaction manager's planning,
effort, and continual contact
with key decision-makers,
investors, and users, as well as
contact with ancillary professionals. This ongoing process
allows for feedback, establishes
a network for problem solving,
provides a means to offer
additional services to the client,
and enhances the transaction
manager's preparedness for the
next assignment.

Site
An area or plot of ground with
defined limits on which a building, project, park, etc., is located
or proposed to be located.

Site
An area of land with a defined
boundary.

Value
Value engineering: A discipline
of engineering that studies
the relative monetary values
of various materials and construction techniques, including
the initial cost, maintenance
cost, energy usage cost, replacement cost, and life expectancy.

Schedule of values: A statement
furnished by the contractor
to the architect reflecting the
portions of the contract sum
allotted for the various parts
of the work and used as the
basis for reviewing the
contractor's applications for
progress payments.

Value
The architectural commentator
Paul Finch (2002) has suggested
that, in the context of
development economics, value
is satisfaction minus price.

Valuation: Ascribing monetary
value to something.

Appendix

Aalbers, Manuel and Brett Christophers, "Centring Housing in Political Economy." *Housing, Theory and Society* Vol. 31, No. 4 (2014): 373–394.

ABC News. "Transcript: Freedom Partners Forum: Ted Cruz, Rand Paul and Marco Rubio in Conversation with ABC's Jonathan Karl." January 26, 2015. http://abcnews.go.com/Politics/transcript-freedom-partners-forum-ted-cruz-rand-paul/story?id=28491534.

Acharya, Viral V., Matthew Richardson, Stijn Van Nieuwerburgh, and Lawrence J. White. *Guaranteed to Fail: Fannie Mae, Freddie Mac, and the Debacle of Mortgage Finance.* Princeton: Princeton University Press, 2011.

Aizpún, Carlos Labarta. "Revisitando a Schindler, Comprendiendo a Gehry, Los Angeles 1921–1978." *Revista de Arquitectura* 14 (2012): 71–80.

Albert, Joseph D. "A Retrospective on the Intellectual Environment Surrounding the Establishment of the American Real Estate Society." *Journal of Real Estate Research* Vol. 12, No. 2 (1996): 123–128.

Alofsin, Anthony. *Frank Lloyd Wright: The Lost Years, 1910–1922: A Study of Influence.* Chicago: University of Chicago Press, 1993.

Angotti, Tom. *New York for Sale: Community Planning Confronts Global Real Estate.* Cambridge, MA: MIT Press, 2008.

Anti-Discrimination Center. *Cheating On Every Level. Anatomy of the Demise of a Civil Rights Consent Decree.* Last modified May 6, 2014. http://www.antibiaslaw.com/sites/default/files/Cheating_On_Every_Level.pdf.

Appadurai, Arjun, ed. *The Future as Cultural Fact: Essays on the Global Condition.* New York: Verso Books, 2013.

Aravena, Alejandro, and Andres Iacobelli, eds. *Elemental: Incremental Housing and Participatory Design Manual.* Ostfildern: Hatje Cantz, 2012.

Archer, Wayne, and Marc Smith. "Explaining Location Patterns of Suburban Offices." *Real Estate Economics* Vol. 31, No. 2 (2003): 139–164.

Architizer. "Rendering Redux." Accessed August 10, 2015. http://architizer.kinja.com/tag/rendering-redux.

Arrighi, Giovanni. *Adam Smith in Beijing: Lineages of the 21st Century.* London and New York: Verso Books, 2007.

Ashenfelter, Orley C. "Comparing Real Wages." NBER Working Paper 18006. Cambridge, MA: National Bureau of Economic Research, 2012.

Atkinson, Anthony B. *Inequality: What Can Be Done?* Cambridge, MA: Harvard University Press, 2015.

Baird-Remba, Rebecca. "Balancing Cost and Beauty: Architects Talk Affordable Housing Design." *New York YIMBY*, May 1, 2015. http://newyorkyimby.com/2015/05/balancing-cost-and-beauty-architects-talk-affordable-housing-design.html.

Bandes, Susan J., ed., *Affordable Dreams: The Goetsch-Winckler House and Frank Lloyd Wright.* East Lansing: Michigan State University Press, 1991.

Banham, Reyner. "A Home is not a House." *Art in America*, April 1965: 70–79.

Banner, Stuart. *American Property: A History of How, Why, and What We Own.* Cambridge, MA: Harvard University Press, 2011.

Barboza, David. "Chinese City Has Many Buildings, but Few People." *New York Times*, October 20, 2010.

Barkan, Joshua. "Chapter 3: Personhood," *Corporate Sovereignty: Law and Governance under Capitalism.* Minneapolis: University of Minnesota Press, 2013.

Bauer, Catherine. *Modern Housing.* New York: Houghton Mifflin, 1934.

Bauman, John F., Roger Biles, and Kristin M. Szylvian, eds. *From Tenements to the Taylor Homes: In Search of an Urban Housing Policy in Twentieth Century America.* University Park: The Pennsylvania State University Press, 2000.

Beal, George. "The Place of Planning in the Architectural Curriculum." *Journal of Architectural Education* Vol. 12, No. 1 (1956): 18–24.

Beauregard, Robert. "The Texture of Property Markets: Downtown Housing and Office Conversions in New York City." *Urban Studies* Vol. 42, No. 13 (2005): 2431–2445.

Beauregard, Robert. *When America Became Suburban.* Minneapolis: University of Minnesota Press, 2006.

Becker, Gary S. *The Economics of Discrimination.* Chicago: University of Chicago Press, 1957.

Beckert, Sven. *The Monied Metropolis: New York City and the Consolidation of the American Bourgeoisie, 1850–1896.* Cambridge, UK: Cambridge University Press, 2001.

Behrens, Carl F. *Commercial Bank Activities in Urban Mortgage Financing*. New York: National Bureau of Economic Research, 1952.

Bell, Jeannine. *Hate Thy Neighbor: Move-In Violence and the Persistence of Racial Segregation in American Housing*. New York: NYU Press, 2013.

Ben-Joseph, Eron. "Workers' Paradise: The Forgotten Communities of World War I." MIT School of Architecture and Planning. Accessed March 25, 2014. http://web.mit.edu/ebj/www/ww1/ww1a.html.

Benjamin, John, G. Donald Jud, and Daniel Winkler. "The Supply Adjustment Process in Retail Space Markets." *Journal of Real Estate Research* Vol. 15, No. 3 (1998): 297–308.

Bergdoll, Barry, and Peter Christensen. *Home Delivery: Fabricating the Modern Dwelling*. New York: Museum of Modern Art, 2008.

Bergdoll, Barry, and Reinhold Martin, eds. *Foreclosed: Rehousing the American Dream*. New York: Museum of Modern Art, 2012.

Berle, Adolf A., and Gardiner C. Means. *The Modern Corporation & Private Property*. New York: Macmillan, 1932.

Bernstein, Peter L. *Against the Gods: The Remarkable Story of Risk*. New York: John Wiley and Sons, 1996.

Biles, Roger. "A Mormon in Babylon: George Romney as Secretary of HUD, 1969–1973." *Michigan Historical Review* Vol. 38, No. 2 (Fall 2012): 63–89.

Black, Roy T., Neil G. Carn, Julian Diaz III, and Joseph S. Rabianski. "The Role of the American Real Estate Society in Defining and Promulgating the Study of Real Property." *Journal of Real Estate Research* Vol. 12, No. 2 (1996): 183–193.

Blackmar, Elizabeth. "Of REITS and Rights: Absentee Ownership on the Periphery." In *City, Country, Empire: Landscapes in Environmental History*, edited by Edited by Jeffry M. Diefendorf and Kurk Dorsey, 81–98. Pittsburgh: University of Pittsburgh Press, 2005.

Blakely, Edward J. and Mary Gail Snyder. *Fortress America: Gated Communities in the United States*. Washington, D.C.: Brookings Institution Press, 1997.

Bleecker, Samuel E. *The Politics of Architecture: A Perspective on Nelson A. Rockefeller*. New York: Routledge Press, 1981.

Block, Ralph J. *Investing in REITs: Real Estate Investment Trusts*. 4th ed. Princeton: Bloomberg Press, 2011.

Bloom, Nicholas Dagen, Fritz Umbach, and Lawrence J. Vale, eds. *Public Housing Myths: Perception, Reality, and Social Policy*. Ithaca and London: Cornell University Press 2015.

Bloom, Nicholas Dagen. *Public Housing That Worked: New York in the Twentieth Century*. Philadelphia: University of Pennsylvania Press, 2008.

Bloomberg Business. "China Slowdown Brings Ordos Bust as Li Grapples With Credit." July 15, 2013. http://www.bloomberg.com/news/articles/2013-07-15/china-slowdown-sends-ordos-to-bust-as-li-grapples-with-credit.

Blundell Jones, Peter, Doina Petrescu, and Jeremy Till, eds. *Architecture and Participation*. London and New York: Spon Press, 2005.

Bolton, Megan, Elina Bravve, Emily Miller, Sheila Crowley, and Ellen Errico. *Out of Reach 2015*. Washington, D.C.: National Low Income Housing Coalition, 2015.

Bonnet, Odran, Pierre-Henri Bono, Guillaume Chapelle, and Etienne Wasmer. "Does housing capital contribute to inequality? A comment on Thomas Piketty's Capital in the 21st Century." Discussion Paper 2014–07. Paris: Economics Department, Science Po and LIEPP, April 17, 2014.

Bosma, Koos. *Housing for the Millions, John Habraken and the SAR (1960–2000)*. Rottterdam: NAi Publishers, 2000.

Boston Landmarks Commission. "Review and Application Information, Instructions and Fees." Accessed June 24, 2015. http://www.cityofboston.gov/landmarks/process.asp.

Boston Redevelopment Authority. "Inclusionary Development Design Guidelines." Last modified July 2009. http://www.bostonredevelopmentauthority.org/housing/faqs.

Boston Redevelopment Authority. "Information Requirements for BCDC Presentation." Accessed June 24, 2015. http://www.bostonredevelopmentauthority.org/planning/urban-design/boston-civic-design-commission.

Boston, William. "REITs Gear Up in Germany: New Coalition Is Set to Scrap 2007 Rules Limiting Industry." *The Wall Street Journal*, April 12, 2015. http://www.wsj.com/articles/SB125546154759483019.

Botein, Hilary Ann. *"Solid Testimony of Labor's Present Status:" Unions and Housing in Postwar New York City*. PhD diss., Columbia University, 2005.

Botein, Hilary. "New York State Housing Policy in Postwar New York City. The Enduring Rockefeller Legacy." *Journal of Urban History* 35, No. 6 (2009): 833–852.

Bowly Jr., Devereux. *The Poorhouse: Subsidized Housing in Chicago 1985–1976*. Edwardsville: Southern Illinois University Press, 1978.

Brähmig, Horst-Dieter. "Entwicklung und Perspektiven der Stadt Hoyerswerda." *Stadtumbau Ost, Superumbau Hoyerswerda*, edited by Michael Klaus, 13–16. Dresden: Sächsische Akademie, 2006.

Bratt, Rachel G. "The Quadruple Bottom Line and Nonprofit Housing Organizations in the United States," *Housing Studies* Vol. 27, No. 4 (2012): 438–456.

Brealey, Richard A., Stewart C. Myers, and Franklin Allen. *Principles of Corporate Finance*. 9th ed. New York: McGraw-Hill, 2007.

Bredderman, Will. "Deputy Mayor: Prevailing Wages Would Cost City 17,000 Affordable Apartments." *New York Observer*, June 1, 2015. http://observer.com/2015/06/deputy-mayor-prevailing-wages-would-cost-city-17000-affordable-apartments/.

Brett, Deborah L., and Adrienne Schmitz. *Real Estate Market Analysis: Methods and Case Studies*. 2nd ed. Washington D.C.: Urban Land Institute, 2009.

Bristol, Katherine G. "The Pruitt-Igoe Myth." *Journal of Architectural Education* Vol. 44, No. 3 (1991): 163–171.

Brooks, Charlotte. *Alien Neighbors, Foreign Friends: Asian Americans, Housing, and the Transformation of Urban California*. Chicago: University of Chicago Press, 2009.

Brown, S.J., and C.H. Liu, eds. *A Global Perspective on Real Estate Cycles*. New York: Springer, 2001.

Brueckner, Jan. *Lectures on Urban Economics*. Cambridge, MA: MIT Press, 2011.

Brueggeman, William, and Jeffrey Fisher. *Real Estate Finance & Investments*. 14th ed. Homewood: Irwin, 2011.

Bryant, Willis R. *Mortgage Lending: Fundamentals and Practices*. New York: McGraw-Hill, 1956.

Buck, Brennan. "A Short History of Building as Asset." *Log* No 18 (Winter 2010): 5–13.

Burd-Sharps, Sarah, and Kristen Lewis. *Geographies of Opportunity: Ranking Well-Being by Congressional District*. The Measure of America Series of the Social Science Research Council, April 2015.

Calder, Lendol Glen. *Financing the American Dream: A Cultural History of Consumer Credit*. Princeton: Princeton University Press, 1999.

Calem, Paul S., Kevin Gillen, and Susan Wachter. "The Neighborhood Distribution of Subprime Mortgage Lending." *The Journal of Real Estate Finance and Economics* Vol. 29, No. 4 (December 2004): 393–410.

Caplin, Andrew, Sewin Chan, Charles Freeman, and Joseph Tracy. *Housing Partnerships: A New Approach to a Market at a Crossroads*. Cambridge, MA: MIT Press, 1997.

Caplovitz, David. *The Poor Pay More: Consumer Practices of Low-Income Families*. New York: Free Press, 1967.

Caramellino, Gaia. "Housing is Everybody's Business (1930–1934)." In *William Lescaze: A European architect in the New Deal*. Newcastle: Cambridge Scholars Publishing, 2015.

Caro, Robert A. *The Power Broker: Robert Moses and the Fall of New York*. New York: Vintage Books, 1975.

Carson, E. Ann. "Prisoners in 2013." Bureau of Justice Statistics, U.S. Department of Justice. September 30, 2014. http://www.bjs.gov/content/pub/pdf/p13.pdf.

Case, Bradford, William Goetzmann, and Geert Rouwenhorst. "Global Real Estate Markets: Cycles and Fundamentals." Yale ICF Working Paper No. 99–03, March 1999. http://papers.ssrn.com/sol3/papers.cfm?abstract_id=157019.

Case, Karl, and Robert Shiller. "Is There a Bubble in the Housing Market?" Brookings Papers on Economic Activity, 2003 (2): 299–362.

Case, Karl E., Robert J. Shiller, and John Quigley. "Stock Market Wealth, Housing Market Wealth, and Consumption," unpublished paper, 2001.

Castillo, Greg. *Cold War on the Home Front: The Soft Power of Midcentury Design*. Minneapolis: University of Minnesota Press, 2010.

Chaban, Matt. "Goldstein, Hill & West: How New York's Most Anonymous Architects Have Taken Over the Skyline." *New York Observer*, October 16, 2012.

Chakrabarti, Vishaan. *A Country of Cities: A Manifesto for an Urban America*. New York: Metropolis Books, 2013.

Chakrabarty, Dipesh. "On Conjoined Histories." *Critical Inquiry*, Vol. 41, No. 1 (Autumn 2014): 1–23.

Chan, Melissa. "China's Empty City." Al Jazeera, November 10, 2009. Accessed August 10, 2015. http://www.aljazeera.com/news/asia-pacific/2009/11/2009111061722672521.html.

Chovanec, Patrick. "China's Real Estate Riddle." *An American Perspective from China*, June 11, 2009. Accessed June 24, 2015. https://chovanec.wordpress.com/2009/06/11/chinas-real-estate-riddle/.

Citizens Housing and Planning Council. "Making Room." Accessed June 15, 2015. http://makingroomnyc.com.

City and County of San Francisco, Mayor's Office of Housing & Community Development, "Inclusionary Housing Program." Accessed June 29, 2015. http://sf-moh.org/index.aspx?page=263.

Climber, Adam. "Charles Percy, Former Ill. Senator, Dead at 91." *New York Times*, September 17, 2011.

Clinton, Hillary Rodham. "Keynote Speech by the Honorable Hillary Rodham Clinton." New America Foundation. May 16, 2014. http://www.newamerica.net/conference2014/keynote_by_the_honorable_hillary_rodham_clinton.

Coates, Ta-Nehisi. "The Case for Reparations," *The Atlantic*, June 2014.

Cohen, Lizabeth. *A Consumer's Republic: The Politics of Mass Consumption in Postwar America*. New York: Alfred A. Knopf, 2003.

Cohen, Lizabeth. *Making a New Deal*. New York: Cambridge University Press, 1990.

Cohen, Patricia. "Middle Class but Feeling Economically Insecure." *New York Times*, April 10, 2015.

Colean, Miles L. *The Impact of Government on Real Estate Finance in the United States*. New York: National Bureau of Economic Research, 1950.

Colomina, Beatriz. *Domesticity at War*. Cambridge, MA: MIT Press, 2007.

Congress of the New Urbanism, ed. Accessed June 12, 2015. https://www.cnu.org/.

Copeland, Thomas E., J. Fred Weston, and Kuldeep Shastri. *Financial Theory and Corporate Policy*. 4th ed. Upper Saddle River: Prentice Hall, 2005.

Costello, James, et al. "Real Estate Risk: A Forward-Looking Approach." *Real Estate Finance* Vol. 18, No. 3 (2001): 20–28.

Cowie, Jefferson. *Capital Moves: RCA's Seventy-Year Quest for Cheap Labor*. Ithaca, NY: Cornell University Press, 1999.

Curbed. "Upper West Side 'Poor Door' Rentals Start At $833/Month." Accessed June 9, 2015. http://ny.curbed.com/tags/40-riverside-boulevard.

Dasso, Jerome. "Real Estate Education at the University Level." *Recent Perspectives in Urban Land Economics*, University of British Columbia (September 1976): 177–178.

Dasso, Jerome, and Alfred A. Ring. *Real Estate: Principles and Practices*. 11th ed. Englewood Cliffs: Prentice Hall, 1989.

Dasso, Jerome, and Lynn Woodward. "Real Estate Education: Past, Present, and Future: The Search for a Discipline." *Real Estate Economics* Vol. 8, No. 4 (1980): 404–416.

Davies, Pearl Janet. *Real Estate in American History*. Washington, D.C.: Public Affairs Press, 1958.

Davis, John Emmaeus, ed. *The Community Land Trust Reader*. Cambridge, MA: Lincoln Institute of Land Policy, 2010.

Day, Jared. *Urban Castles: Tenement Housing and Landlord Activism in New York City 1890-1943*. New York: Columbia University Press, 1999.

de Graaf, Reinier. "Architecture is now a tool of capital, complicit in a purpose antithetical to its social mission." *Architectural Review*, April 24, 2015.

De Grazia, Victoria. *Irresistible Empire: America's Advance through Twentieth-Century Europe*. Cambridge, MA: Belknap Press, 2005.

De Souza, Flávio, and Roger Zetter. "Urban land tenure in Brazil: from centralized state to market processes of housing land delivery." In *Market Economy and Urban Change: Impacts in the Developing World*, edited by Roger Zetter and Mohamed Hamza, 163–184. Sterling, VA: Earthscan, 2004.

DeFilippis, James, and Susan Saegert, eds. *The Community Development Reader*. New York: Routledge, 2012.

DeNavas-Walt, Carmen and Bernadette D. Proctor. "Income and Poverty in the United States: 2013." United States Census Bureau. Accessed August 10, 2015. https://www.census.gov/content/dam/Census/library/publications/2014/demo/p60–249.pdf.

Deng, Yongheng, Stephen L. Ross, and Susan M. Wachter. "Racial differences in homeownership: the effect of residential location." *Regional Science and Urban Economics* Vol. 3, No. 5 (Sept. 2003): 517–556.

DesignIntelligence. "FXFowle Architects." Accessed June 24, 2015. http://www.di.net/almanac/firms/fxfowle-architects/.

DesignIntelligence. "Kohn Pedersen Fox." Accessed June 24, 2015. http://www.di.net/almanac/firms/kohn-pedersen-fox/.

Diaz, David R. Barrio Urbanism: Chicanos, Planning, and American Cities. New York: Routledge, 2005.

Diefendorf, Jeffry M. "Berlin on the Charles, Cambridge on the Spree: Walter Gropius, Martin Wagner, and the rebuilding of Germany." In Kulturelle Wechselbeziehungen im Exil—Exile across Cultures, edited by Helmut F. Pfanner, 343–357. Bonn: Bouvier Verlag Herbert Grundmann, 1986.

DiPasquale, Denise and William C. Wheaton. Urban Economics and Real Estate Markets. Upper Saddle River, NJ: Prentice Hall, 1995.

Dreier, Peter, John Mollenkopf, and Todd Swanstrom. Place Matters: Metropolitics for the Twenty-First Century. 3rd ed. Lawrence: University Press of Kansas, 2014 [2001].

Duany, Andres, and Jeff Speck with Mike Lydon. The Smart Growth Manual. New York: McGraw Hill, 2010.

Dumasoya, Maya. "The Problem with Mixed-Income Housing." Jacobin, May 21, 2014. https://www.jacobinmag.com/2014/05/the-problem-with-mixed-income-housing/.

Dunn-Haley, Karen. The House that Uncle Sam Built: The Political Culture of Federal Housing Policy, 1919–1932. PhD diss., Stanford University, 1995.

Dunster, David. "Selling Mies." In Chicago Architecture: Histories, Revisions, Alternatives, edited by Charles Waldheim and Katerina Rüedi, 93–102. Chicago: University of Chicago Press, 2005.

Edel, Matthew, Elliott D. Sclar, and Daniel Luria. Shaky Palaces: Home Ownership and Social Mobility in Boston. New York: Columbia University Press, 1984.

Eichler, Ned. The Merchant Builders. Cambridge: MIT Press, 1982.

Ellen, Ingrid Gould, and Margery Austin Turner. "Do neighborhoods matter? Assessing recent evidence." Housing Policy Debate Vol. 8, No. 4 (1997): 833–866.

Elsingaa, Maria, Mark Stephens, and Thomas Knorr-Siedow. "The Privatisation of Social Housing: Three Different Pathways." In Social Housing in Europe, edited by Kathleen Scanlon, Christine Whitehead, and Melissa Fernández Arrigoitia, 389–414. Oxford: John Wiley & Sons, 2014.

Elson, Robert T. Time Inc.: the Intimate History of a Publishing Enterprise. New York: Atheneum, 1968.

Ely, Richard T. Ground Under Our Feet: An Autobiography. New York: Macmillan Co, 1938.

Enterprise Community Partners. "Our Story." 2013. Accessed January 14, 2015. http://enterprisecommunity.com.

Esperdy, Gabrielle. Modernizing Main Street: Architecture and Consumer Culture in the New Deal. Chicago: University of Chicago Press, 2008.

Fabozzi, Frank J., Franco Modigliani, and Michael Ferri. Foundations of Financial Markets and Institutions. Englewood Cliffs, Prentice Hall, 1994.

Fainstein, Susan S. "Feminism and Planning: Theoretical Issues." In Gender and Planning: A Reader, edited by Susan S. Fainstein and Lisa J. Servon, 120–138. New Brunswick: Rutgers University Press, 2005.

Fainstein, Susan. The City Builders: Property Development in New York and London, 1980–2000. 2nd ed. Lawrence, KS: University Press of Kansas, 2001.

Fischel, William A. Do Growth Controls Matter? A Review of Empirical Evidence on the Effectiveness and Efficiency of Local Government Land Use Regulation. Cambridge, MA: Lincoln Institute of Land Policy, 1990.

Fisher, Ernest M. Urban Real Estate Markets: Characteristics and Financing. New York: National Bureau of Economic Research, 1951.

Fisher, Roger, William L. Ury, and Bruce Patton. Getting to Yes: Negotiating Agreement Without Giving In. New York: Penguin Books, 2011 [1981].

Fishman, Robert. "New Urbanism." In Planning Ideas that Matter: Livabiliy, Territoriality, Governance, and Reflective Practice, edited by Bishwapriya Sanyal, Lawrence J. Vale, and Christina D. Rosan, 65–90. Cambridge, MA: MIT Press, 2012.

Fishman, Robert. Urban Utopias in the Twentieth Century: Ebenezer Howard, Frank Lloyd Wright, and Le Corbusier. New York: Basic Books, 1977.

Flint, Barbara J. Zoning and Residential Segregation: A Social and Physical History, 1910–1940. PhD diss., University of Chicago, 1977.

Floyd, Charles F. and Marcus T. Allen. Real Estate Principles, 7th ed. Chicago: Dearborn Real

Estate Education, 2002.

Fogelson, Robert M. *Bourgeois Nightmares: Suburbia, 1870–1930*. New Haven: Yale University Press, 2007.

Forsyth, Ann. *Reforming Suburbia: The Planned Communities of Irvine, Columbia, and the Woodlands*. Berkeley: University of California Press, 2005.

Foster, Thomas B., and Rachel Garshick Kleit. "The Changing Relationship Between Housing and Inequality, 1980–2010." *Housing Policy Debate* Vol. 25, No. 1 (2014): 16–40.

Foucault, Michel. *Society Must Be Defended. Lectures at the Collège De France, 1975–76*. Edited by Mauro Bertani and Alessandro Fontana; general editors, François Ewald and Alessandro Fontana; translated by David Macey. New York: Picador, 2002.

Foucault, Michel. *Security, Territory, Population: Lectures at the Collège De France, 1977–78*. Edited by Michel Senellart; general editors, François Ewald and Alessandro Fontana; translated by Graham Burchell. New York: Picador, 2007.

Fraser, Steve. *The Age of Acquiescence: The Life and Death of American Resistance to Organized Wealth and Power*. New York: Little, Brown and Company, 2015.

Freestone, Robert, and Marco Amati, eds. *Exhibitions and the Development of Modern Planning Culture*. Surrey, UK: Ashgate, 2014.

Freund, David. *Colored Property: State Policy and White Racial Politics in Suburban America*. Chicago: University of Chicago Press, 2007.

Friedman, Jack P., J. Bruce Lindeman, and Jack C. Harris. *Dictionary of Real Estate Terms*. 5th ed. Hauppauge, NY: Barron's Educational Series Inc, 2000.

Friedman, Mildred. *Frank Gehry: The Houses*. New York: Rizzoli, 2009.

Friedman, Yael. "Lessons from Rockaway: What to Save from the Flood." *Urban Omnibus*, March 20, 2013. http://urbanomnibus.net/2013/03/lessons-from-rockaway-what-to-save-from-the-flood/.

Froot, Kenneth A. "The Market for Catastrophe Risk: A Clinical Examination." *Journal of Financial Economics*, Vol. 60, No. 2–3 (May 2001): 529–571.

Froyen, Hubert-Paul. "Molenvliet - Wilgendonk: Experimental Housing Project, Papendrecht, The Netherlands. Frans van der Werf, architect." *The Harvard Architectural Review* Vol. 1 (Spring 1980): 160–169.

Fry, Richard, and Rakesh Kochhar. "America's wealth gap between middle-income and upper-income families is widest on record." Pew Research Center, December 17, 2014. Accessed June 2, 2015. http://www.pewresearch.org/fact-tank/2014/12/17/wealth-gap-upper-middle-income/.

Fulcrum (Jack Self & Shumi Bose), eds. *Real Estates: Life Without Debt*. London: Bedford Press, 2014.

Gabriel, Stuart, and Frank Nothaft. "Rental Housing Markets, the Incidence and Duration of Vacancy, and the Natural Vacancy Rate." *Journal of Urban Economics* Vol. 49, No. 1 (2001): 121–149.

Gage, Daniel D. "Status of Collegiate Real Estate Training." *Journal of Property Management* (Spring 1946): 175–184.

Galatas, Roger with Jim Barlow. *The Woodlands: The Inside Story of Creating a Better Hometown*. Washington, D.C.: The Urban Land Institute, 2004.

Gallagher, Leigh. *The End of the Suburbs: Where the American Dream is Moving*. New York: Penguin, 2013.

Gebeloff, Robert, and Shaila Dewan. "Measuring the Top 1% by Wealth, Not Income." *New York Times*, January 17, 2012. Accessed August 9, 2015. http://economix.blogs.nytimes.com/2012/01/17/measuring-the-top-1-by-wealth-not-income/?_r=0.

Gelpi, Rose-Maria, and Francois Julien-Labruyere. *The History of Consumer Credit: Doctrines and Practices*. New York: St. Martin's Press, 2000.

Geltner, David, Norman G. Miller, Jim Clayton, and Piet Eichholtz. *Commercial Real Estate Analysis and Investments*. 2nd ed. Mason, Ohio: Thompson South-Western, 2007.

George, Henry. *Progress and Poverty*. New York: The Modern Library, 1879.

Gibbs, Robert. *Principles of Urban Retail Planning and Development*. Hoboken: Wiley and Sons. 2012.

Gilman, Charlotte. *The Home: Its Work and Influence*. New York: McClure, Phillips, 1903.

Glaeser, Edward L., and Todd Sinai, eds. *Housing and the Financial Crisis*. Chicago: The University of Chicago Press, 2013.

Glaeser, Edward L. *Cities, Agglomeration, and Spatial Equilibrium*. New York: Oxford University Press USA, 2008.

Glaeser, Edward. "There are Worse Things in Housing Policy than Poor Doors." Discussion 12: "The Dream Revisited: The Poor Door Debate." Furman Center, March 31, 2015. http://furmancenter.org/research/iri/glaeser.

Global Times. "When the Ordos Bubble Bursts." *People's Daily Online*, July 12, 2013. Accessed June 11, 2015, http://en.people.cn/90778/8323346.html

Goldstein, Barbara, ed. *Arts & Architecture: The Entenza Years*. Cambridge, MA: MIT Press, 1989.

Goldstein, Matthew. "Another Shadow in Ferguson as Outside Firms Buy and Rent Out Distressed Homes." *New York Times*. September 3, 2014. Accessed June 1, 2014. http://dealbook.nytimes.com/2014/09/03/another-shadow-in-ferguson-as-outside-firms-buy-and-rent-out-distressed-homes/.

Gornick, Janet. "Inequality: It Maters." *Folio* (Winter 2013).

Gotham, Kevin Fox. *Race, Real Estate, and Uneven Development: The Kansas City Experience, 1900–2000*. Albany: State University of New York Press, 2014 [2002].

Gotham, Kevin Fox. "Separate and Unequal: The 1968 Housing Act and the Section 235 Program." *Sociological Forum*, Vol. 15, No 1 (2000): 13–37.

Gottesdiner, Laura. *A Dream Foreclosed: Black America and The Fight for A Place to Call Home*. Westfield, NJ: Zuccotti Park Press, 2013.

Gowans, Alan. *The Comfortable House: North American Suburban Architecture, 1890–1930*. Cambridge, MA: MIT Press, 1986.

Graeber, David. *Debt: The First 5,000 Years*. Brooklyn: Melville House Publishing, 2011.

Graaskamp, James A. "Redefining the Role of the University Education in Real Estate and Urban Land Economics." *The Real Estate Appraiser* (March–April 1976): 23–26.

Grebler, Leo, David M. Blank, and Louis Winnick. *Capital Formation in Residential Real Estate: Trends and Prospects*. Princeton: Princeton University Press, 1956.

Grebler, Leo. *The Role of Federal Credit Aids in Residential Construction*. New York: National Bureau of Economic Research, 1953.

Green, Richard K. "Housing Markets, Prices and Policies." In *The Oxford Handbook of Urban Economics and Planning*, edited by Nancy Brooks, Kieran Donaghy, and Gerrit-Jan Knapp. New York: Oxford University Press, 2012. 419–437.

Green, Richard K. and Susan M. Wachter. "The American Mortgage in Historical and International Context." *Journal of Economic Perspectives* Vol. 19, No. 4 (2005): 93–114.

Green, Richard K. and Susan M. Wachter. "The housing finance revolution." In *Proceedings – Economic Policy Symposium – Jackson Hole*. (Kansas City, MO: Federal Reserve Bank of Kanses City, 2007): 21–67.

"Greendale: A Planned Community in the Great Depression." The Living New Deal: Still Working for America. Department of Geography, University of California, Berkeley. December 6, 2012. Accessed April 7, 2014. http://livingnewdeal.berkeley.edu/tag/greenbelt-towns/.

Gropius, Walter, and Martin Wagner. "Program for City Reconstruction." *Architectural Forum* 79 (July 1943): 75–86.

Gropius, Walter, and Martin Wagner. "Cities' Renaissance." *Kenyon Review* Vol. 5, No. 1 (Winter 1943): 12–33.

Gross, Jenny. "Once A Housing Project, Now Prime London Real Estate." *Wall Street Journal*, November 6, 2012. Accessed June 30, 2015. http://www.wsj.com/articles/SB10001424052970203922804578080943633004554.

Gruenstein Bocian, Debbie, and Robert G. Quercia. *Lost Ground, 2011: Disparities in Mortgage Lending and Foreclosures*. Center for Responsible Lending, 2011. http://www.responsiblelending.org/mortgage-lending/research-analysis/Lost-Ground-2011.pdf.

Guggenheim, Michael. "Immutable Mobiles: Building Conversion as a Problem of Quasi-technologies." In *Urban Assemblages: How Actor-Network Theory Changes Urban Studies*, edited by Ignacio Farías and Thomas Bender, 161–178. London and New York: Routledge, 2010.

Guthrie, Doug, and Michael McQuarrie. "Privatization and Low-Income Housing in the Untied States since 1986." *Research in Political Sociology* Vol. 14 (2005): 15–50.

Gyger, Helen. *The Informal as Project: Self-Help Housing in Peru*. PhD diss., Columbia University, 2012.

Gyourko, Joseph, and Donald B. Keim. "What Does the Stock Market Tell Us About Real Estate Returns?" *Journal of the American Real Estate and Urban Economics Association* Vol. 20, No. 3 (1992): 457–485.

Gyourko, Joseph, and Jeremy Siegel. "Long-Term Return Characteristics of Income-Producing Real Estate." *Real Estate Finance* Vol. 11, No. 1 (Spring 1994): 14–22.

Gyourko, Joseph, and Peter Linneman. "Analyzing the Risk of Income-Producing Real Estate." *Urban Studies* Vol. 27, No. 4 (August 1990): 497–508.

Gyourko, Joseph, and Todd Sinai. "The REIT Vehicle: Its Value Today and In the Future." *Journal of Real Estate Research* Vol. 16, No. 3 (1998): 251–269.

Gyourko, Joseph. "Understanding Commercial Real Estate: How Different Is It from Housing Really." *Journal of Portfolio Management* Vol. 35, No. 5 (2009): 23–37.

Habraken, N. John. *Supports: An Alternative to Mass Housing.* London: Urban International Press, 1972.

Hackworth, Jason. "Progressive activism in a neoliberal context: the case of efforts to retain public housing in the United States." *Studies in Political Economy,* Vol. 75 (2005), 29–51.

Hall, Craig. *Timing the Real Estate Market: How to Buy Low and Sell High in Real Estate.* New York: McGraw-Hill, 2003.

Hanlon, James. "Success by Design: HOPE VI, New Urbanism, and the Neoliberal Transformation of Public Housing in the United States." *Environment and Planning* Vol. 42, No. 1 (2010): 80–98.

Harloe, Michael. *The People's Home?: Social Rented Housing in Europe and America.* Oxford, UK and Cambridge, MA: Blackwell, 1995.

Harris, Dianne. *Little White Houses: How the Postwar Home Constructed Race in America.* Minneapolis: University of Minnesota Press, 2013.

Harris, Neil. *Chicago Apartments: A Century of Lakefront Luxury.* New York: Acanthus Press, 2004.

Harris, Richard. *Building a Market: The Rise of the Home Improvement Industry, 1914–1960.* Chicago: University of Chicago Press, 2012.

Harris, Richard. *Unplanned Suburbs?: Toronto's American Tragedy, 1900 to 1950.* Baltimore: Johns Hopkins University Press, 1996.

Harriss, C. Lowell. *History and Policies of the Home Owners' Loan Corporation.* New York: H. Wolff Book Manufacturing Company, 1951.

Harvey, David. "The New Urbanism and the Communitarian Trap." *Harvard Design Magazine,* Winter/Spring 1997, 1–3.

Harvey, David. *Spaces of Global Capitalism: Towards a Theory of Uneven Geographical Development.* New York: Verso, 2006.

Hayden, Dolores. *Redesigning the American Dream: Gender, Housing, and Family Life.* New York: WW Norton & Company, 2002.

Hays, Allen. *The Federal Government and Urban Housing: Ideology and Change in Public Policy.* Albany: State University of New York Press, 2012 [1985].

Heathcott, Joseph. "The Strange Career of Public Housing: Policy, Planning, and the American Metropolis in the Twentieth Century." *Journal of the American Planning Association* Vol. 78, No. 4 (2012): 360–375.

Heathcott, Joseph. "Black Archipelago: Politics and Civic Life in the Jim Crow City." *Journal of Social History* Vol. 38, No. 3 (Spring 2005): 705–736.

Heathcott, Joseph. "The City Quietly Remade: National Programs and Local Agendas in the Movement to Clear the Slums, 1942–1952." *Journal of Urban History* Vol. 34, No. 2 (January 2008): 221–242.

Heathcott, Joseph, and Maire Agnes Murphy. "Corridors of Flight, Zones of Renewal: Industry, Planning, and Policy in the Making of Metropolitan St. Louis, 1940–1980." *Journal of Urban History* Vol. 31, No. 2, (January 2005): 151–189.

Hecht, Ben. *Developing Affordable Housing: A Practical Guide for Non-Profit Organizations.* 3rd ed. Hoboken: Wiley and Sons, 2006.

Hegedüs, József, Martin Lux, and Nora Teller, eds. *Social Housing in Transition.* New York: Routledge, 2013.

Hendershott, Patric H., Thomas G. Thibodeau, and Halbert C. Smith. "Evolution of the American Real Estate and Urban Economics Association." *Real Estate Economics* Vol. 37, No. 4 (2009): 559–560.

Henderson, A. Scott. *Housing and the Democratic Ideal. The Life and Thought of Charles Abrams.* New York: Columbia University Press, 2013.

Henselmann, Hermann, "Bemerkungen zu Franziska Linkerhand." *Die Weltbühne* 35 (1974): 1108–1111.

Herbert, Gilbert. *The Dream of the Factory-Made House: Walter Gropius and Konrad Wachsmann.* Cambridge, MA: MIT Press, 1984

Herring Richard J., and Susan Wachter. "Real Estate Booms and Banking Busts: An International Perspective." Center for Financial Institutions Working Papers 99-27. Wharton School Center for Financial Institutions, University of Pennsylvania, 1999.

Higham, John. *Strangers in the Land: Patterns of American Nativism, 1860–1925.* New Brunswick: Rutgers University Press, 1988.

Himmelberg, Charles, Christopher Mayer, and Todd Sinai, "Assessing High House Prices: Bubbles, Fundamentals, and Misperceptions." *Journal of Economic Perspectives* Vol. 19, No. 4 (2005): 67–92.

Hirsch, Arnold R.. *Making the Second Ghetto: Race and Housing in Chicago, 1940–1960.* Chicago: University of Chicago Press, 1998.

Hirsch, Arnold R. "Massive Resistance in the Urban North: Trumbull Park, Chicago, 1953–1966." *The Journal of American History* Vol. 82, No. 2 (1995): 522–550.

Hoffman, Jan. "Shrink to Fit: Living Large in Tiny Spaces." *New York Times*, September 21, 2012.

Hofmann, Tess. "Riffing on renderings: Architects unpack the pretty pictures." *The Real Deal*, February 6, 2015. Accessed May 26, 2015. http://therealdeal.com/blog/2015/02/06/riffing-on-renderings-architects-unpack-the-pretty-pictures/.

Holmes, Thomas. "The Effect of State Policies on the Location of Manufacturing: Evidence from State Borders." *Journal of Political Economy* Vol. 106, No. 4 (1998): 667–705.

Homann, Klaus, Martin Kieren, and Ludovica Scarpa, eds. *Martin Wagner, 1885–1957: Wohnungsbau und Weltstadtplanung: die Rationalisierung des Glücks.* Berlin: Akademie der Künste, 1985.

Hopkins, Robert, Jon A. Southard, Raymond G. Torto, and William C. Wheaton. "Evaluating Real Estate Risk: Debt Applications." *Real Estate Finance* Vol. 18, No. 3 (2001): 29–41.

Hornstein, Jeffrey M. *A Nation of Realtors: A Cultural History of the Twentieth-Century American Middle Class. Radical Perspectives.* Durham: Duke University Press, 2005.

Horwitz, Morton J. "Chapter VI: The Triumph of Contract." In *The Transformation of American Law, 1780–1860*, 160–210. Cambridge, MA: Harvard University Press, 1977.

Hoyt, Homer. *One Hundred Years of Land Values in Chicago: The Relationship of the Growth of Chicago to the Rise in its Land Values, 1830–1930.* Chicago: University of Chicago Press, 1933.

Huang, Xiao. "Special Supplement: More than Grasslands Growing in Ordos." *China Daily*, last modified August 7, 2008. http://www.chinadaily.com.cn/life/2008-08/07/content_6913092.htm.

Huang, Yiping, Jian Chang, and Lingxiu Yang. "China: Beyond the Miracle, Part 3: Bubble Deflation, Chinese Style." *Barclays Capital Emerging Markets Research*, November 8, 2011. Accessed June 24, 2015. http://www.fullertreacymoney.com/system/data/images/archive/2011-11-11/Barclays11-8-11-China-Beyond-the-Miracle-Part-3-Bubble-Deflation-Chinese-Style.pdf.

Hunt, Bradford D. *Blueprint for Disaster: The Unraveling of Chicago Public Housing.* Chicago: University of Chicago Press, 2009.

Hunt, Bradford D. "What Went Wrong with Public Housing in Chicago? A History of the Robert Taylor Homes." *Journal of the Illinois State Historical Society* Vol. 94, No. 1 (Spring 2001): 96–123.

Hunter, Bivens. "Neustadt: Affect and Architecture in Brigitte Reimann's East German Novel Franziska Linkerhand." *The Germanic Review* 2 (2008): 139–166.

Hurd, Richard M. *Principles of City Land Values.* New York: The Record and Guide, 1903.

Hyman, Louis. *Debtor Nation: The History of America in Red Ink.* Princeton: Princeton University Press, 2011.

Hyman, Louis. "American Debt, Global Capital: The Policy Origins of Securitization." In *The Shock of the Global: The 1970s in Perspective*, edited by Niall Ferguson, Charles S. Maier, Erez Manela, and Daniel J. Sargent. Cambridge, MA: Belknap Press, 2010.

Ibbotson, Roger, and Lawrence Siegel. "Real Estate Returns: A Comparison with Other Investments." *Real Estate Economics* Vol. 12, No. 3 (1984): 219–242.

Imperiale, Alicia. "An American Wartime Dream: The Packaged House of Konard Wachsmann and Walter Gropius." In *Offsite: Theory and practice of Architectural Production*, edited by Ryan E. Smith, John Quale and Rashida Ng. ACSA Conference Proceedings, 2012.

"Industrialized House . . . : General Panel Corporation, using a Panel System Developed by Konrad Wachsmann and Walter Gropius, can Fabricate a House in 20 Minutes, Erect it in 38 Man Hours." *Architectural Forum* 86 (1947): 115–120.

"Interbau: Heiliger Otto." *Der Spiegel* 31/1957: 48–53.

Isenberg, Alison. *Downtown America: A History of the Place and the People Who Made It*. Chicago: University of Chicago Press, 2004.

Jackson, Kenneth T. "Race, Ethnicity, and Real Estate Appraisal The Home Owners Loan Corporation and the Federal Housing Administration." *Journal of Urban History* Vol. 6, No. 4 (1980): 419–452.

Jackson, Kenneth T. *Crabgrass Frontier: The Suburbanization of the United States*. New York: Oxford University Press, 1985.

Jacobs, Jane. *The Death and Life of Great American Cities*. New York: Random House, 1961.

John, G. Donald Jud, and Daniel Winkler. "The Supply Adjustment Process in Retail Space Markets." *Journal of Real Estate Research* Vol. 15, No. 3 (1998): 297–308.

Johnson, David E. *Fundamentals of Land Development: A Real-World Guide to Profitable Large-Scale Development*. Hoboken: J. Wiley and Sons, 2008.

Johnson, Donald L. "Frank Lloyd Wright in Moscow: June 1937." *Journal of the Society of Architectural Historians* Vol. 46, No. 1 (March 1987): 65–79.

Johnson, Philip, and Henry-Russell Hitchcock et al., eds. *Modern Architecture. International Exhibition, New York Feb. 10 to March 23, 1932*. New York: Museum of Modern Art, 1932.

Johnson, Philip, and Mark Wigley. *Deconstructivist Architecture*. New York: The Museum of Modern Art, 1988.

Johnston, David Cay, ed. *Divided: The Perils of our Growing Inequality*. New York: The New Press, 2014.

Joint Center for Housing Studies. *The State of the Nation's Housing 2004*. Cambridge, MA: Harvard University, 2004.

Joint Center for Housing Studies. *The State of the Nation's Housing 2010*. Cambridge, MA: Harvard University, 2010.

Jones, Daniel. *Masters of the Universe: Hayek, Friedman, and the Birth of Neoliberal Politics*. Princeton: Princeton University Press, 2012.

Julian, Elizabeth K., and Michael M. Daniel. "Separate and Unequal—The Root and Branch of Public Housing Segregation." *Clearinghouse Review* 23 (1989): 666–676.

Kamenetz, Anya. *Generation Debt: Why Now is a Terrible Time to be Young*. New York: Riverhead Books, 2006.

Kasperkic Jana. "New York bans 'poor doors' in win for low income tenants." *Guardian*, June 29, 2015.

Katznelson, Ira. *Fear Itself: The New Deal and the Origins of Our Time*. New York: Liveright, 2013.

Keenan, Jesse M. "The Art & Science of Real Estate Development." *Volume* 42 (2014): 12–19.

Kelly, Burnham. *The prefabrication of houses; a study by the Albert Farwell Bemis Foundation of the prefabrication industry in the United States*. New York, NY: The Technology Press of MIT and John Wiley and Sons, Inc., 1951.

Kendall, Leon T., and Michael J. Fishman, eds. *A Primer On Securitization*. Cambridge, MA: MIT Press, 1996.

Kendall, Stephen, and Jonathan Teicher. *Residential Open Building*. London and New York: E & FN Spon, 2000.

Khare, Amy T. "Putting People Back into Place-Based Public Policies." *Journal of Urban Affairs* Vol. 37, No. 1 (2015): 47–52.

Khare, Amy T., Mark L. Joseph, and Robert J. Chaskin. "The Enduring Significance of Race in Mixed-Income Developments." *Urban Affairs Review*, published online before print June 25, 2014, doi: 10.1177/1078087414537608

Kimmelman, Michael. "In a Bronx Complex, Doing Good Mixes With Looking Good." *New York Times*, September 26, 2011.

King, Richie, and Roberto Feldman. "How many months it takes an average worker to earn what the CEO makes in an hour." *Quartz*, December 23, 2013.

Klemek, Christopher. *The Transatlantic Collapse of Urban Renewal: Postwar Urbanism from New York to Berlin*. Chicago: Chicago University Press, 2011.

Kneebone, Elizabeth, and Alan Berube. "Confronting Suburban Poverty in America: Executive Summary." Metropolitan Policy Program at Brookings, 2013. Accessed June 7, 2015.

Kohler, Scott. "Program to Strengthen Business Education: Ford Foundation, 1954." Center for Strategic Philanthropy and Civil Society, Duke University, 2007.

Koloff, Abbott, and Jim Norman. "Massive Fire at Edgewater's Avalon Apartments; Hundreds Evacuated." *North Jersey News*, January 21, 2015. Accessed June 22, 2015. http://www.northjersey.com/news/massive-fire-at-edgewater-s-avalon-apartments-hundreds-evacuated-1.1231207.

Kopczuk, Wojciech, Emmanuel Saez, and Jae Song. "Earnings Inequality and Mobility in the United States: Evidence from Social Security Data Since 1937." *The Quarterly Journal of Economics* Vol. 125, No. 1 (2010): 91–128.

Kossel, Elmar. *Hermann Henselmann und die Moderne: eine Studie zur Modernerezeption in der Architektur der DDR*. Koenigstein: Langewiesche, 2013.

Kostof, Spiro. *The City Shaped: Urban Patterns and Meanings Through History*. London: Thames and Hudson, 1991.

Kramer, Anita. *Retail Development Handbook*. 4th ed. Washington, D.C.: Urban Land Institute, 2008.

Kramer, Carl E. "The Evolution of the Residential Land Subdivision Process in Louisville, 1772–2008." *The Register of the Kentucky Historical Society* Vol. 107, No. 1 (Winter 2009): 3–81.

Krists, Magdolenovv. "Story of Lunik IX." Unpublished and undated paper. Accessed July 3, 2015. https://www.academia.edu/6901291/Story_of_Lunik_IX

Krugman, Paul. Columns. *New York Times*. http://www.nytimes.com/column/paul-krugman.

Krugman, Paul. Blog. *New York Times*. http://krugman.blogs.nytimes.com.

Lasner, Matthew Gordon. "Architect as Developer and the Postwar U.S. Apartment, 1945–1960." *Buildings & Landscapes* Vol. 21, No. 1 (Spring 2014): 27–55.

Lasner, Matthew Gordon. *High Life: Condo Living in the Suburban Century*. New Haven: Yale University Press, 2012.

Lefcoe, George. *Real Estate Transactions, Finance, and Development*, 6th ed. Newark: Lexis-Nexis, 2009.

Lepore, Jill. "Richer and Poorer: Accounting for Inequality." *The New Yorker*, March 16, 2015.

Lewis, Michael. *Liar's Poker*. New York: Penguin Books, 1989.

Light, Jennifer S. *From Warfare to Welfare?: Defense Intellectuals and Urban Problems in Cold War America*. Baltimore: Johns Hopkins University Press, 2003.

Linklater, Andro. *Owning The Earth: The Transforming History of Land Ownership*. New York: Bloomsbury, 2013.

Linneman, Peter, and Stan Ross. "Real Estate Private Equity Funds." *Wharton Real Estate Review* Vol. 6, No. 1 (Spring 2002): 5–22.

Linneman, Peter. "The Equitization of Real Estate." *Wharton Real Estate Review* Vol. 10, No. 2 (Fall 2006): 5–26.

Linneman, Peter. *Real Estate Finance and Investments: Risks and Opportunities*. 3rd ed. Philadelphia: Linneman Associates, 2011.

Lisa McGirr, *Suburban Warriors?: The Origins of the New American Right*. Princeton: Princeton University Press, 2001.

Loeb, Carolyn. *Entrepreneurial Vernacular: Developers' Subdivisions in the 1920s*. Baltimore: Johns Hopkins University Press, 2001.

Loew, Stuart and Sasha Tsenkova, *Housing Change in East and Central Europe: Integration or Fragmentation?* Aldershot, UK/Burlington, VT: Ashgate, 2003.

Loewen, James W. Sundown Towns. New York: Simon and Schuster, 2005.

Long, Charles. *Finance for Real Estate Development*. Washington, D.C.: Urban Land Institute, 2011.

Long, Herman H., and Charles S. Johnson. *People vs. Property: Race Restrictive Covenants in Housing*. Nashville: Fisk University Press, 1947.

Lubenau, Anne-Marie. "On the Road with the Rudy Bruner Award: Via Verde – Bronx, NY." *Metropolis*, April 11, 2013.

Lubin, Gus. "TIMBER! Home Prices Are Crashing In China's Most Famous Ghost City." *Business Insider*, December 6, 2011. Accessed June 11, 2015. http://www.businessinsider.com/home-prices-ordos-2011-12?IR=T.

Lucarello, Fosco, and Mariabruna Fabrizi. "The Trellick Tower: Rise and Fall of a Modern Monument." *San Rocco Magazine* 5 (Fall 2012): 108–114.

Lusht, Kenneth M. *Real Estate Valuation: Principles and Applications*. New York: McGraw-Hill, 1997.

MacArthur Foundation. "How Housing Matters." Accessed June 15, 2015. http://www.macfound.org/programs/how-housing-matters/.

MacLeish, Archibald. *Housing America*. New York: Harcourt, Brace, 1932.

Macpherson, C. B. "The Meaning of Property." In *Property, Mainstream and Critical Positions*, 1–14. Toronto: University of Toronto Press, 1978.

Malkiel, Burton G. *A Random Walk Down Wall Street: The Time-Tested Strategy for Successful Investing*. 10th ed. New York: W.W. Norton and Company, 2012.

Malpass, Peter. *Housing and the Welfare State: The Development of Housing Policy in Britain.* New York: Palgrave MacMillan, 2005.

Malpezzi, Stephen. "The Wisconsin Program in Real Estate and Urban Land Economics: A Century of Tradition and Innovation." Department of Real Estate and Urban Land Economics, University of Wisconsin, 2009.

Malpezzi, Stephen, and Susan M. Wachter. "The Role of Speculation in Real Estate Cycles." Zell/Lurie Real Estate Center Working Paper #401, June 2002.

Mann, Bruce H. *Republic of Debtors: Bankruptcy in the Age of American Independence.* Cambridge, MA: Harvard University Press, 2002.

Marc, Angélil, Rainer Hehl, and Something Fantastic, eds. *Minha Casa – Nossa Cidade!* Berlin: Ruby Press, 2014.

Marcuse, Peter. "The New Urbanism: The Dangers so Far." *disP - The Planning Review* Vol. 36, No. 140 (2000): 4–6.

Marcuse, Peter. *The Myth of the Benevolent State: Towards a Theory of Housing.* New York: Columbia University, Graduate School of Architecture and Planning, 1978.

Martin, Reinhold. "Fundamental #13: Real Estate as Infrastructure as Architecture." *Places Journal*, May 2014. https://placesjournal.org/article/fundamental-13/.

Martin, Reinhold, Leah Meisterlin, and Anna Kenoff, eds. *The Buell Hypothesis.* New York: The Temple Hoyne Buell Center for the Study of American Architecture, 2011.

Martin, Reinhold, Raphael Sperry, Amit C. Price Patel, Liz Ogbu, and Tom Angotti. "The Housing Question." Debate. *Places Journal*, June 2012. https://placesjournal.org/article/the-housing-question/.

Massey, Douglas and Nancy A. Denton. *American Apartheid: Segregation and the Making of the Underclass.* Cambridge, MA: Harvard University Press, 1998.

Massey, Douglas S., Len Albright, Rebecca Casciano, Elizabeth Derickson, and David N. Kinsey. *Climbing Mount Laurel: The Struggle for Affordable Housing and Social Mobility in an American Suburb.* Princeton: Princeton University Press, 2013.

Massey, Jonathan. "Risk and Regulation in the Financial Architecture of the American House." In *Governing by Design: Architecture, Economy, and Politics in the Twentieth Century*, edited by Aggregate Architectural History Collaborative, 21–46. Pittsburgh: University of Pittsburgh Press, 2012.

Matlack, J. L., and J. L. Vigdor. "Do Rising Tides Lift All Prices? Income Inequality and Housing Affordability." NBER Working Paper 12331. Cambridge, MA: National Bureau of Economic Research, 2006.

Maxwell, David O. "HUD's Project Selection Criteria: A Cure for Impermissible Color Blindness." *Notre Dame Law Review* Vol. 48, No. 1 (1972): 92–104.

McCann, Philip. *Modern Urban and Regional Economics.* 2nd ed. New York: Oxford University Press USA, 2013.

McEntire, Davis. *Residence and Race: Final and Comprehensive Report to the Commission on Race and Housing.* Berkeley: University of California Press, 1960.

McGirr, Lisa. *Suburban Warriors.* Princeton, NJ: Princeton University Press, 2002.

McHarg, Ian. *Design with Nature.* Garden City, NY: Natural History Press for the American Museum of Natural History, 1969.

McMillen, Daniel, and John McDonald. "Reaction of House Prices to a New Rapid Transit Line: Chicago's Midway Line, 1983–1999." *Real Estate Economics* Vol. 32, No. 3 (2004): 463–486.

Meisterlin, Leah, ed. *Comments on Foreclosed.* New York: The Temple Hoyne Buell Center for the Study of American Architecture, 2012.

Mertins, Detlef. *Mies.* London: Phaidon, 2014.

Miles, Mike E., Gayle L. Berens, Mark J. Eppli, and Marc A. Weiss. *Real Estate Development: Principles and Process.* 4th ed. Washington D.C.: Urban Land Insitute, 2007.

Mills, Edwin S. and Bruce W. Hamilton. *Urban Economics.* 5th ed. Upper Saddle River: Prentice Hall, 1997.

Mironova, Oksana. "The Value of Land: How Community Land Trusts Maintain Housing Affordability." *Urban Omnibus*, April 29, 2014. http://urbanomnibus.net/2014/04/the-value-of-land-how-community-land-trusts-maintain-housing-affordability/.

Mitchell, Thomas W. *From Reconstruction to Deconstruction: Undermining Black landownership, political independence and community through partition sales of tenancies in common.* Research Paper No. 132, Land Tenure Center, University of Wisconsin-Madison, 2000. http://minds.wisconsin.edu/handle/1793/21887.

Mitchell, Timothy. "Economentality: How the Future Entered Government." *Critical Inquiry* Vol. 40, No. 4 (2014): 479–507.

Mohl, Raymond A. "Shifting Patterns of American Urban Policy since 1900." In *Urban Policy in Twentieth Century America*, edited by Arnold R. Hirsch and Raymond A. Mohl, 1–45. New Brunswick: Rutgers University Press, 1993.

Morris, Charles R. *The Two Trillion Dollar Meltdown: Easy Money, High Rollers, and the Great Credit Crash*. New York: Public Affairs, 2008.

Mortice, Zach. "2012 Twenty-Five Year Award: Gehry Residence." American Institute of Architects. Accessed July 1, 2015. http://www.aia.org/practicing/awards/2012/twenty-five-year-award/.

Nascimento, D. M. "N.J. Habraken Explains the Potential of the Open Building Approach in Architectural Practice." *Open House International*, Vol. 37, No. 4 (2012): 5–13.

National Association of Home Builders."Housing's Contribution to Gross Domestic Product (GDP)." Accessed May 1, 2015. http://www.nahb.org/en/research/housing-economics/housings-economic-impact/housings-contribution-to-gross-domestic-product-gdp.aspx.

National Low-Income Housing Coalition. "Affordable Housing is No-where to be Found for Millions." *Housing Spotlight* 5, No. 1 (2015).

Neto, Paulo Nascimento, Tomás Antonio Moreira, and Zulma Das Graças Lucena Schussel. "Housing Policy. A Critical Analysis on the Brazilian Experience." *Comunicação e Meio Ambiente* Vol. 5, No. 3 (December 22, 2012): 65–76.

New York Times Editorial Board. "Big Business's Critical Role on Anti-Gay Laws." *New York Times*, April 4, 2015.

Newman, Katherine. *Falling From Grace: The Experience of Downward Mobility in the American Middle Class*. New York: Free Press, 1988.

Newman, Oscar. *Defensible Space: Crime Prevention through Urban Design*. New York: Collier, 1973.

Newman, Sandra J. "Housing Allowances American Style: The Housing Choice Voucher Program." In *Housing Allowances in a Comparative Perspective*, edited by P. A. Kemp, 87–106. Bristol: Policy Press, 2007.

Nichols, J.C. "Housing and the Real Estate Problem." *Annals of the American Academy of Political and Social Science* Vol. 51 (Jan. 1914): 132–139.

Nicolaides, Becky. *My Blue Heaven: Life and Politics in the Working-Class Suburbs of Los Angeles, 1920–1965*. Chicago: University of Chicago Press, 2002.

Nightingale, Carl H. *Segregation: A Global History of Divided Cities*. Chicago: University of Chicago Press, 2012.

Nuijsink, Cathelijne. "Nothing is Happening here." *Mark: Another Architecture* No. 36 (2/2012): 148–155.

NYC Department of Housing Preservation & Development. "Bronxchester Request for Proposals." Accessed June 24, 2015. http://www1.nyc.gov/site/hpd/developers/rfp-rfq-rfo-archives/Bronxchester-RFP.page.

NYC Department of Housing Preservation & Development. "New Construction Guidelines." August 1, 2000. Accessed June 15, 2015. http://www1.nyc.gov/assets/hpd/downloads/pdf/developers/new-constr-guidelines.pdf.

NYC Housing Development Corporation. "HDC Closes on a 904-Unit Frank Gehry Designed Tower in Lower Manhattan." *Real Estate Rama*, April 1, 2008. http://newyork.realestaterama.com/2008/04/01/hdc-closes-on-a-904-unit-frank-gehry-designed-tower-in-lower-manhattan-ID0259.html.

Nypels, Erwin. *Statement on Housing and Physical Planning Rental Policy, Tweede Kamer der Staten-Generaal, 45ste Vergadering*, February 17, 1982.

O'Connor, Thomas H. *Building A New Boston: Politics and Urban Renewal, 1950–1970*. Boston: Northeastern University Press, 1995.

O'Sullivan, Arthur. *Urban Economics*. 8th ed. New York: McGraw-Hill/Irwin, 2012.

Oates, Wallace. "Property Taxation and Local Public Spending: The Renter Effect." *Journal of Urban Economics* Vol. 57, No. 3 (2005): 419–431.

Oberlander, H. Peter, Eva Newbrun, and Martin Meyerson. *Houser: The Life and Work of Catherine Bauer*. Vancouver: UBC, 1999.

OECD. "Better Life Index." Accessed June 15, 2015. http://www.oecd.org/betterlifeindex.

OECD. "Income Distribution and Poverty." Accessed June 15, 2015. http://stats.oecd.org/Index.aspx?DatasetCode=IDD.

Oliver, Melvin. *Black Wealth/White Wealth: A New Perspective on Racial Inequality*.

New York: Routledge, 1995.

Olsen, Joshua. *Better Places, Better Lives: A Biography of James Rouse.* Washington, D.C.: The Urban Land Institute, 2003.

Oosterman, Arjen, ed. "Art & Science of Real Estate." *Volume* 42. 2014.

Orlebeke, Charles J. "The Evolution of Low-Income Housing Policy, 1949 to 1999." *Housing Policy Debate* Vol. 11, No. 2 (2000): 489–520.

Osman, Suleiman. *The Invention of Brownstone Brooklyn: Gentrification and the Search for Authenticity in Postwar New York.* New York: Oxford University Press, 2011.

Oxfam. *Working for the Few: Political Capture and Economic Inequality.* January 20, 2014. Accessed June 12, 2015. https://www.oxfam.org/sites/www.oxfam.org/files/bp-working-for-few-political-capture-economic-inequality-200114-en.pdf.

Patnaude, Art. "Netherlands Plots a Housing-Market Overhaul." *Wall Street Journal,* May 13, 2014.

Pavlov, Andrey, and Susan M. Wachter. "Real Estate Crashes and Bank Lending," *Wharton Real Estate Review* Vol. 9, No. 1 (Spring 2005): 62–68.

Pavlov, Andrey, and Susan M. Wachter. "Robbing the Bank: Non-recourse Lending and Asset Prices." *The Journal of Real Estate Finance and Economics* Vol. 28, No.2–3 (2004): 147–160.

Peca, Stephen. *Real Estate Development and Investment: A Comprehensive Approach.* Hoboken, NJ: Wiley, 2009.

Peiser, Richard, and David Hamilton. *Professional Real Estate Development: The ULI Guide to the Business.* 3rd ed. Washington D.C.: Urban Land Institute, 2012.

Perin, Constance. *Everything in Its Place: Social Order and Land Use in America.* Princeton: Princeton University Press, 2014 [1977].

Pew Research Center. *Fewer, Poorer, Gloomier: The Lost Decade of the Middle Class.* Washington, D.C.: Pew Social & Demographic Trends, 2012.

Pew Research Center. *Most Say Government Policies Since Recession Have Done Little to Help Middle Class, Poor.* March, 2015.

Piketty, Thomas. *Capital in the Twenty-First Century.* Translated by Arthur Goldhammer. Cambridge, MA: Harvard University Press, 2014.

Piketty, Thomas, and Emmanuel Saez. "Income Inequality in the United States, 1913–1998." *The Quarterly Journal of Economics* CXVIII (1), updated to 2013: 1–39. Accessed June 16, 2015. http://eml.berkeley.edu/~saez/.

Pitzke, Marc. "Luxuswohnen in New York: Arme müssen durch die Hintertüre." *Spiegel Online,* October 30, 2014. http://www.spiegel.de/wirtschaft/poor-doors-new-yorks-luxusimmobilien-mit-tueren-fuer-arme-a-998732.html.

Plunz, Richard. *The History of Housing in New York City: Dwelling Type and Social Change in the American Metropolis.* New York: Columbia University Press, 1990.

Polanyi, Karl. *The Great Transformation.* Boston: Beacon Press, 1957 [1944].

Pollakowski, Henry O., and Susan M. Wachter. "The Effects of Land-Use Constraints on Housing Prices." *Land Economics* Vol. 66, No. 3 (August 1, 1990): 315–324.

Poorvu, William J., and Jeffrey L. Cruickshank. *The Real Estate Game: The Intelligent Guide to Decision-Making and Investment.* New York: The Free Press, 1999.

Porter, Michael E. "Location, Competition, and Economic Development: Local Clusters in a Global Economy." *Economic Development Quarterly* Vol. 14, No. 1 (February 2000): 15–34.

Putnam, Robert D. *Our Kids: The American Dream in Crisis.* New York: Simon & Schuster, 2015.

Radford, Gail. *Modern Housing for America: Policy Struggles in the New Deal Era.* Chicago: University of Chicago Press, 1996.

Randel, James A. *Confessions of a Real Estate Entrepreneur: What It Takes to Win in High-Stakes Commercial Real Estate.* New York: McGraw-Hill, 2005.

Rangan, V. Kasturi, John A. Quelch, Gustavo Herrero, and Brooke Barton, eds. *Business Solutions for the Global Poor: Creating Social and Economic Value.* Cambridge, MA: Harvard University Press, 2005.

Rapoza, Kenneth. "China's Housing Bubble Past, And Its Future." *Forbes,* November 11, 2011. Accessed June 11, 2015. http://www.forbes.com/sites/kenrapoza/2011/11/08/chinas-housing-bubble-past-and-its-future/.

Ratcliff, Richard. *Real Estate Analysis.* New York: McGraw Hill, 1961.

Reimann, Brigitte. *Franziska Linkerhand,* Berlin: Aufbau-Verlag, 1998 [1974].

Reimann, Brigitte, and Hermann Henselmann. *Briefwechsel.* Berlin: Verlag Neues Leben, 1994.

Rendering. CLOG. 2012. 2nd ed.

Renner, Andrea. *Housing Diplomacy: US Housing Aid to Latin America, 1949–1973*. PhD diss., Columbia University, 2011.

Rich, Damon. "Liquidation of Architecture." *Perspecta* 42 (2010): 46–54.

Richard Shearer & Associates. *City of Ferguson: Vision 2015 Plan Update*. August 1998.

Right to Rise, 2015. "What we Believe." Accessed June 15, 2015. https://righttorisepac.org/what-we-believe/.

Rilling, Donna. *Making Houses, Crafting Capitalism: Builders in Philadelphia, 1790–1850*. Philadelphia: University of Pennsylvania Press, 2000.

Ritchie, Alan. "Foreword." *NYSR Portfolio of Architectural & Interior Rendering* Vol. 5 (2004–2005), 1.

Roback, Jennifer. "Wages, Rents, and the Quality of Life." *Journal of Political Economy* Vol. 90, No. 6 (1982): 1257–1278.

Rodgers, Daniel T. *Atlantic Crossings: Social Politics in a Progressive Age*. Cambridge, MA: Harvard University Press, 1998.

Rome, Adam. "Building On the Land: Toward an Environmental History of Residential Development in American Cities and Suburbs, 1870–1990," *Journal of Urban History* Vol. 20, No. 3 (May 1994): 407–434.

Rome, Adam. *Bulldozer in the Countryside: Suburban Sprawl and the Rise of American Environmentalism*. New York: Cambridge University Press, 2001.

Rosenthal, Rob, and Maria Foscarinis. "Community Development Corporations: challenges in supporting a right to housing." In *A Right to Housing: Foundation for a New Social Agenda*, edited by Rachel G. Bratt, Michael E. Stone, and Chester Hartman, 340–359. Philadelphia: Temple University Press, 2006.

Rosenthal, Stuart, and Robert Helsley. "Redevelopment and the Urban Land Price Gradient." *Journal of Urban Economics* Vol. 35, No. 2 (1994): 182–200.

Rothstein, Richard. "Race and Public Housing: Revisiting the Federal Role." *Poverty & Race* Vol. 21, No. 6 (2012): 1–16.

Rothstein, Richard. "The Making of Ferguson: Public Policies at the Root of its Troubles." Economic Policy Institute Report, October 15, 2014.

Rothwell, Jonathan. "Housing Costs, Zoning, and Access to High-Scoring Schools." Washington, D.C.: The Brookings Institution. 2012. http://www.brookings.edu/research/papers/2012/04/19-school-inequality-rothwell.

Roulac, Stephen E. "Requisite Knowledge for Effective Property Involvements in the Global Context." In *Real Estate Education Throughout the World: Past, Present and Future*, edited by Karl-Werner Schulte, 3–24. New York: Springer Science+Business Media, 2002.

Rowlands, David T. "Some Reflections on Real Estate and Urban Economics." *Proceedings*, American Real Estate and Urban Economics Association, Vol. II (1967): 5–11.

Ryan, Brent. *Design after Decline: How America Rebuilds Shrinking Cities*. Philadelphia: University of Pennsylvania Press, 2014.

Saez, Emmanuel, and Gabriel Zucman. "Wealth Inequality in the United States since 1913: Evidence from Capitalized Income Tax Data." NBER Working Paper 20625. Cambridge, MA: National Bureau of Economic Research, 2014. Accessed June 5, 2015. http://gabriel-zucman.eu/files/SaezZucman2014.pdf.

Sagalyn, Lynne B. "Conflicts of Interest in the Structure of REITs." *Real Estate Finance*, Vol. 13, No. 2 (June 1996): 34–51.

Sampson, Robert J. *Great American City: Chicago and the Enduring Neighborhood Effect*. Chicago: University of Chicago Press, 2011.

Sassen, Saskia. *The Global City: New York, London, Tokyo*. Princeton: Princeton University Press, 1991.

Satter, Beryl. *Family Properties: How the Struggle over Race and Real Estate Transformed Chicago and Urban America*. New York: Henry Holt, 2009.

Schindler, Susanne, and Juliette Spertus. "A Few Days in the Bronx: From Co-op City to Twin Parks." *Urban Omnibus*, July 25, 2012. http://urbanomnibus.net/2012/07/a-few-days-in-the-bronx-from-co-op-city-to-twin-parks/.

Schindler, Susanne. "Architecture vs. Housing: The Case of Sugar Hill." *Urban Omnibus*, September 3, 2014. http://urbanomnibus.net/2014/09/architecture-vs-housing-the-case-of-sugar-hill/.

Schuman, Tony. "Labor And Housing In New York City: Architect Herman Jessor and the Cooperative Housing Movement." Unpublished and undated paper. New Jersey Institute of Technology.

Schwartz, Alex. *Housing Policy in the United States: An Introduction.* 3rd ed. New York: Routledge, 2014 [2006].

Schwartz, Herman. "Anglo-America as Global Suburbia: Political Economy and Endogenous Multiculturalism." In *Anglo-America and its Discontents: Civilizational Identities beyond West and East,* edited by Peter Katzenstein, 56–78. New York: Routledge, 2012.

"Seeding the First CLTs: New Communities, Inc." *Roots & Branches: A Gardener's Guide to the Origins and Evolution of the Community Land Trust.* Accessed June 16, 2015. http://greenfordable.com/clt/the-guide/early-hybrids-breeding-and-seeding-the-clt-model/georgia-seedbed.

Service Employees International Union. *Troubling Developments: The History of Safety Problems, Law-Breaking Contractors, and Unaffordable Health Insurance at AvalonBay Communities.* 2012. Accessed June 22, 2015. http://www.seiu32bj.org/wp-content/uploads/2012/09/AVB-White-Paper.pdf.

Shapiro, Thomas M. "Race, Homeownership and Wealth." *Washington University Journal of Law & Policy* 20 (2006): 53–74.

Shiller, Robert J., and Allan N. Weiss. "Home Equity Insurance." *Journal of Real Estate Finance and Economics,* Vol. 19, No. 1 (1999): 21–47.

Shiller, Robert J. *Finance and the Good Society.* Princeton: Princeton University Press, 2012.

Shiller, Robert J. *Irrational Exuberance.* Princeton: Princeton University Press, 2000.

Shiller, Robert J. *The New Financial Order: Risk in the 21st Century.* Princeton: Princeton University Press, 2003.

Shilton, Leon, and Craig Stanley. "Spatial Patterns of Headquarters." *Journal of Real Estate Research* Vol. 17, No. 3 (1999): 341–364.

Shukla, Vibhooti, and Paul Waddell. "Firm Location and Land Use in Discrete Urban Space: A Study of the Spatial Structure of Dallas-Fort Worth." *Regional Science and Urban Economics* Vol. 21, No. 2 (1991): 225–253.

Sinai, Todd, and Nicholas Souleles. "Owner Occupied Houisng as Insurance Against Rent Risk." Unpublished paper. Wharton School, University of Pennsylvania, May, 2001.

Singer, Audrey. "Migration and the Metropolis." Washington, D.C.: The Brookings Institution, 2013. http://www.brookings.edu/research/articles/2013/04/migration-metropolis-singer.

Singer, David Andrew. *Regulating Capital: Setting Standards for the International Financial System.* Ithaca, NY: Cornell University Press, 2007.

Sirota, David. *Essentials of Real Estate Finance.* 12th ed. New York: Kaplan Publishing, 2009.

Smith, Adam James. "'Re-education' campaigns teach China's new ghost city-dwellers how to behave." *Guardian,* November 6, 2014.

Smith, David. "Johannesburg's Ponte City: 'the tallest and grandest urban slum in the world' – a history of cities in 50 buildings, day 33." *Guardian,* May 11, 2015. http://www.theguardian.com/cities/2015/may/11/johannesburgs-ponte-city-the-tallest-and-grandest-urban-slum-in-the-world-a-history-of-cities-in-50-buildings-day-33.

Smith, Preston H. *Racial Democracy and the Black Metropolis: Housing Policy in Postwar Chicago.* Minneapolis: University of Minnesota Press, 2012.

Smithson, Alison and Peter. *Changing the Art of Inhabitation.* London: Artemis, 1994.

Snowden, Kenneth A. "Mortgage Banking in the United States, 1870–1940," Special Report of the Research Institute for Housing America, Mortgage Bankers Association, October 28, 2013.

Snowden, Kenneth A. "The Anatomy of a Residential Mortgage Crisis: A Look Back to the 1930s." Working Paper, The National Bureau of Economic Research, July 2010.

Snowden, Kenneth A., and Jonathan Rose. "The New Deal and the Origins of the Modern American Real Estate Loan Contract." Working Paper, The National Bureau of Economic Research, September 2012.

Somerville, C. Tsuriel. "The Industrial Organization of Housing Supply: Market Activity, Land Supply and the Size of Homebuilder Firms." *Real Estate Economics* 27, No. 4 (1999), 669–695.

Song, Yan, and Gerrit-Jan Knaap. "New Urbanism and Housing Values: A Disaggregate Assessment." *Journal of Urban Economics* 54, No. 2 (2003): 218–238.

Sorkin, Michael. "Little Boxes," *The Nation,* July 29, 2014.

Space Caviar (Joseph Grima, Andrea Bagnato, Tamar Shafrir), ed. *SQM: The Quantified Home.* Ennetbaden: Lars Müller Publishers, 2014.

Steffen, Will, Paul J. Critzen, and John R. McNeill, "The Anthropocene: Are Humans Now Overwhelming the Great Forces of Nature?" *AMBIO* 36 (Dec. 2007): 614–21.

Spertus, Juliette. "Luxury for All?" *Bauwelt* (October 2012): 26–29.

Steil, Justin, and James Connolly. "Can the Just City be Built from Below?: Brownfields, Planning, and Power in the South Bronx." In *Searching for the Just City: Debates in Urban Theory and Practice*, edited by Peter Marcuse et al., 172–193. London and New York: Routledge, 2009.

Stein, Samuel. "De Blasio's Doomed Housing Plan." *Jacobin*, Issue 15/16 (Fall 2014). https://www.jacobinmag.com/2014/10/de-blasios-doomed-housing-plan/.

Stern, Robert A. M., David Fishman, and Jacob Tilove. *Paradise Planned: The Garden Suburb and the Modern City*. New York: The Monacelli Press, 2013.

Stevens, Sara Kathryn. *Developing Expertise: The Architecture of Real Estate, 1908–1965*. PhD diss., Princeton University, 2012.

Stiglitz, Joseph E. "Of the 1%, by the 1%, for the 1%." Vanity Fair, May 2011.

Stiglitz, Joseph E. *The Great Divide: Unequal Societies and What We Can Do About Them*. New York: W.W. Norton & Co., 2015.

Stiglitz, Joseph E. *The Price of Inequality: How Today's Divided Society Endangers Our Future*. 2nd ed. New York: W.W. Norton & Co., 2013 [2012].

Sugawara, Toru, and Tetsuya Abe. "China faces a rapid-growth hangover." *Nikkei Asian Review*, December 11, 2014. Accessed July 8, 2015. http://asia.nikkei.com/magazine/20141211-Turn-of-the-commodities-wheel/Cover-Story/China-faces-a-rapid-growth-hangover.

Sugrue, Thomas J. *Origins of the Urban Crisis: Race and Inequality in Postwar Detroit*. 3rd ed. Princeton: Princeton University Press, 2005 [1992].

Sugrue, Thomas J. "The Structures of Urban Poverty: The Reorganization of Space and Work in Three Periods of American History." In *The Underclass Debate: Views from History*, edited by Michael B. Katz, 85–92. Princeton: Princeton University Press, 1993.

Sugrue, Thomas J., and Kevin M. Kruse, eds. *The New Suburban History*. Chicago: University of Chicago Press, 2006.

Szylvian, Kristin M. *The Mutual Housing Experiment: New Deal Communities for the Urban Middle Class*, Philadelphia: Temple University Press, 2015.

Talamo, John. *The Real Estate Dictionary*. 6th ed. South Bend, IN: Financial Publishing Co., 1999.

Talbott, John R. *The Coming Crash in the Housing Market: 10 Things You Can Do Now to Protect Your Most Valuable Investment*. New York: McGraw-Hill, 2003.

Tan, Michael, and Cara Meng. "Overseas Investment by Chinese Individuals - Current Legislation and Recent Developments." *TaylorWessing China Alerter*, October 2011. Accessed July 8, 2015. http://www.taylorwessing.com/newsletter/china/china-alerter-october-2011/overseas-investment-by-chinese-individuals-current-legislation-and-recent-developments.html.

Taverne, Ed. "Rise and Fall of the 'Second Socialist City' Hoyerswerda-Neustadt: An Architectural Historian's Reaction to Franziska Linkerhand (1974), a Novel by Brigitte Reimann." In *Ideals in Concrete: Exploring Central and Eastern Europe*, edited by Cor Wagenaar and Mieke Dings, 117–124. Rotterdam: Nai Publishers, 2005.

The Brookings Institution Metropolitan Policy Program. *State of Metropolitan America: On the Front Lines of Demographic Transformation*. Washington, D.C.: The Brookings Institution, 2010.

The Center for Urban Pedagogy. *What is Affordable Housing?: NYC Edition*. Envisioning Development Series. New York: The Center for Urban Pedagogy, 2009.

Titman S., and A. Warga. "Risk and the Performance of Real Estate Investment Trusts: A Multiple Index Approach," *AREUEA Journal* Vol. 14, No. 3 (1986): 414–431.

Thomas, June Manning, and Marsha Ritzdorf, eds. *Urban Planning and the African American Community: In the Shadows*. Thousand Oaks: Sage Publications, 1997.

Thompson, H.A. "Why Mass Incarceration Matters: Rethinking Crisis, Decline, and Transformation in Postwar American History." *The Journal of American History* Vol. 97, No. 3 (2010): 703–734.

Thorsnes, Paul. "Internalizing Neighborhood Externalities: The Effect of Subdivision Size and Zoning on Residential Lot Prices." *Journal of Urban Economics* Vol. 48, No. 3 (2000): 397–418.

Travis, Jeremy, Bruce Western, and F. Stevens Redburn. *The Growth of Incarceration in the United States: Exploring Causes and Consequences*. Washington, D.C.: The National Academies Press, 2014.

U.S. Census Bureau. "2009–2013, 5-Year American Community Survey." Accessed June 15,

2015. http://factfinder.census.gov/.

U.S. Census Bureau. "American Housing Survey (AHS): About." Accessed August 10, 2015. http://www.census.gov/programs-surveys/ahs/about.html.

U.S. Census Bureau. "Current Population Survey (CPS), Definitions." Accessed June 14, 2015. http://www.census.gov/cps/about/cpsdef.html.

U.S. Census Bureau. *Statistical Abstract of the United States: 1973*, (94th ed.). Table No. 1167: Occupied Housing Units – Tenure, and Population per Occupied Unit, by Race of Household Head and by Residence: 1900 to 1970. Washington, D.C.

U.S. Census Bureau. *Statistical Abstract of the United States: 1976*, (97th ed.). Table No. 1269: Housing Units, by Geographic Region: 1950 to 1974. Washington, D.C.

U.S. Census Bureau. *Statistical Abstracts Section 31: 20th Century Statistics*. Table No. 1428: Housing Units – Historical Trends for Selected Characteristics: 1940 to 1997. https://www.census.gov/prod/99pubs/99statab/sec31.pdf.

U.S. Department of Health and Human Services. "Frequently Asked Questions." Accessed August 10, 2015. http://www.hhs.gov/answers/.

U.S. Department of Housing and Urban Development. "Low-Income Housing Tax Credits." Accessed July 8, 2015. http://www.huduser.org/portal/datasets/lihtc.html.

U.S. Department of Housing and Urban Development, Office of Policy Development and Research. "Mixed Messages on Mixed Incomes." *Cityscape: A Journal of Policy Development and Research* Vol. 13, No. 2 (2013). http://www.huduser.org/portal/periodicals/cityscpe/vol15num2/index.html

Ulfstjerne, Michael Alexander. *Un-real Estate: The Social Life of Temporary Wealth in China.* PhD diss., Københavns Universitet, Det Humanistiske Fakultet, 2015.

Urban Land Institute. "About ULI." Accessed July 15, 2015. http://uli.org/about-uli/

Urban Land Institute. "ULI Case Studies: New York by Gehry at 8 Spruce Street," November 2014. Accessed August 10, 2015. http://uli.org/publications/case-studies/.

Urban Land Institute. "ULI Case Studies: Via Verde," January 2014. Accessed August 10, 2015. http://uli.org/case-study/uli-case-studies-via-verde/.

Urban, Florian. *Tower and Slab: Histories of Global Mass Housing.* New York: Routledge, 2012.

Vale, Lawrence J. *From Puritans to Public Housing: Public Housing and Public Neighborhoods.* Cambridge: Harvard University Press, 2000.

Vale, Lawrence J. *Purging the Poorest: Public Housing and the Design-Politics of Twice-cleared Communities.* Chicago: University of Chicago Press, 2013.

Vallye, Anna. "The Collaboration between Gropius and Martin Wagner." *Design And The Politics Of Knowledge In America, 1937–1967: Walter Gropius, Gyorgy Kepes.* PhD diss. Columbia University, 2011.

Veblen, Thorstein Bunde. *Absentee Ownership. Business Enterprise in Recent Times: The Case of America.* New Brunswick: Transaction Publishers, 2009 [1926].

Vermeersch, Peter. *The Romani Movement: Minority Politics and Ethnic Mobilization in Contemporary Central Europe.* New York: Berghahn Books, 2006.

Verplanck, Gulian C. *An Essay on the Doctrine of Contracts: Being an Inquiry How Contracts are Affected in Law and Morals, by Concealment, error, or Inadequate Price.* New York: G. & C. Carvill, 1825.

Von Hoffman, Alexander. "Calling Upon the Genius of Private Enterprise: The Housing and Urban Development Act of 1968 and the Liberal Turn to Public-Private Partnerships." *Studies in American Political Development* 27 (October 2013): 165–194.

Vornovitsky, Marina Alfred Gottschalck, and Adam Smith. *Distribution of Household Wealth in the U.S.: 2000 to 2011.* U.S. Census Bureau. https://www.census.gov/people/wealth/files/Wealth%20distribution%202000%20to%202011.pdf.

Waddell, Paul, Brian Berry, and Irving Hoch. "Residential Property Values in a Multinodal Urban Area: New Evidence on the Implicit Price of Location." *Journal of Real Estate Finance and Economics* Vol. 7, No. 2 (1993), 117–141.

Wagenaar, Cor and Mieke Dings, eds. *Ideals in Concrete: Exploring Central and Eastern Europe.* Rotterdam: Nai Publishers, 2005.

Wagner, Martin. *Potemkin in West-Berlin.* Berlin: City Presse, 1957.

Wainwright, Oliver. "Poor doors are not the worst thing about social housing." *Guardian Arts and Design Blog*, July 30, 2014. Accessed August 10, 2015. http://www.theguardian.com/artanddesign/architecture-design-blog/2014/jul/30/poor-door-social-housing-apartheid.

Wasik, John F. "You Too Can Be a Global Real Estate Investor." *New York Times*, April 24, 2015.

Weaver, Robert C. *The Negro Ghetto.* New York: Russell & Russell, 1948.

Weiss, Marc A. "Researching the History of Real Estate." *Journal of Architectural Education* Vol. 11, No. 3, (Spring 1988): 38–40.

Weiss, Marc A. "The Origins and Legacy of Urban Renewal." In *Urban and Regional Planning in an Age of Austerity*, edited by P. Clavel, J. Forrester, and W. Goldsmith, 53–80. New York: Pergamon Press, 1980.

Weiss, Marc A. *The Rise of the Community Builders: The American Real Estate Industry and Urban Land Planning*. New York: Columbia University Press, 1987.

Western, Bruce, and Becky Pettit. "Incarceration and Social Inequality." *Daedalus* 139.3 (2010): 8–19.

"What Is a House?" series. *The Journal of the American Institute of Architects*. Washington, DC: Octagon, 1918.

"What Percent Are You?" *New York Times*, January 14, 2012. Accessed August 25, 2015. http://www.nytimes.com/interactive/2012/01/15/business/one-percent-map.html.

Wheaton, William, and Gleb Nechayev. "The 1998–2005 Housing 'Bubble' and the Current 'Correction': What's Different This Time?" *Journal of Real Estate Research* Vol. 30, No. 1 (2008): 1–26.

Wheaton, William. "Real Estate 'Cycles': Some Fundamentals." *Real Estate Economics* Vol. 27, No. 2 (1999): 209–230.

Whitsett, Ross. "Urban Mass: A Look at Co-Op City." *The Cooperator*, December 2006. Accessed July 1, 2015. http://cooperator.com/articles/1354/1/Urban-Mass/Page1.html.

Wiedemer, John P., Joseph E. Goeters, and J. Edward Graham. *Real Estate Investment*. 7th ed. Mason: South-Western Cengage Learning, 2011.

Wiese, Andrew. *Places of Their Own: African American Suburbanization in the 20th Century*. Chicago: University of Chicago Press, 2004.

Wilson, William Julius. *The Truly Disadvantaged: The Inner City, the Underclass, and Public Policy*. Chicago: University of Chicago Press, 1987.

Witt, Susan, and Robert Swann. "Land: Challenge and Opportunity." In *Rooted in the Land: Essays on Community and Place*, edited by William Vitak, and Wes Jackson, 244–252. New Haven: Yale University Press, 1996.

Wolf, Peter M. *Land in America: Its Value, Use and Control*. New York: Pantheon, 1981.

Wood, Elizabeth. "Realities of Urban Development." *Journal of Housing* (January 1994): 12–14.

World Bank. "GINI Index (World Bank estimate)." http://data.worldbank.org/indicator/SI.POV.GINI

Wotapka, Dawn. "Builders' Dream Home Sold for a Song at Foreclosure Auction." *Developments: Real Estate News and Analysis from The Wall Street Journal*. January 19, 2010. Accessed July 1, 2015. http://blogs.wsj.com/developments/2010/01/19/builders-dream-home-sold-for-a-song-at-foreclosure-auction/.

Wright, Frank Lloyd. *An Autobiography*. New York: Horizon Press, 1977.

Wright, Frank Lloyd. *The Disappearing City*. New York: William Farquhar Payson, 1932.

Wright, Frank Lloyd. *The Living City*. New York: Horizon Press, 1958.

Wright, Frank Lloyd. *When Democracy Builds*. Chicago: University of Chicago Press, 1945.

Wright, Gwendolyn. *Building the Dream: A Social History of Housing in America*. New York: Pantheon Books, 1981.

Wurster, Catherine Bauer. "The Social Front of Modern Architecture in the 1930s." *Journal of the Society of Architectural Historians* Vol. 24, No. 1 (1965): 48–52.

WXY, William Morrish, and Tygron. *10 Steps To Creating a Conversation: Community Design for Affordable Homes and Sustainable Places*. WXY Studio, 2014. http://wxystudio.com/uploads/1400014/141342100269/10StepsToCreatingAConversation.pdf

Wyly, Elvin, C. S. Ponder, Pierson Nettling, Bosco Ho, Sophie Ellen Fung, Zachary Liebowitz, and Dan Hammel. "New Racial Meanings of Housing in America." *American Quarterly* Vol. 64, No. 3 (Sept. 2012): 571–604.

Zipp, Samuel. *Manhattan Projects: The Rise and Fall of Urban Renewal in Cold War New York*. New York: Oxford University Press, 2012.

Zukin, Sharon. *Loft Living: Culture and Capital in Urban Change*. New Brunswick: Rutgers University Press, 2014 [1982].

Zukin, Sharon. *Landscapes of Power: From Detroit to Disneyworld*. Berkeley: University of California Press, 1991.

HOUSE HOUSING

AN UNTIMELY HISTORY OF ARCHITECTURE AND REAL ESTATE

House Housing: An Untimely History of Architecture and Real Estate is an ongoing, multi-year research project conducted by the Temple Hoyne Buell Center for the Study of American Architecture at Columbia University. The initiative seeks to encourage a public, historically informed conversation about the intersection of architecture and real estate development. The untimeliness of this history, as indicated by the project's title, is twofold. First, it returns us to financial matters widely discussed in the immediate aftermath of the 2008 foreclosure crisis but now largely abandoned by mainstream discourse. Second, it discloses surprising repetitions of themes, tendencies, and actions—reminding us that the economic infrastructures on which architecture rests are the outcome of such repetitions, rather than an a priori, natural ground. These infrastructures locate housing at the center of the current economic regime, with the United States as an influential node in a transnational network.

House Housing consists of a growing body of research that draws on multimedia sources. The results, which include this book, have appeared in numerous locations as exhibitions, panel discussions, and publications, and relate to different institutional frames. Overall, *House Housing*'s objects of inquiry range from architect-designed houses to prefabricated apartment blocks to suburban gated communities. All of these architectures are analyzed in light of their position at the intersection of design, policy, and finance. New narratives emerge out of surprising juxtapositions.

The *House Housing* website, focusing on evidence, analysis, and clear sourcing, reflects the Center's dialogic approach to research while creating opportunities for interested parties to join in. In this way, *House Housing* aims not only to craft what we see as a much needed and heretofore unwritten history of architecture and real estate, but also to support the Center's mission by generating public scholarship in an open conversation with our various constituencies.

www.house-housing.com

2015   FIRE DESTROYS NEW JERSEY APARTMENT COMPLEX FOR A
SECOND TIME
Event Highlights Distance Between REIT's Owners and Occupants

2012   VIOLENCE ENTERS A GATED COMMUNITY
Teenager is Shot and Killed in The Retreat at Twin Lakes

2011   CONSTRUCTION IN KANGBASHI NEW DISTRICT GRINDS TO A HALT
Housing Prices Plummet As Local Economy Slows and Debtors Default

2010   THE NEW AMERICAN HOME™ FAILS
Model House Intended for Trade Show Foreclosed Before Built

2009   BRAZILIAN GOVERNMENT LAUNCHES *MINHA CASA, MINHA VIDA*
World Bank Endorses the Program While Urging a Greater Role for the
Private Sector

2000   *DWELL* MAGAZINE CLAIMS A NEW FRONTIER
Editors Trace a Course "From the Robie House to Our House"

1997   MAYOR ENDORSES THE RENOVATION OF KOŠICE CITY CENTER
Romani Community Segregated in Luník IX Housing Estate

1995   ST. LOUIS SUBURB COMMISSIONS "VISION 2015 PLAN"
Housing Components Fall Short of Goals

1994   FEDERAL HOUSING POLICY MEETS LOCAL RESISTANCE
New Urbanists' Arrival Postponed on Far Rockaway

1986   FEDERAL LOW-INCOME HOUSING TAX CREDIT APPROVED
Enterprise Foundation Seeks to Reconcile Purpose with Profit

1982   DUTCH PARLIAMENT DEBATES HOUSING POLICY
Industry-backed Group to Investigate "Open Building" Alternatives

1978   ARCHITECT DECONSTRUCTS THE SUBURBAN HOME
Santa Monica House Evolves From Eyesore to Icon

1975   CO-OPERATORS WITHHOLD CARRYING CHARGES FOR NINE MONTHS
Residents Join Ranks to Fight for Continued Affordability in High-Rise
Enclave

1973   NIXON DECLARES MORATORIUM ON HOUSING ASSISTANCE
Wave of Section 235 Foreclosures Cited as One Cause

1939   **FHA DENIES INSURED MORTGAGE FOR EAST LANSING USONIA**
Frank Lloyd Wright Houses are Declared Bad Investments

1937   **ARCHITECT FINDS SIMILARITIES BETWEEN U.S.S.R AND U.S.A.**
Seeks a Form of Private Ownership Based on Freedom and Social
Justice

1934   **CATHERINE BAUER'S *MODERN HOUSING* PUBLISHED**
330-Page Volume Challenges Priorities During the International
Style Era

1933   **PRESIDENT PROMOTES SAVING AS CIVIC RESPONSIBILITY**
Roosevelt's First "Fireside Chat" Addresses Fear and the Banking Crisis

1932   **ARCHITECT PRESENTS BROADACRE CITY AS SOLUTION TO THE
NATION'S HOUSING PROBLEM**
Radical Vision Seeks to Distribute One Acre of Federal Land to Each
Family in Need

1918   **UNITED STATES HOUSING CORPORATION BUILDS HOUSING FOR
WARTIME WORKERS**
Program Abandoned as Role of Government is Questioned

1910   **FRANK LLOYD WRIGHT SELLS HIS VISION FOR SUBURBANIZING
AMERICA**
Berlin-Based Publication Establishes Architect's Reputation in Europe